Career
Diplomacy

More praise for *Career Diplomacy*

"Frank, incisive, and a good read, this book told me many things I never really understood about the foreign service. I don't know how we got along without it."
—John R. Galvin, former supreme Allied Commander in Europe and former commander-in-chief, U.S. European Command

"Harry Kopp and Charles Gillespie have produced an insightful and comprehensive response to the questions, 'What is the foreign service and why do we need it?' This is a required read for anyone contemplating a career in the foreign service."
—Stephen W. Bosworth, dean, Fletcher School of Law and Diplomacy, Tufts University

"A clear, unvarnished look at life in the United States Foreign Service, what works, and what doesn't. *Career Diplomacy* should be must reading for every foreign service officer—and everyone else who represents our country overseas."
—Ann Blackman, author of *Seasons of Her Life: A Biography of Madeleine Korbel Albright*

Career Diplomacy

*Life and Work in the
U.S. Foreign Service*

Harry W. Kopp
Charles A. Gillespie

Georgetown University Press/Washington, DC

Georgetown University Press, Washington, D.C. www.press.georgetown.edu
© 2008 by Georgetown University Press. All rights reserved. No part of this book
may be reproduced or utilized in any form or by any means, electronic or mechanical,
including photocopying and recording, or by any information storage and retrieval
system, without permission in writing from the publisher.

Library of Congress Cataloging-in-Publication Data

Kopp, Harry.
    Career diplomacy : life and work in the U.S. foreign service / Harry W. Kopp,
Charles A. Gillespie.
        p.   cm.
    Includes bibliographical references and index.
    ISBN-13: 978-1-58901-219-6 (alk. paper)
    1. United States. Foreign Service.   2. Diplomatic and consular service, American.
3. United States—Foreign relations administration.   I. Gillespie, Charles A.   II. Title.
    JZ1480.A5K67 2008
    327.73—dc22
    2008004495

♾ This book is printed on acid-free paper meeting the requirements of the American
National Standard for Permanence in Paper for Printed Library Materials.

15   14   13   12   11   10   09   08   9   8   7   6   5   4   3   2
First printing

Printed in the United States of America

In Memoriam

Charles A. Gillespie

1936–2008

Contents

Illustrations   viii
Preface   ix
Acknowledgments   xi

Part I   **The Institution**
1   What Is the Foreign Service?   3
2   History   10
3   The Foreign Service Today   34

Part II   **The Profession**
4   Form and Content   51
5   Stabilization and Reconstruction in Iraq   74
6   Politics and Professionalism   88

Part III   **The Career**
7   Stability and Change   131
8   Foreign Service Functions—Five Tracks   150
9   Assignments and Promotions   168

Part IV   **The Future Foreign Service**
10   Tomorrow's Diplomats   187

Appendices
A   Department of State Organization Chart   198
B   Foreign Service Core Precepts   200
C   Interviews   213
D   Websites   216

Notes   219
Glossary   239
Bibliography   247
About the Authors   253
Index   255

Illustrations

Tables

2.1	State Department Posts and Staffing, 1781–2006	13
2.2	Foreign Service Officers (Generalists)	23
2.3	Spending on International Affairs (Function 150)	30
3.1	The Foreign Service in Round Numbers, 2007	35
6.1	FY 2009 International Affairs Request	104–5
7.1	Foreign Service Pay Scale, 2008—Base Pay	133
7.2	Senior Foreign Service Pay Scale, 2008—Base Pay	133
7.3	Executive Level Pay Scale, 2008	133
7.4	Career Trajectory: Years in Grade and Years in Service	134
7.5	Time in Class, Time in Service	137
7.6	Thirteen Dimensions	142
7.7	Foreign Service Specialists—Jobs and Job Categories	144

Figure

| 6.1 | Organization of a Typical Mission | 114 |

Preface

Career Diplomacy: Life and Work in the U.S. Foreign Service began as a gleam in a general's eye. In 2005 retired U.S. Army general John R. Galvin joined the policy committee of the Una Chapman Cox Foundation, a private foundation dedicated to a strong, professional foreign service. General Galvin, a soldier-diplomat who had commanded allied forces in Europe and had served as dean of the Fletcher School of Law and Diplomacy, wondered out loud whether the foreign service had a book that would guide him through the basics. There is no such book, he was told. "Well, there should be," he said, and Tony Gillespie, another member of the committee, agreed. The Cox Foundation provided some seed money, Ambassador Gillespie recruited former foreign service officer Harry Kopp to work with him on the project, and the result is in these pages.

Whether America's diplomacy succeeds or fails depends to a large extent on its foreign service professionals. *Career Diplomacy* describes the foreign service as an institution, a profession, and a career. It provides a full and rounded picture of the organization, its place in history, its strengths and weaknesses, and its role in American foreign affairs. It is not a polemic. The authors have (mostly) resisted the temptation to tell the world what is wrong and how to set it right.

Readers of this book will come to understand who America's professional diplomats are, the behavior and achievements they reward, and the culture in which they operate. If you are in, or interested in, the service, *Career Diplomacy* will teach you things you did not know. If you are thinking about joining the service, this book will help you make a wise decision.

The authors invite comments to be sent to host@careerdiplomacy.com.

Acknowledgments

The authors are grateful to the many men and women who assisted in this project. We thank of course those whose names appear in the list of interviews; we are equally grateful to those interviewed whose names have been withheld.

The Una Chapman Cox Foundation, a remarkable institution with a remarkable story (www.uccoxfoundation.org), provided support and seed money. The foundation and its principals—chairman Harvie Branscomb Jr., former president Kenton McDonald, president Alexander F. Watson, executive director Clyde Taylor, and trustees Dian VanDeMark and Margo Branscomb—are stalwart friends of the foreign service.

Librarian Sara Schoo and Bill Sullivan of the Ralph Bunche Library at the Department of State made the stacks accessible and the facilities available.

Dan Geisler, Alec Watson, Harry Geisel, John Naland, Tony Motley, Charles Gillespie IV, Lew Allison, Ellen Guidera, and other friends and colleagues read ungainly drafts and offered corrections and improvements from which the book greatly benefited. Georgie Ann Geyer helped get the whole thing started.

The wonderfully efficient Melinda Brouwer verified quotations. Helen Glenn Court, a master of style, edited the manuscript for submission to the press. Richard Brown, director of Georgetown University Press, backed the project from beginning to end.

State Department officials, including Assistant Secretary for Public Affairs Sean McCormack, gave us encouragement, but the department did not request or receive any control over the final product. The authors are solely responsible for the contents of the book, including the mistakes we managed to commit despite the efforts of so many to make sure we got things right.

Part I

•

The Institution

1

·

What Is the Foreign Service?

"Look," he said. "What do we need them for? Especially so many of them." He was talking about members of the U.S. Foreign Service. "What we need to know," he said, "is mostly in the news. What we need to say should come from people in tune with the president, not from diplomats in tune with each other."

The speaker was a businessman with international interests. His listener was a former foreign service officer. His question was serious and deserves a careful answer.

Why does the United States need its foreign service, professionals who spend the bulk of their careers in U.S. embassies and consulates around the globe? Does the work they do need to be done? And if so, could others do it better or more efficiently?

The United States is engaged in regional and global conflicts that are at least as political as they are military. Over 11 percent of our population, more than thirty-one million people, are foreign born. Foreign trade is one-quarter of our economy. Environmental changes, epidemic and pandemic diseases, even financial panics sweep across borders and cannot be controlled unilaterally.

We need to make sense of this world, and we need to make sure the world makes sense of us. We need to understand, protect, and promote our own interests. Whenever and wherever we can, we need to shape events to our advantage. That is why we have a foreign service.

The foreign service is the corps of more than twelve thousand professionals who represent the U.S. government in more than 260 missions abroad and carry out the nation's foreign policies. Its members serve mainly in the Department of State, but also in the Department of Commerce, the Department of Agriculture (USDA), the U.S. Agency for International Development (USAID), and wherever else the U.S. government requires civilian service abroad.

Like the army, the navy, the air force, and the marines, the U.S. Foreign Service is a true service. Its officers are commissioned by the president, confirmed by the Senate, and sworn to uphold and defend the U.S. Constitution. Rank is vested in the person, not in the job. Members of the foreign service, with very few exceptions, are available for assignment anywhere in the world. On average, they spend two-thirds of their careers abroad.

The Mission

The foreign service has a triple mission. The first is representation. In U.S. government jargon, representation often refers to official entertaining, for which the government provides a famously small allowance. But diplomacy is not a dinner party, and representation, as used here, is a condition of foreign service life abroad. A member of the foreign service on overseas duty not only acts on behalf of the U.S. government but lives as a representative of the country as well. On behalf of the United States, the foreign service talks, listens, reports, analyzes, cajoles, persuades, threatens, debates, and above all negotiates. The foreign service reaches into other societies across barriers of history, culture, language, faith, politics, and economics to build trust, change attitudes, alter behaviors, and keep the peace.

The second mission is operations. The foreign service is on the ground, dealing every day with host governments and populations, running U.S. programs, executing U.S. laws, giving effect to U.S. policies, offering protection to American citizens, and supporting the full U.S. official civilian presence overseas.

The third is policy. Members of the foreign service, through their long engagement with foreign societies, are well placed to project the international consequences of what we say and do. They are the government's experts on how America's national interests, defined by our political process, can most effectively be advanced abroad. The service is the government's institutional memory for foreign affairs, able to place policy in historical perspective and project risks, costs, and benefits over the long term.

All three missions are essential. A foreign service that sees its mission as diplomacy, with no role for policy, will wait passively for instructions that may come too late, or not at all. A service that believes it should set policy as well as carry it out will lose the trust of the president and the Congress and become an irrelevant annoyance. A service that neglects hands-on operations will exhaust its energy in interagency meetings and cede its ability to act to more nimble and aggressive organizations.

Representation, operations, and policy are all essential to the grand task the country has asked its diplomats to perform. As soon as she was sworn in as secretary of state in January 2005, Condoleezza Rice spoke to a packed house in the State Department's Acheson Auditorium. "The Department of State is going to be leading a tremendous effort to use our diplomacy literally to change the world," she said. "We're activists in this effort to change the world. Yes, we'll analyze. And, yes, we will report. And, yes, we will come up with great ideas. But we also have to be able to really engage and to get it done. That's the new challenge for diplomacy."[1]

Secretary Rice called this challenge transformational diplomacy. She said of America's diplomats, "We know from experience how hard they work, the risks they and their families take, and the hardships they endure. We will be asking even more of them, in the service of their country, and of a great cause." She set for American diplomacy "three great tasks: First, we will unite the community of democracies in building an international system that is based on our shared values and the rule of law. Second, we will strengthen the community of democracies to fight the threats to our common security and alleviate the hopelessness that feeds terror. And third, we will spread freedom and democracy throughout the globe."[2]

An Institution, a Profession, a Career

This book is descriptive, not prescriptive. Readers looking for polemics for or against transformational diplomacy, or for a program for reform of America's foreign policy, or for a reconstruction of its foreign policy establishment should go elsewhere. What we offer instead is a guide to the foreign service as it is, with a look back at what it was and a look ahead at what it may become. We treat the service in three ways: as an institution, a profession, and a career.

The Institution

The institution is the men and women—and their predecessors and successors—who serve the United States under the Foreign Service Act. But the people and the institution are not the same. Presidents often distrust the foreign service as an institution—President Nixon vowed to ruin it—even as they promote individual members of the service to positions of confidence. Yet the spirit and culture of the service shape its members and, in turn, are gradually shaped by them.

Seven events and decisions have played an especially large role in making the foreign service what it is today. In chronological order, they are

- the nineteenth-century split between diplomats, responsible for state-to-state relations, and consuls, who took care of commercial matters and citizens abroad;
- the reliance, until well into the twentieth century, on the well heeled and well connected;
- the wall, until the 1950s, between officers of the foreign service, who spent their entire careers abroad, and officers of the Department of State, who served only in Washington;
- the marginalization of the foreign service during World War II;
- the attacks, in the late 1940s and early 1950s, on the loyalty of the foreign service to the United States, and the absence of a robust defense;
- the rigor of the competitive entrance examination; and
- the control by existing members of the service of their own promotions and the admission of new members.

These factors have led to a service that, until quite recently, has been elite and clubby, hierarchical, cautious, strong in analysis but less so in operations, deeply patriotic, and deferential to the status quo and the weight of history. Over the past few years, the service has grown in numbers and become more diverse, more skilled in languages, less desk bound, and less obeisant to rank. The depth of patriotic feeling is unchanged.

The Profession

The profession of the foreign service is diplomacy. Among professions, it is an odd one, more like journalism than like law or medicine. It is open to all. Training in the field is available but not required. The skills needed to practice diplomacy at a high level are difficult to master, but they are not esoteric. They can be acquired in many fields, including politics, business, the military, and academia. Some of the best practitioners (and also some of the worst) are outsiders who start at the top.

Virtually every country that has a department of foreign affairs also has a professional diplomatic service, and almost none, save for the United States, employs amateurs in large numbers. Most governments recognize that diplomatic skills, though accessible in many ways, are most surely gained through diplomatic experience. A diplomatic service, with ranks gained by merit, also serves to identify the best talents and temperaments as it weeds out the worst.

Diplomatic professionals are skilled in negotiation, communication, persuasion, reporting, analysis, and management. They recognize ambiguity and dissembling and can practice both when necessary. They know foreign languages, cultures, and interests, and they have learned, for at least some parts of the world, how other governments make decisions and carry them out, and what motivates action and change. Equally important, they have learned how their own government works—its politics, laws, and bureaucratic processes. They know where diplomacy fits in the array of tools the nation can deploy to assert its interests, and they work effectively with military and intelligence professionals in pursuit of common objectives.

One need not be a member of the foreign service to be a skilled diplomat, or even a great one. Outsiders can bring new ideas and new energy. Most important in the U.S. system, outsiders can bring to diplomacy a relationship with the country's political leadership that nonpartisan career diplomats rarely attain. But gifted amateurs and revolving-door diplomats are not enough to do the work the nation demands around the world and around the clock. This book will show that the administration of U.S. laws and programs with international reach, the management of the official U.S. civilian overseas establishment, and the daily negotiation of relationships with foreign governments on matters large and small require a dedicated, professional service.

The Career

A foreign service career is like a good limerick: It has unpredictable content in a predictable form.

The content of a career is a function of specialized knowledge, personal preference, and luck. In the Department of State, the individual's knowledge and the needs of the service for particular skills place each officer in one of five tracks (political affairs, economic affairs, consular affairs, public diplomacy, and management), and each specialist in one of seven categories that cover nineteen kinds of jobs. Most if not all assignments for a particular individual will be in the same track or category. Of course, regional knowledge and language skills heavily influence the location of assignment—except when they don't, and then it's the assignment that drives language instruction and the development of regional expertise. Members of the foreign service must be available for assignment worldwide. Two-thirds of a career is likely to be spent abroad—and more than that for foreign service officers in agencies other than State.

Within these parameters, there is plenty of room for surprise. The next post, the next job, the next boss are rarely predictable. Change is constant, but it is not random. The needs of the service impose constraints, but foreign service personnel make many of the choices that determine the progress of their careers. When you are in the service, you cannot control what positions are open when you are ready to move, but the preferences you express among them weigh heavily on the outcome.

The form or trajectory of a foreign service career has less variation: four or five years in entry-level positions, about twenty years in midlevel positions of increasing responsibility, and, for a few people, several more years in the senior ranks, until mandatory retirement at age sixty-five. Pay and benefits are fixed by Congress, with managers able to intervene only at the margins. The checkpoints for an officer's passage from entry level to midcareer to the senior ranks and eventual retirement are well established, though the requirements for passing through the checkpoints change from time to time and have recently grown more rigorous.

Foreign service takes over a life in a way that few occupations do. Where you live, the food you eat, the languages you hear and use, even the diseases you contract, come with the job. If you have a family, the service is a family affair. Children experience the benefits—and drawbacks—of frequent moves and exposure to many cultures. Opportunities for a spouse to work will be erratic. Hazardous duty is likely to impose a separation of a year or more at some point, or at several points, during a career. Nevertheless, retention rates are high. "In for two, in for twenty" is a fair summation, except when "in for three, in for thirty" is more appropriate.

The personnel system gives strong guidance to new recruits, but it has declining influence as a career progresses. After two or three tours, a member of the foreign service should know how assignments come about (this book will help), and should take responsibility for his or her career. The service is small. In all probability, once you have finished three or four tours, which will take about ten years, anyone interested in you will know you or will need no more than two telephone calls to find someone who does.

By 2008 the term *transformational diplomacy* had become politically charged. It may not outlast the administration that coined it. But in Iraq and in trouble spots around the world, members of the service are deeply engaged in the work of stabilization, reconstruction, and development. The center of gravity of the service has shifted—more missionary, less Metternich.

The shift can be exaggerated. American diplomats for a generation have worked, sometimes with marked success, to move foreign societies toward democratic government, the rule of law, respect for basic human freedoms, and provision of basic human needs. But the change, though some dispute it, is real. The stars of the service in the years ahead will be those who really master critical languages, serve (often without family) in hard and dangerous places, and get things done, not just written.

2

.

History

Like the U.S. Congress, the U.S. Foreign Service has rarely enjoyed the esteem as an institution that its members have enjoyed as individuals. Foreign service personnel are widely respected for their intellect, honesty, energy, courage, and patriotism. The service itself, and the Department of State with which it is so closely identified, have often been held in what the late Arizona congressman Mo Udall called "minimum high regard."

Dean Acheson, secretary of state under President Harry Truman, noted that many Americans did not want to hear too much about the complexities of foreign affairs or the stubborn refusal of foreigners to see the world as we do. When world events fail to follow American desires, he wrote, the "believers in American omnipotence, to whom every goal unattained is explicable only by incompetence or treason," were quick to blame the department and the foreign service.[1] Robert F. Kennedy exemplified this paradox. Traveling abroad in 1962 as attorney general in his brother John's administration, he "made little connection between the Foreign Service people he met overseas, whom he by and large admired, and those working in a State Department he disparaged."[2]

President Nixon felt much the same. Henry Kissinger wrote that Nixon "had very little confidence in the State Department" and did not trust the foreign service, which he felt "had disdained him as Vice President and ignored him the moment he was out of office."[3] In fact, Nixon said he intended "to ruin the foreign service. I mean ruin it."[4] Yet many young foreign service officers, several of whom went on to high office, played critical roles on his White House staff.[5]

Mistrust of the foreign service and the State Department is, as Acheson noted, partly a function of American suspicion of foreigners and, by extension, of those who deal with them. It is also a product of the history of the foreign service. Only in the past fifteen years or so has the foreign service really begun to reflect Main Street America, and only in the past few years have American attitudes toward the service begun to recognize that shift.

Amateurs and Entrepreneurs in the Nineteenth Century

American diplomacy, like the American military, is older than the federal government. Even before adopting a declaration of independence, the Continental Congress established armed forces to fight against the British and commissioned envoys to seek support from other countries. American diplomats, notably Benjamin Franklin, secured the French support that proved vital to military victory and then negotiated favorable terms of peace with Britain. The Constitution later provided not only for raising an army and a navy, but also for naming ambassadors, ministers, and consuls.

The paths of the military and diplomatic establishments quickly diverged. The American military developed a professional structure at West Point in 1802 and at the Naval Academy in 1845. Military service became for many young men an attractive career. American diplomacy, however, remained a part-time and largely amateur affair.

Throughout the nineteenth century, Washington maintained two kinds of representatives. Diplomats handled state-to-state relations. Consuls dealt with commercial matters and the problems of individual American citizens abroad. The diplomats were nearly all men of wealth who served with only token pay and rarely sought or received more than one assignment. Consuls, more numerous and socially less privileged, were often American businessmen living in foreign ports but with political connections strong enough to secure an appointment.[6] Working without salary (Congress authorized the first consular salaries in 1856, but payment was spotty), consuls were entitled to pocket the fees they collected for their services, largely related to merchant shipping. Many found ways to use their official positions to advance their private interests—behavior that was scandalous even by the standards of those days. Other than the spoils system by which they were appointed, members of the diplomatic and consular services had little to do with each other.

The nineteenth-century writings of Mark Twain, Henry Adams, Richard Harding Davis, and others established the pompous ambassador and the raffish consul as popular stereotypes.[7] President Theodore Roosevelt complained that "our ambassadors . . . seem to think that [their] life work is a kind of glorified pink tea party."[8] Ambrose Bierce, noting that defeated candidates of the president's party were often consoled with a consular appointment, defined consul in his *Devil's Dictionary* as "a person who, having failed to secure an office from the people, is given one by the Administration on condition that he leave the country."[9] Secretary of State John Hay complained that the president "will have promised all the consulates in the service; the senators will all come to me and refuse to believe me disconsulate; I shall see all my treaties slaughtered, one by one."[10]

Public familiarity bred public contempt and built support for change. Reforms that had begun in the 1880s created a merit-based civil service and a Civil Service Commission that rolled back use of the spoils system in most domestic federal employment. Between 1895 and 1915, legislation and executive action applied civil service rules to the still separate consular and diplomatic services. Consular salaries were much improved, and salaried consular officials were prohibited from engaging in private business. Consular officials came to be better paid, and by and large more capable, than their diplomatic counterparts. A 1909 executive order instructed the secretary of state to identify, to the president, those career diplomats with the potential to serve as chiefs of missions. Subsequent legislation established a personnel classification system and the principle of promotion by merit.

Toward a Professional Service

By the end of the nineteenth century the United States was a formidable world power with an inferior diplomatic establishment. As late as 1910 the United States had only 121 diplomats stationed abroad, but more than 1,000 consuls (see table 2.1). Domestic State Department employees numbered 234.

In 1913 President Woodrow Wilson (1913–1921) named as his first secretary of state a political rival within his own Democratic party, the venerable prairie populist William Jennings Bryan. Wilson installed him in the weirdly ornate State, War, and Navy Building (now the Eisenhower Executive Office Building) and then ignored him. Wilson ignored the rest of the Department of State as well, and he continued to do so even after Bryan had been replaced. Key foreign policy decisions—to remain neutral when war broke out in Europe in 1914, to join the Allied cause in 1917, and to try to dictate terms of the peace negotiated in 1918—were all taken without regard to the secretary of state or his department. Robert Lansing, Bryan's successor, complained in a 1920 letter to Republican congressman John Jacob Rogers of Massachusetts that the government's organization for foreign affairs, though it served well when "the world [was] free from the present perplexities," needed reform and modernization. Rogers took up the challenge and drafted a bill for sweeping change.[11]

Hearings on the bill made it clear that business and shipping interests, American travelers, and academicians were all dissatisfied with the quality

Table 2.1. State Department Posts and Staffing, 1781–2006

	Diplomatic and Consular Posts		State Department Personnel	
	Diplomatic[a]	Consular[b]	Domestic[c]	Overseas[d]
1781	4	3	4	10
1790	2	10	8	20
1800	6	52	10	62
1810	4	60	9	56
1820	7	83	16	95
1830	15	141	23	153
1840	20	152	38	170
1850	27	197	22	218
1860	33	282	42	281
1870	36	318	65	804
1880	35	303	80	977
1890	41	323	76	1,105
1900	41	318	91	1,137
1910	48	324	234	1,043
1920	45	368	708	514
1930	57	299	714	633
1940	58	264	1,128	840
1950	74	179	8,609	7,710
1960	99	166	7,116	6,178
1970	117	122	6,983	5,865
1980	133	100	8,433	5,861
1990	143	100	10,063	6,783
1999	160	83	12,232	7,158
2006	167	100	11,970	7,577

[a] Embassies and other overseas posts headed by a chief of mission.
[b] Includes overseas posts not headed by a chief of mission.
[c] Includes civil service and foreign service.
[d] Civil service and foreign service, excluding foreign service nationals.
Source: Trask 1981.

of representation abroad. Testimony drew invidious comparisons between polished, efficient European professionals and untrained, ineffective, and sometimes venal American representatives. State Department officials complained that pay was so low that only people of private wealth could enter the diplomatic service. Hugh Gibson, a foreign service professional who was at the time ambassador to Poland, declared that "we are the only great power which consistently excludes from competition for [senior diplomatic] posts any but men of independent means." The language he used set a stereotype that lingers eighty years later. "You hear very frequently about the boys with the white spats," he said, "the tea drinkers, the cookie pushers. . . . Our great problem now is to attract enough men so that we will have a real choice of material and crowd out these incompetents and defectives."[12]

The modern foreign service begins with enactment of the Rogers Act on May 24, 1924. This legislation merged the diplomatic and consular services, setting appointment by competitive examination, promotion by merit, and pay comparable to other government jobs. It established a retirement system, home leave, and other benefits. Subsequent legislation authorized the government to buy or build and operate facilities overseas as missions and consulates, making it possible for citizens without extraordinary wealth to serve as chiefs of mission.

Fragmentation

In the wake of the Rogers Act, the foreign service became more professional but not much less patrician. Many members of the old diplomatic service resisted the reforms, looked down on the consular corps, and failed to acquire the specialized skills that America's rapidly complicating and expanding international interests demanded. Government agencies and private interest groups, feeling ill served, pressed for change. The newly unified service quickly fractured, and many government agencies, including the Treasury, the Commerce Department, the Department of Agriculture, and the Bureau of Mines, sent their employees overseas to work outside the foreign service.

Whether one foreign service can represent all U.S. interests, or whether each government agency with an international interest needs a separate overseas presence, is still unsettled. Fragmentation has followed consolidation and vice versa, with periods of organizational turmoil at each turn of the cycle. Even a barebones history of representation in three areas—trade, information, and foreign aid—illustrates this pattern clearly.

Trade

Not long after the Rogers Act was enacted in 1924, Congress established a separate Foreign Commerce Service (FCS) in the Department of Commerce and a separate Foreign Agricultural Service (FAS) in the Department of Agriculture. As the likelihood of war increased in 1939, these agencies were closed and their functions returned to the Department of State. Congress restored the Foreign Agricultural Service in 1954 and the Foreign Commercial Service in 1980.[13] In the 1960s and 1970s, responsibility for developing trade policy and conducting trade negotiations passed from the State Department to the Office of the U.S. Trade Representative (USTR), a White House agency established by Congress in 1962.[14]

Information

Information and cultural affairs came into the State Department when the Office of War Information was shut down in 1945. The function moved to a new outside entity—the U.S. Information Agency (USIA)—in 1953 but came back to State in 1999. It has lately received new urgency and a new name: public diplomacy.[15]

Foreign Assistance

Foreign aid may have a higher ratio of heated debate per dollar of expenditure than any other federal program. In its deeply muddled bureaucratic history, the program has been in, then out, then in, then out, then half in and half out of the Department of State. Where in the foreign affairs bureaucracy foreign aid fits today is not entirely clear.[16]

Each of these bureaucratic struggles has its context, but the perceived failings of State figured importantly in all of them.

Postwar Promise and Persecution

The department was not a strong agency during World War II. Wartime policy, wrote one historian, "required coordination of political ends and military means." The Department of State, he continued, might have understood political ends, but it was unfamiliar with military means, and so it lacked "the expertise and institutions [needed] to exert dominant influence on the shaping of grand strategy."[17] White House planners rarely consulted the State Department, and President Roosevelt left Secretary Cordell Hull out of most of the conferences where the allies planned the conduct of the war and the shape of the postwar world. The department also created political problems for the president by seeking draft deferments for its officers. That could not have helped its standing.[18]

The end of the war should have changed the State Department's fortunes. President Harry Truman, who assumed office in 1945, looked to the department for advice. In 1947 he named General George C. Marshall, the army's chief of staff, as secretary of state. Marshall was, with Dwight Eisenhower, one of the country's most respected soldiers, and one of its most admired citizens as well. Under Marshall (1947–49) and his successor Dean Acheson (1949–53), the State Department recognized the Soviet challenge in Europe and reacted vigorously with a coherent strategy brilliantly executed: the Marshall Plan, the North Atlantic Treaty Organization (NATO), aid to anticommunist forces in Greece and Turkey, and the Berlin airlift. In the decade from 1940 to 1950, the State Department's Washington-based staff, who served only in Washington, grew from 1,128 to 8,609. At the same time, foreign service personnel, who served only overseas, increased from 840 to 7,710.

For broad sectors of the American public, however, the story of the day was communist victory, not Western defense.[19] The detonation of the first Soviet atomic bomb in September 1949, the flight of the Chinese Nationalist government to Formosa (Taiwan) in December 1949, and North Korea's attack on South Korea in June 1950—all of these events suggested to many that the United States was losing a global battle. In the atmosphere of extreme partisanship that followed the unexpected Democratic sweep of the White House, the Senate, and the House in the elections of 1948, the State Department became the target of a violent political attack.

State was especially vulnerable to an anticommunist witch hunt, because it harbored a number of actual witches. George Kennan, a career foreign service officer generally regarded as the country's leading authority on the Soviet Union, wrote: "The penetration of the American governmental services by members or agents (conscious or otherwise) of the American Communist Party in the late 1930s was not a figment of the imagination of the hysterical right-wingers of a later decade. . . . The Roosevelt administration was very slow in reacting to this situation and correcting it."[20]

In 1945 and 1946, the Department of State dismissed almost three hundred employees for security reasons, including forty who were said to have "close connections or involvement" with foreign powers. Ten more were dismissed in the first half of 1947. One of these was Alger Hiss, alleged to be an agent of the Soviet Union.[21]

In a speech in West Virginia on February 9, 1950, the recklessly ambitious Senator Joseph McCarthy, Republican of Wisconsin, blamed the State Department for communist gains and accused it of treason. "While I cannot take the time," he said, "to name all the men in the State Department who have been named as members of the Communist Party and members of a spy ring, I have here in my hand a list of 205 that were known to the Secretary of State as being members of the Communist Party and who, nevertheless, are still working and shaping policy in the State Department."[22] The State Department, he later told the Senate, was "thoroughly infested with Communists." On the Senate floor a McCarthy supporter, Republican Senator William Jenner of Indiana, called Secretary of State Dean Acheson a "Communist-appeasing, Communist-protecting betrayer of America."[23]

The attacks came to focus on the communist takeover in China and on the performance of a small group of foreign service officers known as the China hands. These officers, many of them sons of missionaries, were fluent in Chinese. Most had spent time during the war with communist forces in China. Over a period of years in the 1940s, they had reported the deteriorating capacity of the nationalist government and the near certainty of a communist victory in the civil war that followed the collapse of the Japanese occupation. They recommended that the United States drop its support for the nationalists and develop a relationship with the communists, to keep the communists from turning to Moscow for support.[24]

McCarthy and his supporters charged the China hands with working to bring about the communist takeover they predicted. In the words of one of their accusers, "the professional foreign service men sided with the Chinese Communist Party."[25]

State had praised the work of the China hands when they were performing it, but did not defend either the officers or their work when they were attacked. Instead, it opened secret investigations and denied the China hands access to their own classified reporting, which was considered evidence against them. George Kennan, who was peripherally involved in these events, described the department's attitude as "pious detachment" that in effect said to the accused: "'Here's what people say about you. Defend yourself if you can. We won't lift a finger on your behalf.'"[26]

In the end, two of the China hands were fired, two were forced to resign or retire, and nearly all of the others were assigned outside of Asia for the remainder of their careers.[27] McCarthy lost his grip on the public imagination—and on political power—when he shifted his target from State to the army and provoked resistance from President Dwight Eisenhower. The Senate censured McCarthy in December 1954. He died of complications of alcoholism three years later.

The foreign service suffered as much from the failure of State's leadership to offer a defense as from McCarthy's attacks. An aide recorded the views of

Secretary of State John Foster Dulles (1953–59): "With the responsibilities I have now, I need broad support in Congress. I regret if injustice must be done to a few Foreign Service officers, but as secretary I must be guided by the larger national interest."[28] Officers drew the lesson that their careers depended on political caution and conventional thinking. These habits of mind entered the culture of the service and persisted for many years. Even now, if a senior foreign officer is publicly attacked, other officers do not necessarily rally around. For the foreign service, wrote one observer, "McCarthy was like a flash bulb witnessed up close, seen much later when one's eyes were closed."[29]

Growing Pains: 1946–80

The absence of trust between the State Department's leadership and its employees affected, or afflicted, the management of both the department and the foreign service. The expansion of America's international power, responsibilities, and presence after World War II presented challenges to management that were unevenly met.

As the United States entered the postwar world, foreign service personnel, who spent virtually their entire careers abroad, had little to do with the civil service personnel who staffed the State Department's domestic positions. One noncareer ambassador complained that foreign service posts, with their "fantastic network of men, women, and typewriters," sent reports to Washington, where "they are placed in files." Then "the home team, having properly disposed of the information from the field, proceeds to write its own endless reports to go forward to the same ultimate fate in the embassies throughout the world."[30]

Blue-ribbon commissions in 1949 and 1954 called for integrating the department's civil and foreign service personnel. Foreign service traditionalists objected, but Secretary Dulles acted on most of the proposals. By the end of the 1950s, about fifteen hundred civil service employees had transferred into the foreign service, and roughly the same number of positions in Washington were designated for foreign service employees. The service as a whole gained in numbers, and foreign service officers, though not foreign service staff, began to expect to spend about a third of their careers in domestic assignments. These changes (called Wristonization after Henry Wriston, author of the 1954 report) improved communication between the department and the field and gave foreign service personnel a much-improved understanding of how policy is formed in Washington.

The service was less successful in meeting the demands of the postwar world for specialized expertise in trade promotion, labor affairs, science and technology, cultural affairs, public relations, international finance, development assistance, international law, and other areas beyond the ken or outside the experience of the typical foreign service officer. Congress hoped to solve this problem by creating, in the Foreign Service Act of 1946, a corps of specialists who would enter the foreign service for limited periods without competitive examination. The concept may have been sound, but its execution was flawed. The reserve officers, as they were called, were haphazardly recruited and poorly integrated into the service.[31] Planning for long-range personnel requirements became increasingly divorced from recruitment and training, and then it collapsed.

Eventually State's personnel system fell into crisis. The Vietnam War was a contributing factor. The Civil Operations and Revolutionary Development Support (CORDS) program, which combined military, CIA, and USAID counterinsurgency programs under a single, CIA-dominated management, sent civilians into rural areas of South Vietnam and created a huge demand for linguists with political skills and physical energy. The State Department stepped up recruitment to supply CORDS with foreign service officers. At the height of the program, more than four hundred foreign service officers were in the field in CORDS, and about one hundred more were in language training.

CORDS was a turning point in the lives and careers of many of the foreign service officers who served in the program. A number of CORDS officers were thoroughly dismayed by U.S. policies and left the service. For those who stayed, the experience taught management, leadership, and operational skills that sometimes led to rapid advancement. CORDS veterans faced a problem, though, as they moved up through the ranks: There were not enough positions to accommodate them all.

By the mid-1970s, the discipline of *up or out*, which the foreign service had borrowed from the U.S. Navy and renamed *selection out*, had grown lax. Officers in higher grades almost never lost their jobs for substandard performance. Without selection out, and with an attractive, inflation-indexed retirement package that encouraged at least a twenty-year career, the service came to have more senior diplomats than places to put them. "At the worst point," according to one of the department's managers, "as many as a hundred and thirty senior officers were unassignable, and thus reduced to 'walking the halls.'"[32] Midgrade officers, many of them veterans of CORDS, resented the senior glut that frustrated their chances for promotion.

Dissatisfaction built pressure for change that coincided with President Carter's efforts to reform the civil service. Immediately following passage of the Civil Service Reform Act in October 1978, the State Department's undersecretary for management gathered a small group of insiders to work closely with key members of Congress (including Senator Claiborne Pell of Rhode Island, a former foreign service officer) to draft what became the Foreign Service Act of 1980. The 1980 act gave the service the shape and structure it has today.[33]

The act created a senior foreign service, a top echelon comparable to the senior executive service that the Civil Service Reform Act had just established. To reduce the surplus of senior officers, it introduced mandatory retirement at sixty-five and cut the time allowed in the senior grades from twenty-two to sixteen years. It also placed foreign service officers and specialists on a single pay scale more comparable to the scale used by the civil service.

Under the act the U.S. Agency for International Development, the Department of Agriculture, the Department of Commerce, and other agencies could use the foreign service personnel system to "carry out functions which require service abroad," but the agencies, not State, retained control over their employees. In the Department of State, both foreign service and civil service employees came under the authority of a single senior official who holds two titles: director general of the foreign service and director of human resources. In recent years, policy has favored closer integration of the department's foreign and civil service personnel.

Gender and Race

The first page of the Foreign Service Act of 1980 says "the members of the Foreign Service should be representative of the American people." The mandate was so prominent because the failing had been so great.

In the 1970s, the department and the foreign service were wrestling, generally unsuccessfully, with the treatment of women and minorities. The foreign service in the first half of the twentieth century was very much a white man's organization. As late as 1970 the corps of foreign service officers was 95 percent male (2,945 of 3,084) and only one percent African American (34 of 3,084). All female foreign service officers were single and, until 1971, required to resign if they wed. The service would almost never assign single women to communist or Islamic countries, for fear in the former case of compromise (vulnerability to sexual blackmail) and in the latter of giving offense to the host government. African American officers were typically and disproportionately assigned to posts in Africa.[34]

Foreign service spouses—that is, wives—were regarded as adjuncts. Only in 1972 did the department recognize in a formal statement (Policy on Wives of Foreign Service Employees) that "the wife of a Foreign Service employee who is with her husband at a foreign post is an individual, not a government employee." The same statement reversed long-standing practice by prohibiting, instead of requiring, consideration of a wife's activities in evaluating her husband's performance.

An internal task force in 1977 worried that women and minorities might not seek foreign service careers because of the image of the service as "elitist, self-satisfied, a walled-in barony populated by smug white males, an old-boy system in which women and minorities cannot possibly hope to be treated with equity in such matters as promotions and senior level responsibilities."[35] Maybe this language wasn't strong enough. The department did little to bring about change until employee grievances escalated into litigation.

The impetus came first from Alison Palmer, who had joined the foreign service in 1958 and began to complain of discrimination in assignments and promotions in 1965. The department rebuffed or ignored her for years. In 1972, however, she filed a successful grievance with the Civil Service Commission and led an equally successful campaign on Capitol Hill to block the department's director of personnel from confirmation as ambassador to Sierra Leone.[36] She then received a promotion.

In 1976 Palmer initiated a class action lawsuit that charged the Department of State with discrimination against women in hiring, assignments, and promotions. Like the suit in Dickens's *Bleak House*, the case threatened to outlast the plaintiffs. After thirteen years of litigation, including one appeal, the U.S. District Court for the District of Columbia found in January 1989 that discrimination had indeed occurred. Under court order, the department offered relief in the form of new assignments and revised performance ratings to about six hundred women foreign service officers. Further litigation regarding bias in the entry exam produced a 2002 decree under which the State Department agreed to allow almost four hundred women foreign service applicants who had failed the written examination between 1991 and 1994 to move on to the oral assessment as if they had passed (for a discussion of the entrance exam, see chapter 8).

African American officers followed the path that the women had blazed. In 1985 Walter Thomas, a black foreign service officer, filed a complaint of discrimination with the Equal Employment Opportunity Commission. The EEOC, whose chairman at the time was future Supreme Court Justice

Clarence Thomas, found that the State Department "typically" discriminated against black officers in assignments, performance evaluations, and promotions. As in Alison Palmer's case, the ruling led to a class-action lawsuit, filed in 1986. Ten years later, the department settled out of court, agreeing to pay $38 million in compensation and to offer retroactive promotions to seventeen of the plaintiffs.

Litigation was not the only pressure brought to bear on the State Department's practices. In the 1980s the EEOC, an independent federal agency charged with enforcement of equal opportunity laws and oversight of policies and practices across the federal government, repeatedly criticized the department's affirmative action plans as inadequate. In 1988 Congress directed the General Accounting Office (GAO), renamed the Government Accountability Office in 2001, to report on the department's recruitment, appointment, assignment, and promotion of women and minorities.

The report was broadly unfavorable. The GAO found that in 1987, of a total of 9,432 foreign service employees (foreign service nationals are excluded), about 65 percent were white men, fewer than 25 percent were white women, 6 percent were black, and 3 percent were Hispanic. The same ratios applied to the 5,163 foreign service officers classified as generalists (see table 2.2). Recruitment efforts were failing to attract greater numbers of minority candidates to take the entrance exam, and those that did were failing at relatively high rates. After four years of service, minority junior officers were much more likely to be denied tenure than white junior officers (men or women). Assignments were skewed, with white men overrepresented in political and economic jobs, white women in consular work, and minority officers in administrative positions. Promotions, however, seemed color-blind and gender-neutral.[37]

In response to the GAO report, the department, not for the first time, pledged increased efforts to recruit and promote women and minorities. By the late 1990s, changes in policies and attitudes began to work their way through the system and have an impact on the numbers.

The expansion of the foreign service under Secretary Colin Powell's Diplomatic Readiness Initiative (DRI) was an opportunity to increase minority hiring. According to a former senior official in the Bureau of Human Resources, minorities had been failing the foreign service written exam in greater proportions than whites, though minorities tended to fare as well as whites in the oral assessment. So, the official said, "we made sure the cut score on the written exam was set low enough to give us a representative sample of minorities at the orals." The change had the desired effect. "Minority intake through the foreign service exam rose from about 12.5 percent

Table 2.2. Foreign Service Officers (Generalists)

Year	Total	Female Total	%	Black Total	%	Hispanic Total	%	Other Total	%
1970	3,084	139	4.5	34	1.1	NA	NA	NA	NA
1987	5,163	1,114	21.6	286	5.5	196	3.8	84	1.6
1994	4,877[a]	1,186	26.1	249	5.5	206	4.5	148	3.3
2005	6,293[b]	2,299	36.5	313	5.0	280	4.5	348	5.6

[a] Of these, 337 are not specified by gender or race-ethnicity and were therefore excluded from the calculation of race-ethnicity percentages.
[b] Of these, eighty-eight are not specified by race-ethnicity and were therefore excluded from the calculation of race-ethnicity percentages.
Source: Bacchus 1983; GAO 1989; Department of State Bureau of Human Resources.

to 19 percent in thirty-six months."[38] By 2005, 49 percent of foreign service entrants were women and 22 percent were racial or ethnic minorities.

Minorities are still underrepresented in the foreign service. The situation is improving at the bottom but deteriorating at the top. Minority officers hired under affirmative action programs in the 1970s and early 1980s are now approaching retirement. Affirmative action programs diminished in the 1980s and 1990s as a matter of both policy and law, and as a result there are not enough minority officers in the middle grades to replace the retirees. One retiring officer called this change "decolorization." The diversity visible in the junior grades in 2007 will take fifteen or twenty years to reach the upper ranks.

Marc Grossman, director general of the foreign service in 2000 and 2001, said in 2005 that "the Alison Palmer lawsuit was one of the best things that happened to the State Department, because it forced the department to change its hiring and promotion practices." Without losing focus on the recruitment and promotion of women, Grossman said, additional effort is going into recruiting and retaining minorities. In particular, the department wants to increase the number of Hispanic Americans, who Grossman said are "woefully underrepresented" in the service. Building a foreign service that is "representative of the American people," as the Foreign Service Act requires, takes constant effort. "We work at this," said Grossman, "every single day."[39]

The Iranian Hostage Crisis

The Iranian hostage crisis of 1979 to 1981 put the foreign service more directly in the public eye than it had been since the McCarthy era. The attention this time was wholly favorable and deeply sympathetic, but a lasting impact of the crisis on the foreign service is hard to discern. The story bears retelling.

The shah of Iran, Reza Pahlavi, ascended to the Peacock Throne in 1941. U.S. support, and especially arms sales and military cooperation, helped to sustain him in that position for almost forty years. By the late 1970s, however, his grip on power was increasingly uncertain. In early 1978, demonstrations in support of Ruhollah Khomeini, an exiled Shiite cleric, brought thousands and then hundreds of thousands of Iranians into the streets. The shah abandoned his throne and fled to Egypt on January 16, 1979. Khomeini arrived in Tehran on February 1.

The revolution came as no great surprise to the foreign service officers serving in the Tehran embassy, nor to those in Washington who read their reports. L. Bruce Laingen, who assumed the post of chargé d'affaires (the person responsible for running an embassy in the absence of an ambassador) in Tehran in June 1979, said that embassy reporting on the shah's deteriorating position had been consistent and correct. In Laingen's view, the White House ignored or discounted foreign service reporting in favor of its own sources, who were closer to the shah than to the situation.[40] The memoirs of Cyrus Vance, then secretary of state, support Laingen's position in a backhanded way. Vance wrote that on November 9, 1978, two months before the shah fled to Egypt, "[Ambassador William] Sullivan sent a message that brought home how far the situation had deteriorated. . . . Sullivan's message corroborated the analysis of some State Department advisers, but caused consternation in the White House."[41]

In the chaos that followed the collapse of the shah's regime, the State Department acted quickly to reduce the American presence in the country. Embassy staff was cut from more than fourteen hundred to about seventy. Private Americans were urged to leave, and more than forty-five thousand did so.[42] Ambassador Sullivan left the post in April.

In late October 1979, the shah, suffering from lymphoma, entered the United States for medical treatment. Large demonstrations against the U.S. embassy began in Tehran a week later. On November 4 the embassy was overrun. Two days later, the provisional government, which might have provided help, itself collapsed. Khomeini, who may or may not have directed the seizure of the embassy, was pleased to keep his prize. Fifty-two hostages were held for 444 days, not for ransom (though the hostage takers demanded the return of the shah for trial in Iran) but to humiliate the United States. Most of the hostages were members of the foreign service. Many of the rest were members of the U.S. armed forces.[43]

The seizure of the embassy in Tehran was not the first assault against American diplomats. In the ten previous years, ten American diplomats had been murdered in eight incidents, and almost fifty more had survived thirty-seven incidents of kidnapping or kidnap attempts.[44] The Tehran attack, however, was different in scope, duration, and drama. The American Broadcasting Company, prodded by Roone Arledge, the imaginative president of its news division, gave extended late-night coverage to the story under the caption "America Held Hostage." The program, which featured foreign correspondent Ted Koppel, found and held a grimly fascinated audience for fourteen months.

A frustrated Carter administration launched a military rescue mission in April 1980 that ended in disaster, aborted in the Iranian desert with the loss of eight servicemen. Secretary Vance, who had opposed the mission, resigned. Tehran released the hostages the moment the administration left office, but only after a complex negotiation, conducted through intermediaries, had both unwound most of the sanctions Washington had imposed and renounced all present and future legal claims by U.S. persons, including the hostages, arising from the affair.[45]

The hostages acquitted themselves throughout the crisis with courage and grace. Many members of the foreign service believed that the stalwart behavior of the hostages and the outpouring of public support would change public and congressional attitudes toward the foreign service. They looked forward to a period of growth in the prestige and policy role of foreign service professionals, and to an increase in the budget of the Department of State. Former foreign service officer Andy Steigman wrote in 1985: "The Iranian hostage crisis suddenly and dramatically made Americans aware of the Foreign Service as they never had been before. By the time the 444 days of captivity were at an end, the United States had a new set of heroes—and the Foreign Service had a new image."[46]

Steigman was right about the heroes but wrong about the image. The public and the Congress embraced the hostages as individuals, but admiration for the way they had borne their ordeal did not carry over to the foreign service as an institution or to diplomacy as a profession. In the Hostage Relief Act of 1980, Congress provided benefits that came to a bit more than $50 per hostage per day, about what the presidential Commission on Hostage Compensation had recommended. The hostage crisis played no role in the legislative history of the Foreign Service Act of 1980, the most fundamental overhaul of the service since its creation in 1924.

Security from Tehran to Beirut to East Africa

The hostage crisis did lead to increased attention to physical security at posts abroad. The department launched a security enhancement program in 1980 to reduce the vulnerability of American overseas facilities to mob violence. Congress gave the department pretty much what it asked for in money and positions: $136 million and the equivalent of thirty-two positions over the six years from 1980 to 1985, levels that seemed quite high at the time but in retrospect were far too modest.

Any sense that the programs in place were adequate to the job ended in 1983. In April of that year, a suicide bomber drove a truck with a ton of explosives into the Beirut embassy, destroying the building and killing sixty-three people, including thirteen members of the foreign service. Six months later, in a similar attack, a suicide bomber drove a truck through wire barriers into the front of the U.S. Marine barracks near the Beirut airport, killing 241 American servicemen.

The Inman Report and the 1986 Act

Policies changed in response. Secretary of State George P. Shultz asked retired Admiral Bobby Ray Inman, a former deputy director of the Central Intelligence Agency, to lead a panel of experts to make detailed recommendations for improving embassy security. The Inman report, published in 1985, led directly to passage of the Omnibus Diplomatic Security and Antiterrorism Act of 1986 (the 1986 act), which provided nearly $2.5 billion for upgrading the physical security at American posts around the world.[47] Secretary Shultz also created, in 1985, the Overseas Security Advisory Council (OSAC), which brought private-sector organizations with an overseas presence (mainly commercial, but also religious, educational, and charitable groups) together with government representatives to address security concerns. OSAC today has more than 3,500 participating members.[48] Congress in 1984 established the Rewards for Justice Program, now administered by the department's Bureau of Diplomatic Security (DS), to provide reward money to those who provide information leading to the prevention or resolution of acts of terrorism and related crimes.

The Inman report led the department to create the Bureau of Diplomatic Security (DS) and the Diplomatic Security Service (DSS).[49] DS took on responsibility for the security of the people, the buildings, and the information at all State Department facilities, whether overseas or in the United States, and for the protection of foreign diplomats and high-level official visitors in the United States. The special agents of the Diplomatic Security Service quickly became by far the largest group of specialists in the foreign service.[50] Unlike their predecessors in the State Department's old Office of Security, DSS special agents are federal law enforcement officers. In 2006 they made more than 1,200 arrests, including 512 overseas in cooperation with local police for crimes involving visa and passport fraud, human trafficking, terrorism, and espionage.[51]

In addition to the DSS special agents, the Bureau of Diplomatic Security has foreign service specialists who are not law enforcement officers. They are the engineers and technicians who develop, install, manage, and maintain the department's technical security programs, and the diplomatic couriers who move classified material securely around the world.

The 1986 act made the secretary of state—and by extension the ambassador or chief of mission—responsible for protecting U.S. citizens abroad, and for the security of U.S. government personnel on official duty in his or her country.[52] To carry out that mandate, beginning in the late 1980s the department sent DSS agents overseas to take charge of security under the chief of mission's authority in virtually every American embassy. These agents kept the title regional security officer (RSO), a holdover from the days when professional security officers were so few in number that each had to cover several posts in several countries. By 2006 the DS bureau had about 450 special agents assigned to 258 embassies, consulates, and other posts worldwide.

Marine Security Guards

One element of post security did not change. The agents working as RSOs could continue to rely on a unique and splendid resource, the Marine Security Guards. Marines have had a role in protecting American diplomats and diplomatic property abroad since the early nineteenth century (William Eaton, American consul in Tunis, played a central role in the war that brought Marines to the shores of Tripoli in 1804), but the modern relationship between the State Department and the Marine Corps began after World War II, formalized in the Foreign Service Act of 1946. Marine guards protect classified material and provide a last, armed line of defense for the embassy and its personnel in the event of attack. They are assigned to most but not all embassies and to a few large constituent posts. They do not provide bodyguard security for the ambassador or other officials, and they have no authority or right to operate outside embassy grounds. The size of a detachment depends on the size of the facility it protects: there must be enough Marine guards to cover critical embassy locations around the clock. All members of the detachment are noncommissioned officers or enlisted personnel, and all are volunteers.

Marines have a vital and visible role in foreign service life. A Marine guard on duty is the first American that an embassy visitor sees. Marines raise and lower the embassy's flag at sunrise and sunset in a brief, emotionally powerful ceremony that brings those within sight of it to a halt. They also bring to the embassy traditions of the corps, including the annual Marine Corps Ball (dress blues, black tie) celebrating the anniversary of the founding of the corps on November 10, 1775. Where security permits, the Marines, all of whom apart from the detachment commander must be single, often entertain American and foreign service national personnel at their quarters, the Marine house, with barbecues, softball games, and parties. But they don't stick around. A Marine guard ordinarily spends three years in the program, one year at each of three different posts.

Many more Marines volunteer for this duty than there are positions available, and the corps applies high standards to make its selection. The exotic nature of the work does not make it cushy. Fourteen Marines have died in the line of duty as Marine security guards.

Accountability

The general acclaim that greeted the Inman commission led the Congress to look for ways to ensure that any future terrorist attacks or security failures would be followed by determinations of what went wrong and efforts to set it right. In the 1986 act, Congress required the secretary of state to convene an accountability review board (ARB), a temporary, ad hoc, independent group of experts armed with subpoena powers, to investigate and report on serious breaches of security at missions abroad involving loss of life and other incidents defined in the act.

Each ARB has an executive secretary, normally a senior foreign service officer. ARB members come from a roster maintained by the State Department's management bureau. Because ARB members need high-level security clearances to do their work, and because "only in exceptional circumstances" may they be federal employees, they are most often recent retirees from the foreign service, the intelligence community, or the military, or former senior noncareer officials with a background in security affairs. Each ARB sends a report to the secretary with findings and, at its discretion, recommendations on policy and personnel. The secretary then reports the recommendations and the department's response to them to the Congress. The ARB report and findings do not go to the Congress.

Ambassador Langhorne A. Motley served as chairman of an ARB that examined a 1987 bombing at the embassy in Lima, Peru. "We were able to figure out where the weaknesses were in that case," he said. "We had the independence we needed. Because we had a mandate from the Congress, we could deal effectively with the highest levels at State and with the other agencies involved. An ARB is a painful exercise, but it's a way to learn from failure."[53]

An amendment enacted at the end of 2005 made the ARB optional in the case of incidents involving loss of life at missions in Iraq and Afghanistan. Ambassador Gib Lanpher chaired three ARBs that investigated incidents that occurred in Iraq before the amendment became law. He was disappointed that the department initiated the amendment, even though the recommendations of his boards were not all adopted: "My boards believed that ARBs would still be useful in the case of Iraq because they bring an independent perspective to security issues outside the normal chain of command," he said. "We heard a lot of dissent and different perspectives that would not have surfaced in-house. Folks really let their hair down with us—and we assured them they would not be named in our reports. The DS people we worked extensively with valued our work and fully cooperated. They saw our effort as enhancing their ability to carry out their mandate."[54]

Worldwide Security Upgrades

Throughout the 1990s Congress continued to appropriate large sums to implement the Inman report, even as funds for other diplomatic purposes were cut and the ranks of the foreign service depleted by attrition (see table 2.3). The construction and retrofitting of embassy buildings to Inman standards, including the recommended setback of at least a hundred feet from roadways, proved harder and more expensive to accomplish than anticipated.

Car bombs struck the embassies in Nairobi and Dar es Salaam on August 7, 1998, killing 220 and injuring many more. Both embassies were older buildings that had not been brought up to Inman standards. Following those attacks, Congress funded an ongoing program of worldwide security upgrades. The program cost about $6.7 billion in its first ten years, and the administration requested another $800 million for FY 2008.

Table 2.3. Spending on International Affairs (Function 150)[a]

Fiscal Year	$ billions
1980	12.8
1981	13.6
1982	12.9
1983	13.6
1984	16.3
1985	17.4
1986	17.7
1987	15.2
1988	15.7
1989	16.6
1990	19.1
1991	19.7
1992	19.2
1993	21.6
1994	20.8
1995	20.1
1996	18.3
1997	19.0
1998	18.1
1999	19.5
2000	21.3
2001	22.5
2002	26.2
2003	27.9
2004	38.9
2005	35.6
2006	31.4
2007	32.6
2008 (estimate)	34.0
2009 (requested)	39.5

[a] Amounts in current dollars. Supplemental appropriations are not included. Function 150 and other budget matters are discussed in chapter 6.

Security demands have changed the face of American diplomacy. Embassies were once typically located in city centers, close to pedestrian and vehicular traffic. The U.S. Information Agency ran libraries and cultural centers that were easily, even eagerly, accessible to the public. After the Inman report the department began to move embassies from downtown to suburban areas, easier to protect but harder for people to reach. Libraries and cultural centers were closed, partly for security reasons and partly for lack of funding.

Whenever possible buildings were set back from roadways and guarded by walls, moats, and other barriers. Access, such as that to the State Department building in Washington, was restricted by identity checkpoints and metal detectors. In some places diplomats who lived scattered around the city were moved into compound housing adjacent to embassy offices.

Foreign service officers often complain that high levels of security make their work more difficult. It is harder for them to get to where they need to be, in the middle of the political, economic, and cultural life of the country, and it's harder for people—visa applicants, students, importers, members of the media—to get to them. The complaint is valid, but no one disputes the need to reduce the risk of another Beirut or another Nairobi. The 1998 East Africa embassy bombings resolved the tension between security and convenience decisively in favor of the former. The effort of agencies with an overseas presence is less to balance safety against other goals, and more to find new ways to carry out their missions that are consistent with high levels of security.

Diplomatic Readiness: Do More with More

Over the two decades following the Iranian hostage crisis, the motto for management in the foreign service was "do more with less." Especially in the 1990s, the administration's search for budget cuts and the desire to realize a "peace dividend" at the end of the cold war led to reductions in spending on international affairs and national security. Looking back on the period Defense Secretary Robert Gates saw "the gutting of America's ability to engage, assist, and communicate with other parts of the world."[55] Foreign service responsibilities grew, but foreign service ranks did not. Each year from 1993 to 2001, the State Department brought in too few new foreign service officers to replace departures. Staffing gaps became chronic, especially in the middle grades, and performance declined. In USAID, staffing levels that had reached fifteen thousand during the Vietnam war fell to around three thousand. The U.S. Information Agency was closed down entirely in 1999, its functions and personnel folded unhappily into the State Department.

The political disintegration of the Soviet Union and then Yugoslavia in the 1990s left twenty countries where only two had been. The strain of opening and staffing posts in these newly independent states left vacancies and exposed weaknesses throughout the service. By 2001 the staffing deficit left empty desks at more than seven hundred foreign service and six hundred civil service positions.[56] Training and leave were routinely curtailed.

Recruiting seemed unlikely to repair the damage. Primarily for budgetary reasons, entering classes in the 1980s and 1990s were small. Candidates who passed the exams faced a wait of two years or more to receive an appointment—and, of course, some of the best candidates found other things to do with their lives. Twice in the 1990s, the foreign service canceled the written exam. In 2000, the exam attracted only about eight thousand candidates, about half the usual number. The management consulting firm McKinsey and Company, in a widely read report titled *The War for Talent*, warned the department that foreign service had lost much of its attraction. McKinsey predicted that increasing numbers of officers would leave for private-sector employment. A blue-ribbon Overseas Presence Advisory Panel (OPAP), convened by Secretary of State Madeleine Albright in 1999, found "insecure and decrepit facilities, obsolete information technology, outmoded administrative and human resource practices, poor allocation of resources, and competition from the private sector." The panel concluded that these conditions placed America's diplomatic representation "near a state of crisis."[57]

Marc Grossman, then director general of the foreign service and head of human resources for the Department of State, remembered this period well. "There were gaps everywhere. We were spending huge amounts of time arguing over transfers—when you were going to leave post and when I was going to come. I couldn't send you to training because you had to be at post on such-and-such a day. The military didn't have this problem. I learned that our military colleagues have built a 15 percent float into staffing levels in every unit to cover transfers and training. I knew we had to do the same thing."[58]

Twenty years earlier, a small group of insiders had put together the early drafts of the Foreign Service Act of 1980. In 2000, Grossman assembled a similarly small group to draft the reforms that became the Diplomatic Readiness Initiative (DRI). With encouragement from Secretary Albright, Grossman and what he called his skunk works developed a plan for a rapid and dramatic increase in the size of the foreign service.[59] Then came the election.

"I was driving with a carful of kids through Bull Run Park to see the Christmas lights," Grossman recalled, "when Secretary-designate Powell called my cell phone. He said, 'I'm coming into the building tomorrow, and after I call on the secretary I want to call on you.' I said, 'If you call on me, there'll be a riot, so I'll call on you.'"

Grossman laid out the problem and his proposed solution: an increase in staffing to eliminate vacancies and provide a 15 percent float for training and transfers, 1,158 additional people, at a cost of $100 million per year.[60] Powell was enthusiastic. "'This is great,' the secretary-designate told me. 'We'll do it over three years.' And he took up the idea in his confirmation hearing and kept at it throughout his term. At the end of the three years we had all the positions we asked for."[61]

The DRI rebuilt the foreign service. "I never liked 'do more with less,'" Grossman said, "'Do more with more' had greater appeal." Thousands of other foreign service officers agreed with him. The recruitment budget, under $100,000 in 2001, jumped to more than $1.5 million, which gave the service the ability to aim recruitment efforts at underrepresented segments of the population. The number of candidates taking the foreign service exam rose from eight thousand to more than twenty thousand. The average hiring delay fell from twenty-seven months to nine months, and refusals of job offers fell from 25 percent to 2 percent. New testing procedures reduced the mismatch in skills between entrants and jobs and gave greater weight to critical languages like Arabic, Urdu, and Chinese. A boost in funding for the Foreign Service Institute, the State Department's training facility, allowed officers to receive more extensive and more frequent training at every level, including instruction in tradecraft for junior officers, added time for training in hard languages, and new courses in leadership and management. Measured by student hours, training expanded by 25 percent between 2000 and 2004.[62]

The DRI was under way before September 11, 2001. Planning did not include the demands of Afghanistan, or Iraq, or the need for more security personnel and visa officers. The DRI added 1,069 new foreign service personnel and created and filled more than two hundred new civil service positions. In addition, Congress approved the hiring of another 561 consular officers and 608 specialists in diplomatic security. By 2005, the service was bigger by more than two thousand than it had been four years earlier.[63]

The new hires raised the quality of the foreign service and made it more youthful. "In a way we were beneficiaries of the collapse of the dot–com boom," said Grossman. "We had been competing with dot–coms for these young people, and suddenly a shot at a pension didn't seem so bad." More than 50 percent had master's degrees, more than 10 percent had degrees in law. They moved quickly into midcareer positions, often directly from basic training.

"They came to us with new thoughts," Grossman continued. "They have a different sense of hierarchy. They want a flatter organization. They have a different sense of training—they think it's the employer's responsibility to provide a professional education. They speak more languages, they've been to more places. They have a very different sense of the balance of work and family. And they are much more technologically adept. They bring huge pressure on us to modernize. They will be our revolutionaries, throughout the system. They will insist that we change."

3
·

The Foreign Service Today

This book opened with a question: "What do we need them for?" The answer in the Foreign Service Act of 1980 is dry but clear. The foreign service, it says, exists to "represent the interests of the United States in relation to foreign countries and international organizations," to "provide guidance for the formulation and conduct of programs and activities of the Department [of State] and other agencies," and to "perform functions on behalf of any agency or other Government establishment (including any establishment in the legislative or judicial branch) requiring their services."[1]

The Department of State is the government's lead agency in foreign affairs, and the secretary of state is the president's chief foreign policy adviser (to be sure, on any given issue both the department and the secretary have plenty of competition). The Foreign Service Act says that "the Secretary of State shall administer and direct the Service," but other agencies, including the USAID, Agriculture, and Commerce, "may utilize the Foreign Service personnel system."

No matter what agency they work for, all foreign service personnel are paid on the same salary scale and have access to the same retirement, insurance, and other benefits. An interagency Foreign Service Board, set up in 1982, is supposed to ensure "maximum compatibility" among the personnel systems of the foreign service agencies. But within the limits of the law, each agency establishes its own rules and policies for recruitment, hiring, training, assignment, and promotion. Exchanges of personnel between foreign service agencies are rare, and personnel transfers from one agency to another rarer still.

The foreign service and the civil service are civilian institutions established by law to ensure that the work of government is carried forward professionally, without partisanship or taint of corruption. Their similarities of purpose and design are great, but the differences in their missions lead to important differences in the rights and obligations that each service offers to and demands of its members. Four features in particular distinguish the foreign service.

Table 3.1. The Foreign Service in Round Numbers, 2007

Agency	U.S. Personnel	Remarks
Department of State	11,500	Generalists, 6,600 Specialists, 4,900
Agency for International Development	1,300	
Department of Commerce	200	Foreign Commercial Service
Department of Agriculture	250	Foreign Agricultural Service, 175 Animal and Plant Health Inspection Service, 75
Total	13,250	

First is *rank in person*. Members of the foreign service, like members of the military, have a personal rank that determines base pay. Rank in the regular foreign service is designated by a number, starting at nine and rising to one. Members of the senior foreign service have ranks designated with titles: counselor, minister-counselor, and career minister. Rank is in the person, and pay is linked to rank. In the civil service, however, rank and pay are in the position, not in the person. The Office of Personnel Management (OPM) maintains a general schedule (GS) of pay grades, and each civil service position in the federal government has a pay grade associated with it. A civil service employee who changes jobs may end up with a pay raise or a pay cut, depending on whether the new job has a higher or lower pay grade than the old one. A foreign service employee who changes jobs keeps the same base salary.[2]

Second is *worldwide availability*. Members of the foreign service may be sent anywhere in the world. They can expect to spend about two-thirds of their careers abroad. They have a voice in choosing their assignments, but in the end they must respond to the needs of the service. Civil service personnel, however, are routinely assigned to domestic positions only; overseas assignments are voluntary and exceptional. In mid-2007, about two hundred members of the civil service were assigned abroad.

Third is *up or out*. After a certain number of years in grade without promotion, or years in service without advancement to the senior ranks, a foreign service officer faces mandatory retirement. Officers may also be forced to retire for substandard performance (selection out). Civil servants face no such requirements.

Fourth is *early retirement* at the option of the employee. Foreign service personnel may retire as early as age fifty with twenty years of service.

Retirement in the civil service is ordinarily at age fifty-five with thirty years of service, or at sixty with twenty years of service. In congressional testimony over many years, the foreign service has defended its more generous retirement benefits by pointing to the hardship of worldwide availability and the insecurity of up or out. Congress has agreed.

The Department of State

Understanding the foreign service begins with the Department of State. The two organizations are distinct but inseparable.

There is no better introduction to the Department of State than a visit to the building that has housed it since 1947.[3] Over the years, the building and the department, like a pet and its owner, have come to resemble each other. Like the department, the Harry S Truman Building, more often called Main State, is somewhat removed from Washington's federal center. It stands about two miles west of the White House in a part of town called Foggy Bottom, a name beloved of columnists looking for an easy joke. The building covers more than two city blocks, but there is nothing grand about it. Like a diplomatic communiqué, it is featureless and forgettable in shape, color, and material. The windows do not open.

Approach the department from any direction and you will encounter Jersey walls, concrete planters, steel bollards, and dragon's teeth that force pedestrians to choose between a slalom course around the barriers or a mogul course over them. Visitors must pass through metal detectors even before they enter the marble lobby, where they queue twice, once to check in with a receptionist and again to wait for an escort. When a VIP shows up, protocol officers and security personnel clear a path through the crowd.

The security is certainly not excessive. The State Department is an obvious target for terrorists looking for symbols of America's international reach, and it has been repeatedly stung by spectacular security failures. In 1985, even though security had been tightened following the attacks on the U.S. embassy and Marine barracks in Beirut two years earlier, a visitor managed to bring a rifle into the building and murder his mother, a secretary, near the office of Secretary of State George P. Shultz. In 1998 a recording device, believed to have been planted by a Russian agent, was found in a conference room used by the secretary of state and other senior officials. In 2000 a laptop computer containing highly classified information disappeared from a conference room in a secure area. Neither the computer nor the culprits were ever found.

At either end of the lobby are memorials to foreign service personnel who lost their lives in the line of duty. On the left as you enter, a plaque bears the names, dates, and places of death of ninety-seven officers who died while on active duty "under heroic or tragic circumstances," from William Palfrey, lost at sea in 1780, to Robert R. Little, killed in Vietnam in 1968. Most died of disease or in natural disasters. A newer plaque on the opposite wall bears, as of July 2007, the names of 128 persons "serving their country abroad in foreign affairs" who died "under heroic and inspirational circumstances," from Stephen Miller in Vietnam in 1968 to Margaret Alexander in Nepal in 2006. Most of these died in warfare or terrorist attacks. Six of those listed died in Iraq.[4]

The flags of the countries with which the United States has diplomatic relations hang from a gallery above the lobby in English-language alphabetical order, from Afghanistan to Zimbabwe. Among the missing flags are Cuba's, Iran's, and North Korea's.

The building is a grid with windowless corridors. Visitors and even employees routinely lost their way until 1974, when Nancy Maginnes Kissinger, wife of the then secretary, asked that each corridor be blazed in a different color.

Physically and bureaucratically, the State Department is hierarchical. Vertical location in the building, indicated by the first digit of the room number, is a rough indication of vertical location in the department's chain of command (see appendix A):

- secretary
- deputy secretary
- undersecretary
- assistant secretary (who heads a bureau)
- deputy assistant secretary
- office director (whose office may have more than one division)
- deputy office director
- division chief

Offices of the secretary of state, the deputy secretary, and the undersecretaries are on the seventh floor, with the highest-ranking officials in the offices closest to the secretary. The executive secretariat, which manages information for the seventh-floor principals, is also based there, as is the operations center, a 24/7 hub for crisis management. "The trick to this place," said one old hand, "is to get as close as you can to the center of power without stepping inside the circle of abuse."

For practical purposes, the seventh is the top floor. For ceremonies, however, the eighth floor offers a balcony with a magnificent view and reception rooms that private donors have furnished with artifacts of America's early diplomatic history: the desk on which the Treaty of Paris was signed in 1783, a Houdon bust of Benjamin Franklin dated 1778, an 1816 portrait of John Quincy Adams painted when the future president was minister to Great Britain.

Most assistant secretaries are on the sixth floor. Surrounded by their deputies, they occupy office suites with conference rooms, sitting areas, and, for the boss, a private washroom. Proximity counts. The front offices of the six geographic bureaus, and the office of the foreign service's director general, are directly below the offices of the secretary of state and the other principals. Assistant secretaries who lead other bureaus make do with less prized territory.

Most office directors and below are on floors five, four, and three. The second floor holds the department's press and public affairs operations and much of the machinery and equipment that service the rest of the building. The first floor holds the protocol office, the cafeteria, two large auditoriums, several smaller conference rooms, and the family liaison office.

Washington jargon gives buildings human powers and characteristics: The White House says, the Pentagon wants, Treasury insists, Commerce drags its feet. In the Department of State, this kind of language is applied to floors—and to letters. Letter codes designate all State Department offices. The secretary of state is S. The executive secretariat is S/ES, which manages information flow to seventh-floor principals like P, the undersecretary for political affairs, or M, the undersecretary for management. The Bureau of East Asian and Pacific Affairs is EAP, the Office of Japanese Affairs (also called the Japan desk) is EAP/J, and so forth. It is quite possible for the seventh floor to be furious when S/ES bounces a memo that P tasked to EAP back to J, because the sixth floor did not sign off.[5]

Readers with a sense of geometry may wonder how the pyramid of State's hierarchy fits into the cube of the Main State building. The question has a three-part answer.

First and most obvious is that high-ranking officials have larger offices. The office of the secretary of state would probably hold some two dozen employees if it were on the third or fourth floors.

Second and most important is that State's pyramid is not steep. The department is seriously top heavy. In Washington it has about fifty officials with the rank equivalent to assistant secretary or above—roughly one for every 650 employees.[6] The Treasury Department, by contrast, has only thirty such officials—roughly one for every 4,500 employees. The big-shot-to-small-fry ratio at State is affected by the large number of high-ranking officials with narrowly defined jobs and relatively small staffs. State has, for example, an assistant secretary for verification, compliance, and implementation (of arms control agreements); an assistant secretary for democracy, human rights, and labor affairs; an assistant secretary for population, refugees, and migration; a senior coordinator for international women's issues; and a global AIDS coordinator. Some of these posts were created at high levels in response to public or congressional pressure, or to provide the incumbents with the rank needed to deal on an equal footing with foreign counterparts.

One organizational result of the proliferation of assistant secretaries is the proliferation of even higher officials to oversee them. State has six undersecretaries and two deputy secretaries to Treasury's three and one.

Third and most promising is that the cube isn't big enough to hold the pyramid. Offices are a jumble of cubicles and warrens, and some spill out into the corridors. Many more are housed outside the building entirely, in the forty-five State annexes around Washington linked to Main State by shuttle buses. C. Northcote Parkinson, the British aphorist and student of large organizations, once observed that a bureaucracy that fits in its building is in serious trouble. "Perfection of planned layout," he wrote, "is achieved only by institutions on the point of collapse." By this standard, the Department of State is full of vigorous good health. The hierarchy of the building, like the hierarchy of the foreign service, keeps breaking down under pressure from below.

As of June 2007, ten of the department's fifty top officials were career members of the foreign service. The highest ranking were Deputy Secretary John D. Negroponte and Undersecretary for Political Affairs Nicholas Burns. Ambassador Burns's post, undersecretary for political affairs, is traditionally reserved for a member of the career foreign service.

Three members of the career foreign service have served as deputy secretary of state: Walter Stoessel (1982–83), Lawrence Eagleburger (1989–92), and John Negroponte (2007–). Lawrence Eagleburger was nominated as secretary of state and confirmed by the Senate in time to serve six weeks in that position, from December 1992 to January 1993. He is the only foreign service officer to hold that office.

"The Foreign Service, the Civil Service, and Foreign Service Nationals"

State employs about 57,000 people, including about 19,000 U.S. citizens and 38,000 foreign staff. Of the Americans, about 11,500 work in Washington and 7,500 work overseas. Essentially all of the 38,000 non-Americans work abroad. These include foreign service nationals, or FSNs, directly hired by U.S. missions abroad, as well as local citizens hired under personal-service agreements. Foreign service nationals and other local hires are almost always nationals of the country in which they live and work, but a few resident Americans and third-country nationals also work in U.S. missions overseas. Locally employed staff (LES) may also include family members of American employees at the mission.

Except for about two hundred civil servants on one-time overseas assignments, the 7,500 Americans who work for the State Department overseas are almost all members of the foreign service. There are only 11,500 Americans in the State Department's foreign service, so it is easy to calculate that, on average, a member of State's foreign service spends about two-thirds of his or her career outside the United States. Additionally, U.S. missions overseas employ a small but growing number of private Americans, either foreign service family members or Americans residing overseas. Foreign service nationals and locally hired Americans are sometimes counted together under the LES rubric.

State's foreign service personnel are either generalists (about 6,600) or specialists (about 4,900). The generalists, more often called foreign service officers, or FSOs, get most of the public's attention. In an embassy, they are the political, economic, public affairs, consular, and management officers. The specialists handle communications and information, take care of the money, maintain the buildings, organize and provide security, manage the personnel system, and in general keep things running and humming.

Not included in any of these numbers are foreign service retirees who return to work, receiving their pension plus salary up to their last salary level. Because they are paid a salary only "when actually employed," they carry the acronym WAE. At the beginning of 2007 State had about seven hundred of these WAE personnel back in harness, more than 5 percent of the workforce, and about half of the fourteen hundred retirees who had notified the department of their availability for assignment.

State also employs about eight thousand members of the civil service. Inside the department, foreign service and civil service employees do the same kind of work in the same bureaucratic structure. A foreign service officer or specialist may report to a civil service boss, or vice versa—but they operate under different rules, with different rights and obligations. The foreign service is governed by the Foreign Service Act of 1980.[7] The civil service is covered by the Civil Service Reform Act of 1979, as amended. The director general (DG) of the foreign service is also the director of human resources for State, and so has responsibility for the department's civil service as well as foreign service employees. But when the DG makes decisions affecting the department's civil servants, he or she must follow the regulations and policies of the Office of Personnel Management, an independent federal agency that administers nearly two million civil service employees throughout the federal government. The DG has a freer hand with the foreign service.

On formal occasions the leadership of the Department of State refers to the department's staff as "the foreign service, the civil service, and foreign service nationals." Repetition of this phrase is intended to emphasize the integration of these three categories of employees into a single team. The phrase is hard to say, but it is nonetheless easier said than done. The prejudices and resentments that marred the conversion of civil service employees to foreign service status in the 1950s and 1960s are long gone, but the real differences in the personnel systems constrain managers and affect attitudes.

Other Agencies

The Department of State is not the only place where members of the foreign service work. The U.S. Agency for International Development employs about thirteen hundred foreign service officers and five thousand foreign service nationals in its worldwide operations. The U.S. Department of Agriculture's Foreign Agricultural Service, which promotes the export of American food and agricultural products, has about 175 foreign service officers working in U.S. embassies and consulates as agricultural counselors and attachés.[8] The U.S. Commercial Service, the trade promotion arm of the Department of Commerce, includes about 230 foreign service officers—the Foreign Commercial Service—who staff positions abroad as commercial counselors, senior commercial officers, and attachés, and more than a thousand foreign service nationals. There are some foreign service personnel employed in the Peace Corps and the International Broadcasting Bureau (IBB), which includes the Voice of America, Radio Marti, and Radio Sawa. Many active-duty members of the foreign service work under various arrangements elsewhere in government or in the private sector, for the National Security Council staff, the Department of Defense, other federal agencies, the U.S. Congress, state and local governments, and for-profit and nonprofit corporations, but they remain employees of their home agencies, to which they normally return.

The Foreign Service Act of 1980 lays down a few basic rules that apply to all foreign-service agencies, among them rank-in-person, worldwide availability, up-or-out, and early retirement. The American Foreign Service Association (AFSA) is the professional association of the U.S. Foreign Service and represents foreign service employees in collective bargaining with their employers, the departments of State, Commerce, and Agriculture, the Agency for International Development, and the IBB.[9] AFSA is one of the few unifying elements in a service whose agency employment rules and personnel systems have little in common beyond the basic structures of the 1980 act. For example, the Department of State hires mainly through competitive examination and requires a period of probation before granting full employment, called tenure. Other agencies do things differently. Part III of this book describes the career paths open to the State Department's foreign service personnel in detail. The foreign service in other agencies is dealt with in summary in the section below.

Agency for International Development

After the State Department, the Agency for International Development, referred to as either AID or USAID, employs the largest number of foreign service personnel—about 1,300 foreign service officers and about 4,700 foreign service nationals in field missions in eighty-nine countries (2007). The agency has about seventeen hundred positions in the United States, filled by twelve hundred civil service and five hundred foreign service personnel.

AID is the most operational of the foreign service agencies. In 2007, spending on employee salaries and other direct operating costs was less than seven percent of appropriations. The rest went to programs.[10] Its foreign service officers run programs, manage budgets, and try to accomplish fairly specific objectives over relatively short periods of time. Some foreign service people in State do similar work, but at AID programs and operations are the rule, rather than the rarity.

When President Kennedy established AID in 1961, its personnel were not part of the career foreign service. AID was created as a temporary agency, and most people working for it were not expected to stay for the length of their career. Foreign assistance, though, evolved into a permanent feature of

U.S. foreign policy. By 1980, when the Foreign Service Act was rewritten, AID clearly needed a permanent staff of skilled professionals ready to serve throughout the developing world. The extension of the foreign service to AID in the 1980 act provoked no controversy.

Not so the agency's mission. The battles in Congress and within the administration over how much to spend on foreign aid and how and where to spend it make the agency vulnerable to sharp swings in funding and frequent reorganization (see chapter 2, note 16). Douglas Broome, the AID senior labor management advisor at the American Foreign Service Association, saw scores of these battles during his career at AID.

> *The budgets for programs and for operations—for the staff and infrastructure needed to manage the programs—are rarely synchronized, especially given how quickly operating funds are expended, in the year they are appropriated, with program funds frequently staying in the pipeline, to be spent only over several years. Programs may be expanding while the capacity to manage them is shrinking, which can lead to poor management and waste. Or programs may be shrinking while staff is growing, which can lead to reorganizations, hiring freezes, and other dislocations. The administrators who come in to run this agency have an impossible task.*[11]

Like the foreign service in the Department of State, AID's foreign service lost positions in the mid-1990s. State let its foreign service ranks shrink through attrition, hiring fewer new officers than were needed to replace retirements and resignations. AID stopped hiring entirely in 1995 and then laid off about two hundred active-duty civil service and foreign service personnel, and as many as eight hundred foreign service nationals. Government workers call layoffs a reduction in force, or RIF. In 1996, AID riffed 10 percent of its American employees and pulled out of more than twenty-five countries. In the federal government, a 10 percent RIF is carnage. Around the same time, AID's Washington headquarters moved from crowded but comfortable offices in the Harry S Truman Building to spartan cubicles in the new Ronald Reagan Building. Many in AID worried that the agency was in terminal decline.

Not so. The *National Security Strategy* issued in September 2002, the document that presented the doctrine of preventive war, also defined development as a component of national security, along with defense and democracy.[12] It assigned to development the most ambitious national security goals: shoring up weak states like Afghanistan that might become safe harbors for terrorists, supporting strategic states like Pakistan that are allies in the war on terrorism, transforming vulnerable states through support for the infrastructure of democracy and free markets, responding to humanitarian needs and crises, and addressing global concerns like the spread of HIV/AIDS. Between 2001 and 2004, U.S. foreign aid budgets doubled.

AID had no counterpart to the State Department's diplomatic readiness initiative, but the new attention to, and funding for, foreign assistance programs restored the agency's prestige. In early 2006 Secretary Rice announced a number of changes that reflected the new national security strategy and pointed to a bigger role for AID in carrying out U.S. foreign policy. Most important, the administrator of AID, the agency's top official, was given the additional title of director of foreign assistance and charged with creating and directing "consolidated policy, planning, budget and implementation mechanisms and staff functions" for all U.S. foreign assistance programs, including those run by agencies other than AID. The director of foreign assistance had a rank equivalent to deputy secretary of state and was given a splendid suite in the renovated Marshall wing at Main State (see note 3). In keeping with departmental practice, which calls the secretary S and her deputy D, the new position also acquired a letter, an unfortunate F.[13]

Douglas Broome said that some AID officers reacted to this news with fear that their agency would be absorbed by the Department of State and their programs politicized. Some outside of AID had a different view. Ambassador L. Craig Johnstone, who handled budgets and resource allocation at the State Department in the late 1990s, observed that AID people have learned how to run big programs. That is a skill that the State Department generally lacks, he said, and in an era of transformational diplomacy, one that it badly needs. Closer integration of AID and State, said Johnstone, could make both agencies stronger.[14]

AID's foreign service personnel system differs from State's in several respects. First, there is no written entry exam. Candidates for AID's foreign service positions respond to job offers published on the agency's website, and if their paperwork looks good they will be interviewed. Successful candidates have five years to achieve tenure, a decision made by a tenuring board. Like foreign service officers in the Department of State, tenured officers can expect to spend about twenty years in the middle grades. The most successful will then go on to the senior foreign service. Although AID hires people with specialized skills—agricultural economists, sanitation engineers, experts in small business finance—AID does not divide its foreign service into generalists and specialists.

Historically, promotions have come a bit faster for AID officers than for their counterparts at State. Despite the increasing integration of the two entities, this pattern may persist for a number of years. AID has a shortage of midlevel officers—a legacy of the hiring freeze of the mid-1990s—and that vacuum will be filled by the junior officers who now make up 40 percent of AID's foreign service. If Craig Johnstone is right, the demand for foreign service officers who have run complex programs and managed large budgets is likely to increase. That could mean increased responsibilities and professional opportunities for AID's best people.

Commerce and the Foreign Commercial Service

The Commerce Department is a giant grab bag of an agency. Domestic functions that have no obvious relationship to each other account for the great bulk of the department's $6.5 billion budget and its forty thousand employees. The largest unit, with 30 percent of the staff and 50 percent of the budget, is the National Oceanic and Atmospheric Administration, which includes the National Marine Fisheries Service and the National Weather Bureau. Twenty-five percent of the staff and 17 percent of the budget go to the Census Bureau. Twenty percent of the staff work in the Patent and Trademark Office, which in budget scoring costs less than nothing because the revenue the office generates from fees exceeds its outlays.

The lack of coherence among the department's agencies and administrations briefly made it a target of fiscal conservatives. In 1995 Republican members of the House of Representatives, in the majority for the first time in fifty years and feeling their oats, proposed closing the Commerce Department, killing some of its functions and assigning the rest elsewhere. Their effort failed, but Commerce management has run a bit scared ever since. The department, including the Foreign Commercial Service, devotes considerable effort to documenting and justifying its performance.

Inside the Commerce Department, the Foreign Commercial Service operates out of the International Trade Administration (ITA), which has about 6 percent of the department's budget and 7 percent of its staff. The FCS is headed by an assistant secretary, one of four reporting to the head of ITA, the undersecretary for international trade. The FCS, which operates in about 150 overseas posts in about ninety countries, is part of the U.S. Commercial Service, which also maintains 107 offices in the United States. The annual budget for the entire commercial service, foreign and domestic, is about $250 million.

The Foreign Commercial Service protects U.S. commercial interests and promotes U.S. exports of goods and services. Its overseas locations are chosen to cover the regions offering the best prospects for U.S. trade and investment. Where the FCS is absent, foreign service officers from State handle commercial work.

The Commerce Department and its Foreign Commercial Service have a difficult relationship. Commerce's foreign service personnel are a bit lost among the forty thousand members of the civil service that staff the agency's domestic positions, including the domestic field offices of the U.S. Commercial Service. There are about two hundred foreign service officers at Commerce, and nearly all of them are overseas. There are only eight positions for foreign service officers at FCS Washington headquarters, and opportunities for service in the domestic field offices are rare. The Commerce Department frequently waives rules that limit consecutive years of service overseas, simply because it has no stateside positions for its foreign service personnel.

Ambassador Charles Ford, a member of the FCS from its inception, wrote that "the Foreign Service has yet to find a comfortable coexistence with the Civil Service culture of the Commerce Department and its International Trade Administration." In contrast to the foreign service components of AID, Agriculture, and of course State, Ford said that senior foreign service officers at Commerce "have no real opportunity to serve in program and policy positions in Washington." Ford also said that although the budget for the Foreign Commercial Service doubled between the mid-1990s and 2005, administrative overhead (now 25 percent of outlays) took much of the increase, and foreign service staffing levels remained constant.[15]

The Foreign Commercial Service recruits new officers every other year. There is no written exam. Candidates who successfully complete an online screening process are invited to a day-long oral assessment exercise, and perhaps 20 to 30 percent of those will receive conditional job offers, with a waiting period from offer to entry that may run as long as two years.

New recruits to the Foreign Commercial Service on average begin their careers at a higher pay grade than junior foreign service officers at the Department of State. Because the FCS has relatively few junior or senior positions, a twenty-year career in the foreign service at Commerce is likely to begin at a higher level and end at a lower one than at State.

Agriculture and the Foreign Agricultural Service

Like the Department of Commerce, the Department of Agriculture maintains a small foreign service in a huge domestic agency. USDA employs about

110,000 people. Its Foreign Agricultural Service (FAS) has about 175 foreign service officers, 150 foreign service nationals, and 600 civil service personnel.[16] Like AID, the Foreign Agricultural Service administers billion-dollar programs on a million-dollar budget. To be precise, in fiscal year 2006 the foreign agricultural service had an operating budget of $217 million. FAS programs, including export credits and credit guarantees, market development programs, and food aid, were budgeted at $5.1 billion.

The foreign agricultural service represents American agriculture, and increasingly the U.S. food industry, around the world. Its central mission is exports, but the work goes well beyond trade promotion. "Traditionally we think of our job in three parts," said Chuck Alexander, a thirty-year veteran of the service. "We do policy, reporting, and market development. All of these are changing now. Going forward we'll be putting more emphasis on policy, on getting access to markets, and we'll leave market development more and more to the private sector."[17]

Reporting is changing as well. "Reporting is critical to policy," Alexander said, "because it leads to analysis. In the past we focused on maintaining our database, providing raw data. But we've got to do more sectoral, big-picture analysis. For example, what do rising oil prices mean for global demand for ethanol, and what does that mean for sugar prices, and what does that mean for U.S. policy? Can we get rid of our sugar import quotas? We need to look at these global connections. It's pretty interesting stuff."

FAS stands out among foreign service agencies in several ways. It is small: "Everybody knows everybody. Nothing we do is ever impersonal," said Alexander. It is focused: "We know exactly what we're supposed to do, and we do it." It is well supported: "We have a constituency, American agriculture, that historically has gotten pretty much what it wants on Capitol Hill. And we serve them well." That view is shared by other agencies and by American ambassadors around the world. "In my experience," Alexander said, "no ambassador has ever opposed the addition of an agricultural officer to his staff, or has ever called for a cut. We're highly valued members of the embassy team."

The needs of American agriculture are changing, however, and FAS has had to adapt. The agency's work is more technical than it was a generation ago. "It's biotechnology, avian influenza, bovine spongiform encephalopathy [mad cow disease]. We used to recruit agricultural economists, mostly midwestern farm boys like me," said Alexander. "Now we need a different kind of expertise." FAS no longer insists on a farming background. "If you're overseas talking to farmers, you'd better know something about farming. But if you're going to spend your career in Brussels or Geneva negotiating trade rules and talking to bureaucrats, you don't have to be all that familiar with production agriculture."

Brussels and Geneva are important, but they are not at the center of action. FAS has more people—five—in Beijing than in any other post, and positions are being cut in Western Europe to add to the China contingent. Other new positions are opening in India, Vietnam, and Central America.

Redeployment can only temporarily relieve the shortages that the demand for new positions creates. FAS also needs to grow. Like the other foreign service agencies, FAS lost personnel in the late 1990s. At 175, its American foreign service officer corps is almost 20 percent below its 1995 peak. The service now plans to grow slowly until it reaches a level of around 190 officers around 2015.

As FAS grows, its median age will fall. The employment rules of the Foreign Service Act, including voluntary retirement at age fifty and up-or-out retirement for officers who are not promoted, took effect in the Foreign Agricultural Service in 1984. By 2006, 40 percent of FAS officers were eligible for retirement, and four officers faced mandatory retirement for time in service. These officers in their fifties and sixties will be replaced by officers in their twenties and thirties.

The new foreign service officers will all be people already working in FAS. Alone among the foreign service agencies, FAS does not recruit directly for its foreign service. A candidate must join FAS first in a civil service position, through either an internship or the civil service competitive process, before he or she can apply for entry to the foreign service through written and oral examinations. Proponents of this practice say it ensures compatibility and quality even in the junior ranks. Critics ask why filling foreign service vacancies should depend on civil service vacancies being filled first, especially when the skills required may not match up. They add that new hires coming in through the career intern program spend two years in FAS before achieving permanent civil service status, thereby becoming eligible to apply for the foreign service; that's a long waiting period. Meanwhile, a hiring freeze, induced by tight budgets in the 2004 and 2005 fiscal years and by plans to reorganize much of the department, keeps the pool of potential applicants small. FAS could find that it will have to change its policies or operate below optimal strength for quite a number of years.

Part II

•

The Profession

4

•

Form and Content

Members of the foreign service like to say that they are professionals, and not just in the sense that they are paid for their work. They see diplomacy as a profession—a set of skills to be mastered through apprenticeship and training, with restrictions on entry, advancement by merit, and codes of behavior.

But diplomacy is different from other professions. Unlike the law, medicine, teaching, or preaching, amateurs are allowed to participate. There are no sanctions for being diplomatic without a license.[1] Anyone formally designated by a sending state and accredited by a receiving state is a certified diplomat, with rights and obligations under international law. In the United States, there are only two credentials for service in a high diplomatic position: nomination by the president, and confirmation by the senate.

Professionals are proud of their craft, and when elected officials name political friends as ambassadors or assistant secretaries, career diplomats fret. Career foreign service personnel tend to presume that political appointees, at least those without credentials, are incompetent until proven otherwise. The ratio of career to political appointees under President Kennedy was about two to one, and that rough standard has prevailed ever since. The American Foreign Service Association—which is simultaneously the professional society for American diplomats and the collective-bargaining agent for American foreign service personnel at State, Commerce, Agriculture, and USAID—keeps count, and sometimes it speaks out on the subject.[2]

The numbers game has its silly side. After all, the foreign service is a career. It is diplomacy that is the profession, and you do not have to belong to the foreign service to be a professional diplomat. Zalmay Khalilzad, the highly regarded American ambassador to Afghanistan (2003–5), Iraq (2005–7), and the United Nations (2007–) moves between think tanks like RAND and Cambridge Energy Research Associates, and government service with the National Security Council staff, the Department of State, and the Department of Defense; he is not a member of the foreign service, but

51

diplomacy has become his profession. Peter Galbraith left the staff of the Senate Foreign Relations Committee to become U.S. ambassador to Croatia (1993–98), where he was credited with putting together the agreement that ended the Muslim-Croat war. He later worked in East Timor for the United Nations. Robert Gallucci, who led the nuclear negotiations with North Korea during the Clinton administration, was a State Department civil servant with no overseas experience; he later became dean of the Georgetown University School of Foreign Service. Richard Holbrooke, ambassador to Germany (1993–94) and to the United Nations (1999–2001) and twice assistant secretary of state (for East Asian affairs, 1977–81, and for European affairs, 1994–96), joined the foreign service in 1962 but resigned a decade later. The Department of State considers Ambassador Holbrooke a noncareer appointee.[3] Ambassador Dennis Ross, who with various titles was the chief U.S. negotiator on Middle East issues from 1988 to 2000, came into government from an academic background and was not a foreign service officer. Richard Armitage, Colin Powell's deputy secretary of state (2001–5), is a U.S. Navy veteran who under presidential assignment in the 1990s handled diplomatic missions in the Philippines, the Middle East, and the former Soviet Union. Under the last eight secretaries of state, from Haig to Rice, three of the nine undersecretaries for political affairs, traditionally the highest post held by a career foreign service officer, have been noncareer appointees.[4]

The United States is one of the few countries to make widespread use of nonprofessionals in high diplomatic posts. The Philippines does so, perhaps as a legacy of American colonial rule. Poland also sometimes uses nonprofessionals. Presidents in some Latin American, and especially Central American, countries from time to time offer foreign embassies to military and political figures, usually to get them out of the way. Nearly everywhere else, however, the top diplomatic jobs go to people who devote their lives to diplomatic service.

If you don't have to be a professional to be a diplomat, you also don't have to be a diplomat to practice diplomacy. When Hu Jintao, the president of China, came to the United States in April 2006, his first stop was Washington State, not Washington, D.C. He spent his first evening at dinner with Bill and Melinda Gates. "Increasingly," wrote the *Seattle Post-Intelligencer*, "the Microsoft billionaire and his palatial Medina estate serve as an extension of the State Department. Sort of a White House West."[5] Hu's second day in the United States began with a Boeing plant tour and a speech to Boeing employees. President Hu certainly had a diplomatic purpose in arranging these meetings: He intended to confront American protectionism by showing how important China is to companies that create jobs and wealth for hundreds of thousands of Americans. Bill Gates and Jim McNerney, Gates's counterpart at Boeing, were practicing diplomacy as well, trying to influence Chinese policies and purchasing decisions and inevitably affecting the Chinese leader's view of the United States.

Diplomatic Traditions and Protocol

Diplomacy is an ancient practice, but as a profession it is merely old. Harold Nicolson, the British diplomat and scholar, says that the origins of diplomacy "lie buried in the darkness" of prehistory. Modern diplomacy, however, he traces to the France of Louis XIV and Cardinal Richelieu. The French system, as Nicolson named it, replaced the opportunistic scheming of Byzantium and Machiavelli's Italian states with permanent negotiations aimed at "solid and durable relations" that furthered "national interests" and had support in "national opinion." Richelieu and his disciple François de Callières taught that successful negotiation depends on building confidence, which in turn depends on avoidance of lies. Callières urged that diplomacy be treated as a profession, with appointments and advancement according to talent, and with regular payment.[6]

Emerging nation-states in Europe followed the French example. They set up ministries of foreign affairs to centralize policy, and they sent and received permanent resident embassies to conduct negotiations with other states. The formulation of policy in foreign ministries, and the pursuit of policy through resident embassies, dominated diplomatic practice from the eighteenth well into the twentieth century.

Diplomats operating in the French system confronted a number of problems that continue to bedevil foreign service professionals today. Receiving states often regarded embassies with deep suspicion, as nests of spies and agents of subversion. They kept diplomats physically isolated in compounds and socially isolated in endless and expensive rounds of official obligations. (Even where receiving states are less hostile, American foreign service officers today complain that security requirements keep them in compounds, and reporting requirements, often of dubious value, keep them at their desks.) Diplomats also provoked suspicion in their native lands, where their long sojourns among foreigners left them out of touch with domestic matters and vulnerable to charges that they lacked, if not patriotism, then patriotic fervor.

Cut off or estranged from the local population and thrown upon each other's company, diplomats gossiped and pooled information and found they had much in common. The sense of shared hardships produced what Callières called a "freemasonry of diplomacy," a professional bond that operated without regard to country of allegiance.[7]

Immunity

The maligned practice of diplomatic immunity enhances the impression that diplomats of different countries belong to the same odd guild. When private persons, or for that matter most officials, visit or reside in a foreign country, they submit themselves to that country's laws and regulations. If they fail to conform, they risk punishment. Diplomats, however, once they are named by the sending state and accepted by the receiving state, travel in a legal bubble. They are subject to the laws of the state that sends them but exempt from the laws of the state that receives them. This is diplomatic immunity.

Diplomatic immunity may have begun with the pragmatic battlefield custom of providing safe passage to envoys offering terms of surrender. When adhered to, the practice reduced carnage on both sides. Yet adherence from the Greeks forward was erratic. The adage "don't shoot the messenger" is evidence that messengers were sometimes shot. The messengers—the diplomats—had to rely on the uncertain mercy of their enemies. They were eager to find a stronger basis for their security.

By the seventeenth century, as nation-states gained power across much of Europe, the aristocrats and churchmen who carried out most diplomatic missions developed a theory that justified their protection. According to the theory, a diplomat represents a sovereign who rules by divine right as a power independent of all other earthly powers. One sovereign cannot exercise authority over another, and so a diplomat who is properly accredited must be immune from arrest, prosecution, taxation, and all other forms of coercion by the government that receives him. This theory, which became doctrine, facilitated negotiation, flattered the sovereigns, and not incidentally protected the lives and property of the diplomats.

At the Congress of Vienna, the multilateral peace conference that ended the Napoleonic wars in 1815, diplomatic immunity found a home in treaty law. Nearly a hundred and fifty years later, the 1961 Vienna Convention on Diplomatic Relations and the 1963 Vienna Convention on Consular

Relations codified the rights and obligations of sending and receiving states, and of their envoys. These conventions have been ratified by nearly every country in the world.[8]

Under the Vienna conventions, an accredited diplomat, called a diplomatic agent in the language of the conventions, is immune from any form of arrest or detention. His home and its contents are as inviolable as the embassy itself. He is immune from the criminal and, with a few exceptions, from the civil and administrative jurisdiction of the host country. Administrative and technical staff have the same immunities, except those from civil and administrative jurisdiction for acts committed outside the course of their duties. Immunities extend to family members, which can present difficulties for spouses seeking employment outside the embassy.

Immunity is not a license to break the law or a get-out-of-jail free card. The Vienna Convention says: "It is the duty of all persons enjoying such privileges and immunities to respect the laws and regulations of the receiving State. They also have a duty not to interfere in the internal affairs of that State."[9] The sending state may always waive the immunity of any of its diplomats, and a diplomat has no role or recourse with regard to that decision.[10] When a diplomat commits a crime, sometimes the sending state waives immunity, as the Republic of Georgia did when its deputy chief of mission killed a woman in a drunk-driving incident in 1997 in Washington, D.C. Sometimes it does not, as Brazil did not when the son of its ambassador shot a man in a bar in 1992, also in Washington, D.C.

Accreditation, Rank, and Precedence

History and tradition weigh heavily on the diplomatic profession, as well they should. The use of Latin and French terms to describe certain diplomatic practices testifies to their early origins.

When one state prepares to send an ambassador to another, it asks the receiving state for *agrément*—not for agreement. *Agrément* involves a confidential message from the sending to the receiving state: "If we name Smith, will you accept him?" If the answer is no, Smith is never named and therefore never suffers rejection. In American practice today, when the president's choice seems controversial, the Department of State may ask an even more hypothetical question: "If we were to ask you whether, should we name Smith, you would accept him, how would you reply?" If the answer is "we would say yes," then a formal request for *agrément* will follow.[11]

A receiving state recognizes the right of a consular officer accredited to it to perform consular functions by granting an *exequatur,* often in the form of an elaborate stamp or seal on the officer's consular commission.

A receiving state that wants to rid itself of a diplomat it has accredited may declare that person unwelcome, or persona non grata (PNG). No reason need be given, but governments often cite "activities incompatible with diplomatic status," meaning espionage. The U.S. government covers the basic costs of transferring an American diplomat who is declared PNG (or "pinged"). Some insurance companies offer PNG policies that will cover out-of-pocket expenses.

A similar patina of age appears in the terminology and practice of diplomatic rank and precedence, codified at the Congress of Vienna and scarcely changed since.[12] The forms and titles in use in the American foreign service, and in foreign ministries around the world, have a comic-opera quality that contributes to the popular image of the diplomat as a twit with table manners. Diplomats may be ambassadors (in most cases, ambassadors extraordinary and plenipotentiary), chargés d'affaires, ministers, minister-counselors, counselors, and first, second, or third secretaries, attachés, or assistant attachés. Consular officials may be consuls general, consuls, or vice consuls. The pope's representative to a country that has diplomatic relations with the Vatican carries the title of nuncio and is equivalent to an ambassador. Chargé d'affaires denotes an officer in charge of an embassy who is not an ambassador; if he is in charge only temporarily the words *ad interim* are tacked on, a Franco-Latin twofer.

For members of the American foreign service, diplomatic rank will be (but should not be) confused with personal rank, which determines pay (see chapter 7). The senior foreign service has three ranks or grades, called counselor, minister-counselor, and career minister. An officer with the personal rank of counselor may have the diplomatic rank of minister-counselor, or one with the rank of career minister may be sent abroad as an ambassador. A member of the foreign service may be most proud of his personal rank, but to the outside world, it is the diplomatic rank that counts. Diplomatic rank establishes precedence, which may determine where one sits at dinner, or stands in line to greet a dignitary, or—more important—whom one calls upon in host government offices. For diplomats of equal rank, precedence depends on seniority at post, determined by the date of accreditation. In U.S. practice, ties are broken by pay grade.

Precedence is a central element of social protocol, an often mocked but necessary set of written and unwritten rules of behavior for diplomats abroad.

American embassies and the foreign service have become less protocol conscious over the years, but they are hierarchical institutions and rank matters. Officers and staff still rise when the ambassador enters a room, respond promptly and almost always positively to invitations to functions, and remain at those functions until the ambassador leaves or gives them permission to do so.[13]

Accreditation is the recognition by the receiving government of the diplomatic status of the envoy of the sending government. It is the final step in establishing the privileges, immunities, and precedence that a diplomat is accorded under the Vienna conventions. For most diplomats, accreditation is routine. The embassy of the sending state sends a note with names and particulars to the foreign ministry of the host government, which replies with approval and often with identity cards (*carnets*) that diplomats are expected to carry at all times. For ambassadors, however, accreditation usually involves the presentation of credentials, the in-person delivery of a letter from the head of the sending state to the head of the receiving state.

The accreditation ceremony can be elaborate. In the United Kingdom, according to the official website of the monarchy, a new ambassador "is collected from the embassy or residence by a State landau from the Royal Mews" and "escorted by the Marshal of the Diplomatic Corps." During a twenty-minute "audience with The Queen," the ambassador "presents his or her Letters of Credence," and the Queen also greets "his or her suite," which has followed in a separate state landau.[14] In the United States, the president holds a simpler ceremony for newly arrived ambassadors about three or four times a year. Until they have presented their credentials ("letters of credence"), ambassadors are properly called ambassadors-designate.

Local staff, including foreign service nationals, are not accredited but are normally reported to the host government. Foreign service nationals receive no immunities or diplomatic privileges. On the contrary, in some countries they are targets of harassment.

Foreign ministries ordinarily maintain and publish a diplomatic list identifying by name and title all accredited diplomats in the country, just as the State Department does.[15] The embassy tells the ministry where an individual diplomat fits on the list of that embassy's diplomatic personnel. Family members over the age of eighteen are also listed.

In the U.S. foreign service, nearly all generalists (officers) have diplomatic status when posted abroad, as do many foreign service specialists and most civil servants assigned to embassies from nonforeign service agencies. Those without diplomatic status are ordinarily recognized as officials, a title of courtesy that confers no immunity.

Diplomatic accreditation is not automatic. A government may reject any request for accreditation, either through a declaration of persona non grata or through denial or withdrawal of a visa. Some governments formally or informally limit the number of people they will accredit, or prohibit access by diplomats to parts of the country.

The Secret Handshake

As it was in the days of Richelieu, so it is today. Men and women in foreign service, regardless of the country or government they serve, belong to the same profession. They share a secret handshake with their colleagues. It is a blessing and a curse.

Most diplomats acquire, along with foreign languages, cuisines, customs, and diseases, a certain broadmindedness and tolerance, a ready sympathy for foreigners and their points of view. Knowledgeable diplomats, with their common professional ideals and similar experiences, are less likely than amateurs to misunderstand each other. Negotiations between them are thereby facilitated. A professional diplomat who brings an agreement home carries a heavy burden of proof: Did he or she achieve the maximum advantage for national interests, and cede as little as possible to the other side? Especially after it is reached, an agreement negotiated by someone who sees an issue from more than one point of view may be suspected of failing this test.

Secretary of State George Shultz made it a practice to receive newly appointed American ambassadors in his office before they left Washington to take up their posts. He would take them over to a large globe that stood near the secretary's desk and ask them to "show me your country." When they did, Shultz would correct them. "No, that is the country to which you are assigned. Your country is here, the United States of America."[16]

No diplomat can afford to forget, even for a moment, for whom he works and whose interests he serves. It is not the country to which he is accredited, nor the world in general, nor the cause of peace. A diplomat serves his country and its people and its government, and them only.

What Diplomats Do

As old as it is, the essence of the diplomatic profession is hard to pin down. Definitions of a diplomat range from the waggish ("an honest man sent to lie abroad for the commonwealth"), to the pompous ("the voice of their state in foreign lands . . . the peaceable heralds of its power"), to the mundane ("a person appointed by a national government to conduct official negotiations and maintain political, economic, and social relations with another country or countries").[17]

To complicate the matter, the American foreign service defines its personnel by the department they work for, their job description, and their rank or pay grade. The matrix generates scores of pigeonholes but produces more confusion than enlightenment. In fact, just as the foreign service has a triple mission, the diplomatic profession has just three corresponding areas of practice: representation, operations, and policy (see chapter 1).

Representation

The work of representation consists of four verbs: talk, listen, report, negotiate. It depends on the efficient, precise, and persuasive transmission of information from the United States to foreign audiences, and from foreign sources to the U.S. government. The craft—and occasional craftiness—involved can be learned and will improve with practice, but a lively curiosity and high level of social energy are essential to success.

The representational work of the foreign service is often described by analogy: Reporting is like journalism, public diplomacy is like advertising, negotiation is like law or business. These are all misleading.

Foreign service reporting is not journalism. It cannot and should not compete with the mainstream media in speed, immediacy, or shock value, but it can and should provide context and analysis that journalism often does not.

Unlike journalists, foreign service reporters are actors, not observers. Their work is not done when they hit the Send button. Unlike journalism, foreign service reporting has direct implications for policy. It may generate replies in the form of instructions that the reporter then acts upon and carries out. If reports that seek action are merely sent and forgotten, however, they may be merely received and ignored. A foreign service reporter who wants to be heard must make some noise. "In Washington," wrote Henry Kissinger, "ideas do not sell themselves. Authors of memoranda who are not willing to fight for them are more likely to find their words turned into ex post facto alibis than guides to action."[18]

Reporting events is overrated, and so is elegance of style. The value is in the work behind the text. Effective reporting that leads to action is grounded in hard-won experience, based on information not available from other sources, and persuasively presented. Despite the lingering fascination with George Kennan, whose eight-thousand-word telegram from Moscow in February 1946 shaped America's cold war policies for the next forty years, extended analysis is not what Washington wants from the field.[19] Policymakers can consult scores or hundreds of analysts in and out of government, but foreign service work has special value. "The most effective embassies," said Ambassador Barbro Owens-Kirkpatrick, "are those that put a robust list of suggestions for action at the end of every reporting cable, to help Washington know what it should be considering as a course of action."[20] Former National Security Adviser Brent Scowcroft said: "I want to know what our ambassador thinks," since the embassy is best able to interpret events on the ground.[21]

Public diplomacy is not advertising, or marketing, or brand management, and when it strays too far in those directions it often loses its effectiveness.[22] To influence public opinion abroad, the techniques and ethical norms of journalism and education, with their emphasis on information and truth seeking, have proven more successful than those of Madison Avenue, with their emphasis on repetition, hyperbole, and emotional manipulation. Over the years, the flow of personnel into and out of public diplomacy has been primarily with the news media and cultural organizations, though recent leadership in the Department of State has come from the fields of marketing, government relations, and political consulting (undersecretaries Charlotte Beers, Margaret Tutwiler, and Karen Hughes, respectively). The nomination of journalist James K. Glassman as Karen Hughes's successor marks a return to an earlier practice.

The comparison of diplomatic negotiations to law and business has some validity. Like negotiations between buyers and sellers, employers and employees, or litigants seeking a settlement, diplomatic negotiations are an effort to adjust relationships through compromise. Skills developed in one type of negotiation are transferable to another. George Shultz wrote that "a sense of strategy is critical in any negotiation: when to make concessions, when to hold firm, when to let things cool off, when to be intransigent." Shultz considered his training and experience as a labor economist and negotiator excellent preparation for diplomacy.[23]

But diplomatic negotiations present special problems. The gaps between the parties may be unusually wide. Differences of language, history, and culture mean that the parties to a negotiation may have different views of what they are talking about and why. There is a very broad scope for misunderstanding and miscalculation.

Professional diplomats who can bridge these gaps may come to understand each other but lose touch with their domestic masters who make the final decisions. Robert Gallucci, the dean of Georgetown University's School of Foreign Service and a negotiator of the 1994 nuclear agreement with North Korea, said that many Americans will attack any negotiated agreement because they are skeptical of negotiation: "It's an easy sophistry to go from 'We can never compromise our national security,' to 'We can never compromise where national security is concerned,' which means that any negotiation is suspect. I tell students, you have to get the support of the people for your enterprise."[24]

International negotiations often break down between negotiating rounds because, while the parties at the table want agreement and move toward each other, domestic interests in each country, typically not at the table, harden their positions and prevent compromise. Diplomats who do not maintain communication and credibility with domestic interests waste their cross-cultural skills, their training, and their time. Their work will end in failure.[25]

Unlike other talks, diplomatic negotiations are rarely grounded in a body of law accepted by all sides and enforceable by courts of justice armed with police powers. Instead, even the most genteel diplomatic negotiations generally take place in a lawless realm where the final agreement is enforced only by mutual self-interest. There are no courts, no police, and no certain compulsion short of war to ensure that the parties fulfill their obligations. A diplomatic agreement endures only as long as the parties consider it better than the alternatives.

Operations

Operations involve running systems, projects, and programs. The skills required are primarily technical and managerial. Foreign service specialists who run the communications, manage the money, maintain the buildings, and protect the health, welfare, and security of official (and often unofficial) Americans abroad are operational personnel. So are the consular officers, customs and border protection personnel, drug enforcement agents, and others who push the protection of U.S. laws beyond the country's borders. So too are the rising stars of the foreign service, the men and women working on reconstruction and stabilization in Iraq, Afghanistan, and other so-called postconflict situations, organizing the rapid and relatively mishap-free evacuation of Americans from Lebanon in 2006, and running foreign-assistance programs combating poverty, disease, and lawlessness around the world.

Operations are the new growth area of American diplomacy. Until quite recently, the phrase *threat to American security* implied a military or political challenge to American interests, or an economic development that posed a risk to American prosperity. Such threats were and still are met with traditional diplomacy, a mix of inducement and menace conveyed through official representations and designed to change state behaviors. Now the definition has been expanded to include epidemic diseases, environmental depredations, and other natural phenomena that traditional diplomacy, as traditionally exercised, cannot easily address. The events of September 11 revealed the dangers that arise when states fail and governments no longer inhibit the most reckless, barbaric expressions of human hatred. Here too traditional diplomacy, conducted between states, has no effect. Diplomats with the skills and languages to take money and programs into the field and bring about societal changes are likely to be a rising proportion of the foreign service over the next ten or fifteen years, and as long as they are in short supply they are likely to progress faster than their colleagues.

Policy

In the diplomatic history of the United States, with its strong democratic traditions, professional diplomats have rarely achieved the influence over policy that they have attained in other nations. Historian Dexter Perkins has written: "In a sense that is true in no such degree in other nations, American diplomatic action has been determined by the people." As a result, "the professional diplomat has always played a subordinate role" to "men with substantial political experience" who "pay heed to the voice of the great body of citizens" and "shape their decisions with that voice in mind."[26]

For the foreign service, policy involves advising the officials who define national interests and decide what resources should be deployed to secure them. Professional diplomats carry out policies. They try to manipulate events to produce the outcomes policymakers desire; at times, they serve as policymakers. Diplomats in a position to advise on policy must know how to bring their knowledge of foreign cultures, languages, institutions, leaders, aspirations, capabilities, and intents to bear constructively on the questions confronting the policymakers. That requires an understanding of how American foreign policy is made and an awareness of the forces, including the domestic political forces, that are at work on any issue. The value that the foreign service brings to the development of foreign policy is its knowledge of the motivations and levers of power in foreign countries, its sense of the range of possibilities in a negotiation, its ability to predict foreign reactions to a given set of circumstances, and its skill, based in language, personal contact, and a record of honest dealing, at communication without misunderstanding.

Diplomatic Practice, in Practice

The three areas of diplomatic practice—representation, operations, and policy—are bounded by the blurriest of lines. A foreign service officer over the course of a career can expect to train and perform in all three areas.

No foreign service job is confined to one area of practice. A consular officer, faced with the repetitive challenge of applying U.S. law to an endless line of visa applicants, represents the United States on a powerful, personal level to scores of families each day. An AID chief of party (as project managers are called) is thoroughly operational, but he or she is also shaping public opinion and, through control of the disbursement of substantial U.S. resources, shaping U.S. policy as well. A commercial officer who represents U.S. export interests is a source of advice for Washington on U.S. commercial policy and strategy for trade negotiations.

The most successful diplomatic professionals work in representation, operations, and policy at the same time.

Carlucci in Portugal

Frank Carlucci, a career foreign service officer who later served as national security adviser and secretary of defense, came to Portugal as ambassador in January 1975, eight months after a revolution by military officers fed up with colonial wars in Africa had toppled a rightist authoritarian government. In the political vacuum that followed, the country had a series of weak governments (six in two years) that moved successively to the left. Washington became increasingly concerned that Portugal might become the first NATO country to fall under communist control.

Most concerned was Secretary of State Henry Kissinger, who told a conference of American ambassadors in Europe that "the dominance of Communist parties in the West is unacceptable. . . . It is hard to imagine that, if one or the other of these parties takes control of a Western government, it will permit the democratic process to operate and thereby face the possibility that it may itself be removed from office. . . . We must do our utmost to assure the survival of democratic processes and to preserve the Western political orientation of western European countries."[27]

Much of the State Department felt that "it was probably best to write Lisbon off and teach them a lesson" that would dissuade voters in other European countries, especially France and Italy, from following the Portuguese example. Carlucci and his embassy, however, argued for vigorous U.S. support of the country's democratic parties, including in particular the socialists, in the belief that "the electoral process could serve to undermine communist control of the country." This conclusion was not based on faith. Carlucci had personal knowledge of Portuguese politics. "I would make it a goal of meeting at least two or three political figures a day," he told an interviewer in 1999. "I spent many, many hours in long debates and discussions with the prime minister," as well as with the foreign minister and the president. "I would go over and talk to the archbishop quietly, have lunch with him and find out what his views were. . . . I became fairly close to some of the original coup plotters [and] spent a lot of time with them."[28]

He fought for his position against bureaucratic opposition in Washington. He went to Brussels: "I went up to [the U.S. mission to NATO] and participated in the drafting of a cable . . . recommending a military aid package for Portugal, and then went back to Portugal and wrote an endorsement of the USNATO cable." When the State Department said there were no funds, he went back to Washington, to the Office of Management and Budget (OMB), where he had been a deputy director. There he was told he needed congressional support. So he went to members who had Portuguese constituents and secured their backing. "It was unique," Carlucci said, "an ambassador pushing through his own aid program."[29]

Carlucci had experience with aid programs. In 1972 President Nixon had detailed him to supervise relief efforts after a hurricane had caused extensive flooding along the Susquehanna River. While still a foreign service officer, Carlucci had served in the White House in the now defunct Office of Economic Opportunity (OEO), in the Office of Management and Budget, and as an undersecretary in the Department of Health, Education, and Welfare.

He knew President Ford and his chief of staff, Donald Rumsfeld, who had been his direct boss at OEO.

In June 1976, Carlucci used his political connections to arrange a meeting with the president. He then met with Secretary Kissinger, who in Carlucci's account "said something to the effect that the President has asked to see me. . . . At that meeting Henry did say that he would give my policy option a chance, he would back me. So, I told him there was no reason for me to go to the White House. Henry couldn't have been more supportive from that day on."[30]

These extraordinary efforts paid extraordinary dividends. France, Germany, and Britain joined the United States in a program of covert support for the democratic opposition. As Carlucci had predicted, the electoral process worked, a leftwing rebellion in the armed forces failed, and a socialist government took power with a decidedly Western orientation. The Portuguese example had a powerful effect in Spain, where, after the death of Europe's last fascist dictator, Francisco Franco, in November 1975, the transition to democracy was peaceful and the communists were marginalized. Spain joined the North Atlantic alliance in 1982, and no Communist Party members entered the government of any NATO country until well after the collapse of the Soviet Union and the end of the communist military threat.

Could an amateur have done what Carlucci did in Portugal? Not likely. Carlucci's immediate predecessor in Lisbon was an amateur and left behind what the undersecretary of state for management called "the worst embassy in the world."[31] Carlucci spoke Portuguese, which he had learned as a foreign service officer in Brazil in the early 1960s, and had a grasp of the political dynamics in Lisbon. He was a visible, voluble spokesman for the U.S. point of view, and he followed through on programs that established his credibility with key groups. He could navigate around the State Department, Congress, the White House, and NATO. In other words, he had mastered the skills of the profession, and when given the opportunity to perform at a high level, he justified his country's trust.

Happiness Is Multiple Pipelines

The combination Ambassador Carlucci displayed—policy insight with influence on one's own government and successful advocacy overseas—is the trifecta of high-level diplomacy. But diplomacy must adapt to circumstances.

The public diplomacy Carlucci employed relied on media access that is not always available. Despite the emphasis, by Secretary Rice and others, on operations that transform foreign societies from the bottom up, diplomacy that relies almost wholly on official contacts has lost none of its importance. Foreign service reporting and analysis are still the U.S. government's single most important source of intelligence. Government-to-government negotiations and face-to-face encounters with foreign leaders are still the most important tools in foreign relations. They are the tools that the foreign service applied to one of the most fascinating and important geopolitical puzzles of our time.

What may be the world's largest undeveloped reserves of oil and natural gas lie beneath the soil and inland seas of Central Asia and the Caucasus, in eight new countries that for most of the twentieth century were part of the Soviet Union. These countries are poor and erratically governed, with democratic institutions in their infancy or yet to be born. They face pressure from the north from a Russia that seeks to restore its influence in the region, and from the south from an Islamist movement that finds supporters among tribes and clans with little sense of nationhood.

After the Soviet break-up, American policymakers, urged on by the new U.S. embassies in places like Baku, Tbilisi, Almaty, and Ashgabat, saw an opportunity. A commitment by the United States and the West to develop these oil reserves and bring them to market could increase and diversify global supplies; promote economic development and political stability across a volatile, strategically important region; forestall the expansion of Russian and Iranian influence; reduce the political space for violent Islamist extremism; and land some business for U.S. companies. One stone, five birds.

Western energy companies had a strong interest in the region, but even companies accustomed to working in the world's most violent and unstable environments had doubts about investing in the Caucasus or Central Asia. Banks were doubly nervous about project finance. For their part, the new governments and state-owned oil companies in the region lacked experience in international negotiations and faced heavy pressure from Russia, which controlled all existing pipelines, to continue to market through Russian facilities exclusively.

The challenge for the United States was to build private-sector confidence in the possibility of success and persuade governments in the region that fair dealing with Western partners would produce results and revenues that Russian partners could not. Also important was to maintain good relations with Russia throughout the process. Many agencies of the U.S. government were involved in the effort, but the foreign service led the way.

"The foreign service has unique strengths in energy affairs," said Steve Gallogly, director of the Office of International Energy and Commodity Policy in the State Department's Bureau of Economic and Business Affairs:

> First is information. We are in touch with governments and U.S. energy companies all over the world, all the time. We know the latest decree from the government of Peru, the latest projection of refining capacity in Venezuela, the latest estimate of gas reserves in Algeria. Second is access. Governments are mixed up in energy every step of the way, in exploration, development, extraction, production, transport, distribution. Foreign service people, including foreign service nationals, have access to policy people and especially leverage with them that U.S. companies don't have. So U.S. energy companies need to stay close to us. That gives the foreign service an ability to understand and influence how the energy companies behave.[32]

Transportation is the key to developing the resources of Central Asia and the Caucasus. One foreign service officer working on the problem put a bumper sticker on his car: "Happiness is multiple pipelines." But in the end the main U.S. effort aimed at developing an east-west pipeline route from Baku, the capital of Azerbaijan, on the Caspian Sea, through Tbilisi in central Georgia and Erzurum in western Turkey, to Ceyhan, a Turkish port on the Mediterranean. The United States launched an initiative that involved diplomatic efforts in half a dozen countries, as well as constant contact with energy, pipeline, and oilfield service companies, their bankers, and various international organizations. Controlling the initiative presented a managerial challenge that in fact is not unusual in the foreign service.

Because so many countries and agencies were involved, the U.S. government named a special envoy, a senior official outside the usual bureaucratic structure with responsibility for a specific and limited issue. Special envoys don't always succeed. An envoy charged with accomplishing just one goal may easily end up in conflict with those who have other missions and other priorities. But because the Caspian Basin energy project served so many purposes, and because the special envoy was a foreign service professional familiar with the range of issues that the pipeline project would affect, internal conflicts were generally avoided.

The United States between 1996 and 2005 had four special envoys who traveled constantly throughout the region. They came to know the heads of state, the energy ministers, the oil company executives, the engineers, and the financiers. They built confidence through personal commitment and personal trustworthiness, and through an unyielding insistence on transparency.[33]

They worked closely with U.S. embassies in the region and enjoyed strong support from the intelligence community.

"The foreign service really is a team," said Ambassador Steven Mann, special envoy from 2001 to 2005. "The embassies welcomed someone who was following the issue in minute detail. And it didn't hurt that we all knew each other. The ambassadors in that part of the world were all veterans of work on Soviet affairs. We had all been junior officers together. That made our cooperation frictionless."[34]

The work was diplomacy of a high order, practiced at the ministerial and presidential level. "For the countries involved we were the reality check," Ambassador Mann continued. "They would look at the documents and ask us, 'What's the meaning of this provision? What do you think of the environmental arrangements, the security provisions?' And we would tell them."

Over a decade, the U.S. special envoys created the political infrastructure that supported the physical and financial infrastructure of the pipeline itself. In the end, eleven oil companies from eight countries joined the pipeline consortium, and nine oil companies from five countries joined the oilfield operating consortium. Even though U.S. companies have only a 13 percent equity share in the new pipeline, "the United States is strongly identified with the project," Mann explained. "Our name is on it." The Baku-Tbilisi-Ceyhan pipeline, 1,100 miles long, opened May 25, 2005, and began moving 150,000 barrels per day to market. That should rise by 2009 to one million per day, about 5 percent of U.S. consumption.

With the opening of the pipeline, the work of the special envoy for Caspian Basin energy affairs was complete, but Steve Mann's expertise and unique knowledge of the region did not go to waste. He next moved on to become the State Department's special adviser on Europe's frozen conflicts—four unresolved ethnic and secessionist disputes in the former Soviet Union (Nagorno-Karabakh between Armenia and Azerbaijan, South Ossetia and Abkhazia on the borders of Georgia, and Moldova's eastern region of Transdnistria). In that capacity he traveled to many of the same capitals and dealt with many of the same people that he came to know through his work on the pipeline. He built on the trust he enjoyed throughout the region to mediate these disputes, which threaten peace and stability in a volatile and strategic part of the world. "My job gives me the opportunity to work in policy and to execute," Mann said. "I have a free hand to travel to the countries, I decide on the tactics. I have great support from the rest of the State Department, from the Pentagon, and from the intelligence community. It's the best job in the foreign service."

Transformational Diplomacy

What happened in Portugal during Ambassador Carlucci's service there was a transformation of Portuguese politics, which led over time to a thorough transformation of Portuguese and Iberian society. Historians know the temptation, as events recede, to regard what happened as inevitable, part of a set of overwhelming forces that culminate in an inevitable present. But to actors at the time, the moment is in turmoil and the world is full of choice. Portugal in the 1970s was not certain to take the place in modern Europe that it occupies today (2007). Many choices and many acts produced that happy outcome. American diplomacy and Ambassador Carlucci's embassy did not cause the outcome, but they clearly contributed to it, and the United States is safer and more prosperous because of it.

The conviction that democratic reform abroad improves security at home is deeply rooted in American political thought and experience. When communism collapsed in Europe and in the Soviet Union, the risk of a great-power war and nuclear annihilation approached zero. American statesmen drew the lessons that even seemingly frozen societies can change, and that governments that respond to their people are less threatening than those that don't.

Of course these were not new lessons. The United States from its founding embraced universal ideals of human rights, and from the early days of the country's twentieth-century emergence as a global power it sought "a world made safe for democracy."[35] At the same time, Americans enjoyed the strategic benefits of geographic isolation from tumultuous Europe and Asia. Policies aimed at global change were moderated by a popular desire to remain disengaged from foreign troubles, and a recognition that moral power could not run ahead of staying power.

After the attacks of September 11, 2001, changing other societies became a more explicit and important goal of American diplomacy. A White House paper, published in September 2002, said: "The U.S. national security strategy will be based on a distinctly American internationalism that reflects the union of our values and our national interests. The aim of this strategy is to help make the world not just safer but better."[36] A second *National Security Strategy*, published in April 2006, was even clearer: "The goal of our statecraft is to help create a world of democratic, well-governed states that can meet the needs of their citizens and conduct themselves responsibly in the international system. This is the best way to provide enduring security for the American people."[37]

The shift of emphasis in policy implied a change in American diplomacy and in the demands placed upon the foreign service. Traditional diplomacy aims to influence how states relate to other states: "Governments," wrote Henry Adams, "were meant to deal with governments, not with private individuals or the opinions of foreign society."[38] Transformational diplomacy, to use Secretary Rice's phrase, aims also—even primarily—to influence how states behave inside their own borders.[39]

Rice told an audience at Georgetown University's School of Foreign Service that the changing nature of risk in the postcommunist world requires a change in the diplomatic mission: "The greatest threats now emerge more within states than between them. The fundamental character of regimes now matters more than the international distribution of power. . . . We seek to use America's diplomatic power to help foreign citizens to better their own lives and to build their own nations and to transform their own futures."[40] In seeking resources for the Department of State, she told the Congress much the same: "This time of global transformation calls for transformational diplomacy. More than ever, America's diplomats will need to be active in spreading democracy, reducing poverty, fighting terror, and doing our part to protect our homeland."[41]

The first reaction of most members of the professional foreign service was applause, mixed with a sense that appreciation of their work was overdue. "United States foreign policy has been encouraging democracy for a hundred years," said retired Ambassador Tom Boyatt. "And you know what? It's been a huge success."[42] "I think it's what we've been doing all along," Ambassador Rea Brazeal observed. "The Georgetown speech reminded me of the Home Depot slogan: 'You can do it but we'll be there to help.'" Another ambassador with long service in Africa said, "I think we started about fifteen years ago to do what Secretary Rice calls transformational diplomacy." A public diplomacy officer with twenty years of service remarked, "I've been doing transformational diplomacy since the beginning of my career."[43]

Some scoffed. A retired ambassador called "this transformational diplomacy nonsense" a fad or a mistake that would end when Rice and the administration left office. Some saw the risks. What if the host government did not wish to see its country transformed? If the situation were reversed, would the United States government tolerate efforts by foreign diplomats to transform American society—for example, and hypothetically, efforts by the embassy of Saudi Arabia to promote anti-Christian and anti-Semitic instruction in American Islamic schools?[44] Transformational diplomacy risks damaging government-to-government relationships, perhaps severely. It's a risk that the transformers are generally prepared to run.

Whether they regarded transformational diplomacy as part of or counter to usual American diplomatic practice, most members of the foreign service recognized that it had practical implications for their profession and their careers. They saw the shift toward operations and away from reporting and analysis; toward spending more time in civil (or in some countries, clerical) society, and less with foreign government officials; toward a higher premium on speaking foreign languages well, especially the languages of the Middle East and the developing world, and a lesser premium on writing in English. It meant greater stress on public diplomacy; much closer integration of foreign assistance with other elements of foreign policy; and the placement of additional resources—personnel above all—in regions of the world where governments are unstable or weak. Foreign service officers and specialists whose careers were already focused in these areas saw opportunities for more rapid advancement, and those with less experience in the developing or unstable countries became concerned that their work might be undervalued.

Inside the Department of State and the Agency for International Development, the prospect of changing the way the foreign service does its work largely eclipsed discussion of the change in policy and mission. The American Foreign Service Association was swamped with questions from its members. An elaboration of the changes in store for recruitment, hiring, retention, training, assignments, and promotions would take months to emerge and more months to negotiate. The results are discussed in part III of this book, the foreign service as a career.

Fighting AIDS

The President's Emergency Program for AIDS Relief (PEPFAR) is transformational diplomacy at its most successful. The program begins with the recognition that AIDS, beyond the threat it poses to public health and economic development in countries where it is prevalent, is also a matter of national security to the United States. The program's objectives are to improve the treatment and care of those infected or affected and to prevent the spread of the disease, with a focus on fifteen countries (twelve in Africa) where over half of the world's HIV-infected population lives.[45] Achieving these objectives, or just moving toward them, requires changing the behavior of individuals, social groups, and governments. PEPFAR is transformational diplomacy backed by money. Lots of money, in fact—$15 billion over the first five years.

The year 2004, when the first PEPFAR funds were appropriated, was a time of White House and congressional dissatisfaction with the status quo in foreign aid. New approaches were the order of the day. The year before, Congress deliberately placed the new Millennium Challenge Corporation outside of USAID and the Department of State and chartered it to promote economic growth in poor countries. Later that year, with administration support Congress put the U.S. military in the foreign aid business with section 1206 of the Defense Authorization Act, enacted in October 2004 (see chapter 6, note 63). In the same spirit, Randall Tobias, the administration's choice for global AIDS coordinator and first director of PEPFAR, promised "a new way of doing business." Tobias, who had just retired as chief executive of the pharmaceutical company Eli Lilly, wanted to put his own PEPFAR people overseas, to make sure the program would be run as he wanted.

That did not happen. Ambassador Jimmy Kolker, deputy global AIDS coordinator, told the story this way:

> The day after taking office, Tobias left to attend the annual conference of U.S. ambassadors serving in Africa. His deputy John Lange—my predecessor—went with him. Like me, John was a career foreign service officer, a former ambassador to Botswana. He urged Tobias to hold off on his plans. "You already have a staff in the field," John told him. Tobias spent an entire morning with the U.S. ambassadors in the designated focus countries—I was ambassador in Uganda then—and each one of us gave a briefing on AIDS, not just the numbers and ongoing programs, but the different political and cultural factors that affected possibilities for care, treatment, and prevention.
>
> Tobias was impressed. Ambassadors wanted responsibility, authority, and resources to tackle the problem. We were ready to move. The idea of bringing on a new staff just fell away. PEPFAR went in just the other direction, decentralizing decisions and minimizing staff.
>
> The State Department office that manages PEPFAR, the Office of the Global AIDS Coordinator, has just seventy people, running a budget of $15 billion over five years. The bulk of the work is done in the field, by country teams of PEPFAR agencies headed by the ambassador. The main agencies are State, USAID, and the Centers for Disease Control.
>
> The teams write the COPs, I mean the country operating plans, and ambassadors sign off on them. These are detailed plans, sometimes several hundred pages, that set out HIV/AIDS targets and plans to meet them, linked to partners and resource levels. The partners are the local organizations, public

and private, that do the work. The COPs have to be integrated with each country's national HIV/AIDS strategy. All the programs are flexible. We share best practices, but we adapt everything to local circumstances.

This is where the foreign service shines. Our local knowledge of partners, of who's reliable, of what works in the local environment has been tested again and again, and we've passed gloriously. We know the local conditions, constraints, and capabilities. We've been able to make the connection between the scientific and economic data—we've got lots of data—and the public policies that can set priorities and put the data to work.

We give the COPs a technical review and a policy review, but we don't micromanage. We might spend many hours on a review, but the review is also the clearance for the agencies in the program. We give the posts what they determine will achieve best results, within the guidelines that Congress and the administration establish and the limits of the total budget. In my thirty years of experience in the foreign service, what we see in PEPFAR is an unprecedented level of trust in our ambassadors and embassies.[46]

The program has had considerable success. By the middle of fiscal year 2007, halfway through the five-year program, PEPFAR had reached more than 1.1 million people in its fifteen focus countries with antiretroviral treatments and had helped bring care to more than 2 million people infected or affected by the disease. The number of infections averted is hard to measure, especially over such a short period of time, but the Census Bureau has completed baseline studies from which estimates of change from the predicted incidence of AIDS can be calculated. The FY 2009 PEPFAR budget request projects prevention of twelve million new infections over five years.[47] Support in Congress is bipartisan, strong, and growing. The administration announced in May 2007 that it will ask Congress to renew the program for another five years and double its size to $30 billion.

"I have no training in public health," said Ambassador Kolker, "but foreign service skills and foreign service experience give me the perspective I need, and I can learn the rest. I love this work. Maybe I was born for this job."

5
·
Stabilization and Reconstruction in Iraq

The work that ambassadors Carlucci, Mann, and Kolker accomplished was what American diplomats had been doing for many years, at least since the 1960s. Their purpose was to enhance American security and prosperity by achieving objectives that were primarily political (Carlucci), economic (Mann), or humanitarian and developmental (Kolker). Their diplomacy had its transformational aspects—that is, it was intended to a greater or lesser degree to change behavior within states, not between them—but none of them would have used that word to describe it.

The work of American diplomats in Iraq, however, departed from past practice, and ever more sharply as it evolved in the years after the 2003 invasion. The scale of the effort—the Baghdad embassy in 2007 was by far the world's largest, with a budget of close to $1 billion and a staff of well over one thousand—was unprecedented.[1] So was the new and still-evolving relationship between the diplomats and the U.S. military. The stories that follow show how, as the political and security situations deteriorated between 2003 and 2007, U.S. foreign service personnel became more closely integrated with, and dependent on, U.S. and allied military units. The work of the foreign service, which in the immediate wake of the invasion was relatively unstructured and improvisational, became progressively more constrained, with objectives that were more narrowly defined but no less difficult to accomplish.

The foreign service has been called upon to lead in the political stabilization and economic reconstruction of Iraq. The mission is a test of the idea—the soundness of which many doubt—that diplomats can do this work. The test is not fair, because in Iraq conditions are worse, demands greater, success more distant, and pressure more severe than in any other place, and perhaps at any other time. Even so, it is the test on which the service will be judged. Performance will shape the way the service is seen and deployed for years to come.

Provincial Reconstruction Teams

In the months after coalition forces invaded Iraq, diplomats joined with military officers in what came to be known as provincial reconstruction teams (PRTs): small civilian-led groups whose mission was transformational diplomacy at its most dramatic—building a functioning democracy from the bottom up. Initially the teams had substantial financial resources, mostly U.S. cash dollars, and ample security. Nonetheless, they were largely improvisational. They relied on insight, quick-wittedness, luck, and a monopoly on military power. When any of these were lacking, the teams could lose their influence over events.

The teams were disbanded in 2004, reconstituted with a different structure and mission in 2005, and greatly expanded in 2007. Despite false starts and a mixed record, the PRTs may be the model for future cooperation between the foreign service and the military in troubled regions—not necessarily war zones—that present an actual or potential threat to the national security of the United States. The stories below are ground-level, first-person accounts told during or soon after the events they describe occurred. They show, without benefit of hindsight, the range of challenges that confronted the PRTs and their personnel, and they show how foreign service work in Iraq evolved over the grim course of the war.

"Get the Diplomat in Here!"—Provincial Reconstruction in 2003

Toby Bradley, a five-year veteran of the foreign service, arrived in Nasiriyah in September 2003, six months after United States and allied forces crossed the border into Iraq. The Coalition Provisional Authority (CPA) in Baghdad had charged him with setting up a civilian presence in Dhi Qar province that could organize economic reconstruction and turn power over to Iraqi authorities who were yet to be chosen. Bradley recalls:

> *I was the political adviser on what was called a governorate coordination team, headed by a British foreign service officer, John Bourne. An Italian force provided security, and some Romanian troops were there as well. There were five officers in the team when I arrived, and more than a hundred when I left [eight months later]. There were similar teams in seventeen of the eighteen provinces, most of them staffed by military civil-affairs personnel. The idea was that we were the CPA presence, able to nationalize CPA policies and identify problems that needed CPA attention. We were to report on what was*

happening, build up the infrastructure needed for reconstruction, and solve problems or flag them for Baghdad.²

The team in Nasiriyah operated pretty much on its own. "We didn't really have communications," Bradley said.

We had no reliable phone system. We had satellite phones, but we had to be outside to use them, and that raised security issues. So we stayed in touch with Hotmail and Yahoo mail accounts.

I was assigned as the political adviser, but my work was much broader. We'd roll into a town and ask to see the city council. I never knew if two, ten, or a hundred people would show up. I asked them what they wanted to do, how we could help, and get them to set some priorities in the process. It was difficult to get the idea across. They had grown accustomed to receiving whatever policies Baghdad handed down. They had never articulated their needs before. At night I'd report what I'd learned to John Bourne, and he would get the different ministries to work on the issues. There were twenty cities in the province, so I was on the road most of the time.

Bradley and other members of the team organized council elections around Dhi Qar province. "I had no training for this," he recounted, "other than my experience growing up in a democratic society. And I had some Arabic from a six-month State Department course and a tour doing visa and political work in Amman, Jordan." The first election efforts were rocky:

In the town of Ad Dawwayah, Sheikh Saoud, a tribal leader, had taken control, and a cleric who opposed him headed the committee to prepare for elections. The sheik complained to me that the cleric wanted him out—he was right about that—and argued that elections would be unfair and unnecessary. I was completely uncomfortable with the cleric in charge, but told the sheik that I would be there to make sure the vote was honest. I also told him that he had until the day before the voting to decide whether to run.

The day of the election we drove out to the town. An Italian civil affairs military unit had set up a perimeter around the school, with the townspeople inside. No one could leave until they had voted. It was a mess. I literally kept my hand over the ballot box to make sure no one could stuff it.

Then the Italians came to me and said, "There's a sheik outside that wants to speak to you." I entrusted the ballot box to a colleague and walked outside, scared to death. I'm twenty-nine years old, I don't know what I'm doing, my Arabic is limited, and I'm going to confront a sheik and a mob. There were twenty or thirty men, no doubt armed, with banners saying "No to Elections" and "Down with America," all led by Sheikh Saoud. He warned there would be violence if the elections were not stopped. I took a deep breath and decided on my course of action. I shouted to Sheikh Saoud so bystanders could hear: "You had a chance to run in this election, and you chose not to run. Today everyone here with a ration card is equal, everyone with a ration card has the right to vote. Today you have a choice, you can take your right to vote like everyone else, if you have a ration card, or you can go home. And if there is violence, all will know who started it, and who could have prevented it. Any injuries will be on your head."

Sheikh Saoud stood down, and the day passed quietly. We counted votes until one or two in the morning. The ballots weren't printed, each voter had to write in the names of the candidates. A vote for Mohammad would have to be thrown out—was it Mohammad Hassan or Mohammad Ismail? My reading got a lot better that day.

Bradley went on to organize "fourteen or fifteen" elections, learning from mistakes:

In every town we met with all elements of society, former Baathists, clerics, teachers, illiterate people. Even though Dhi Qar is 99 percent Shi'a, there were vast differences of opinion. Through elections and a change in the local-authorities law, we were able to curb the power of mayors, who tended to become strongmen, and shift power to elected city councils, which then chose the mayor. That system brought decisions closer to the people. It introduced checks and balances. It was exciting work. I could see the results of my efforts every day.

The foreign service can do this kind of work. I had no special training, but I learned that the foreign service selection process had identified the skills I needed, the ability to work with foreign cultures. In Iraq, people kept saying, "Get the diplomat in here," because I had a knack for getting local people to solve their problems. I found I could get the Iraqis to tell me what they wanted and then work with them and with the bureaucracy, the CPA in Baghdad, to get things done.

Not enough people are doing this kind of work. A lot of what the foreign service does is answering the mail. Too often going out to talk to people is the extra thing we do, not the central thing. But that mentality is changing. Foreign service officers, especially the new ones coming in, definitely have the skills. Now we need to build on those skills and move them to the heart of our profession.

"The Meetings Were Fairly Hostile"—Political Work, 2005

Toby Bradley and all of the governorate coordination teams left Iraq by June 28, 2004, when the doors of the Coalition Provisional Authority closed and power turned over to an Iraqi-led government intended to lead the country's transition to democracy. But the electoral techniques developed and tested in Dhi Qar province—with the support of the embassy in Baghdad and regional embassy offices (REOs) in Mosul, Kirkuk, Hillah, and Basra—took hold nationally. The year 2005 was the year of the ballot, with the election of a Transitional National Assembly in January, a constitutional referendum in October, and parliamentary elections in December.

Foreign service officer Vincent Campos arrived in Iraq in January 2005 to work on the elections. Campos, a former coast guard officer, came to the embassy in Baghdad's Green Zone on his first tour, four months after his swearing in, as the policy that designated Iraq assignments for more experienced officers began to erode. He had no language training—in fact, he knew no more than a few Arabic phrases—and only a brief introduction to Iraqi culture. He joined a political section of about seventeen officers. Campos said the section head—the political counselor—and his first deputy spoke Arabic (the first deputy spoke it quite well), and the second deputy "had a grasp of the language." Later, "another entry-level officer" came on board with fluent Arabic, but "only a few of the rest had any Arabic at all."[3]

My portfolio included the elections of January 2005, constitution development during 2005, the referendum of October 2005, and the national elections of December 2005 based on the new constitution. I worked on Sunni outreach programs and I was the point of contact for several nongovernmental and international organizations and liaison with USAID. I worked about fourteen or fifteen hours a day, usually from about eight in the morning to ten or eleven at night. We had a half day off a week, like a Saturday or Friday afternoon off.

We lived inside the Green Zone. That's a very large area, about four square miles. The embassy complex, with its own security, is in the former Republican Guard palace that was also the primary location for the multinational force working with the embassy. We had our dining, laundry, living facilities inside the perimeter. The living conditions were tolerable—no, better than that. I had no complaints. We lived in what some called dog boxes, essentially small trailers just big enough for two single beds, a closet to hang clothing, and a very small chest of drawers. There was not really as much room as aboard some Coast Guard cutters. They were small, but even so they were adequate. We really just slept there. The quality of life in general, except for the occasional rain of mortars and bombs, was pretty high, actually.

A lot of our work was inside the Zone. Parliament and a lot of government offices, including the president and the prime minister, were there, along with a few ministries. But work on the elections, and outreach to the Sunnis, took me out of the Zone and out of Baghdad.

I made trips to Kurdistan, Fallujah, Ramadi, Anbar province, Baqubah, some other areas as well. We brought Iraqi election commissioners out from Baghdad to Sunni communities to meet with Sunnis who absolutely distrusted the commissioners and felt the elections were skewed against them.

A typical meeting involved a lot of planning and coordination. Even before a trip, we had to sell the commissioners on making the dangerous trips out and working with the Sunnis. That was my job. Another junior officer from the political section was the primary contact with the Sunni community. A third junior officer was embedded with the U.S. military unit that would work with us in the field.

Once we had a meeting and a date, I had to make it happen from Baghdad. I arranged the schedule, transportation—helos, Suburbans, security, all that. Then we had to make sure that the election commissioners were delivering the right message (their message was consistent with ours), that Sunni votes would count and that they should get involved. At that point, we withdrew and disappeared so that it would in fact be a purely Iraqi event. As the meeting wound down, or if a threat appeared, we got them back to Baghdad.

Those trips were sometimes pretty harrowing. Going to Baqubah our helicopters were shot at and we got hit by an IED [improvised explosive device, or roadside bomb]. We were rained on by mortars in Ramadi, and there were television reports that we'd been taken hostage. That shows how difficult it is to get accurate reporting from the middle of a war zone.

The meetings were typically fairly hostile at the beginning, and sometimes at the end. The Sunnis were not enamored of the Shi'a and felt they were being marginalized. If they were going to get involved, they wanted guarantees. Despite all the voices raised and all the arguments the commissioners generally kept their cool, kept working with Sunni leadership, tribal or political or just as civil society, and in the end they could talk on decent terms with each other. But there were always problems of promises made and not kept, especially in places like Anbar, which was a very difficult environment in which to work. But in the end both sides typically remained very respectful of one another.

In the end we had a huge impact on the elections by making changes in procedures that allowed the Sunnis to participate more fully, which they did. It was a great credit to the foreign service officers in the field and to our military, which was with us every step of the way.

"In Spite of All the Violence"—PRTs, 2006–2007

In late 2005 the regional embassy offices, except in Basra, gave way to provincial reconstruction teams (PRTs), which looked more like Toby Bradley's governorate reconstruction team than the typical consulate office on which the REOs had been modeled. The PRTs had mixed civilian-military staffs, with a foreign service officer in charge. Civilians included personnel from State, USAID, Justice, and Agriculture, outside contractors, and Iraqi employees, joined by a military civil-affairs unit and other military personnel.[4]

Even as the security situation deteriorated, the number of PRTs grew and their mission expanded. By August 2007 there were twenty-five PRTs, ten paired with U.S. military units and others relying on non-U.S. coalition forces or civilian contractors for security, or both. The PRT team leader and the brigade commander shared responsibility: the brigade commander reported to the commanding general, exercised tactical control, and was able to veto any planned movement; the PRT team leader reported to the U.S. ambassador and was in charge of political and economic matters.[5]

The PRT mission, originally limited to fostering economic development and building Iraqi capacity to manage and govern at the municipal and provincial levels, expanded to include political objectives: to bolster moderate political forces, promote reconciliation; and strengthen counterinsurgency efforts. PRTs were called the key to the build element in the clear-secure-build strategy for Iraq.[6] Dan Speckhard, the deputy chief of mission at the Baghdad embassy, described the PRTs as promoting "self-reliance. This is really about transitioning, to Iraqis being able to successfully do the governance and economic work that they need to do in their own provinces." Steven Buckler, a PRT leader, said, "We are working very hard to convince [the Iraqis] to basically change their relationships with one another."[7] Barbara Stephenson, who backstopped the PRTs from her position as deputy coordinator for Iraq in the Department of State, said the teams' first goal is political change—to make the environment more hospitable for moderates, less comfortable for extremists. Then, she indicated, more technical specialists can come in to help with reconstruction, working largely with funding and direction from the Iraqi government.[8]

To call these goals ambitious is an understatement. The grandeur of the mission seems at odds with the modesty of the effort. Total civilian staffing, when all new PRTs are in place, is expected to be just over six hundred people. Total funding for the PRTs in the FY 2008 Iraq supplemental budget request is $679.2 million.[9] But, as one PRT team leader noted, "we don't reconstruct anything. The money flowing from the government of Iraq now dwarfs anything coming through the coalition forces. The coalition funding is less than 10 percent of what goes in."[10]

Foreign service officer Kiki Munshi came out of retirement to head a PRT in Baqubah, Diyala province, in 2006. She told reporters, "I felt a sense of moral obligation to try to help rebuild Iraq." Security problems made things difficult. The PRT was located at Forward Operating Base Warhorse, an army base hit by a car bomb in 2005. Private contractor Blackwater handled security until the Department of State decided the expense was more than the budget could handle and worked out an arrangement with the army. "Life is much easier" with army security, Munshi said, because Blackwater allowed the team only three trips a week off the base. In Muqdadiyah, where a Sunni Muslim cleric had been murdered at a mosque in November 2004, and where U.S. forces arrested twenty people in two bomb-making cells in March 2005, the PRT helped bring local leaders together to sign an agreement to end kidnappings and killings. The agreement collapsed ten days later in a wave of hostage-taking and murder. By February 2007, after a year at Baqubah, Munshi was disheartened enough to quit. A Reuters story quoted her: "In spite of the magnificent and often heroic work being done out there by a lot of truly wonderful people, the PRTs themselves aren't succeeding. The obstacles are too great."[11]

Her successor, John Melvin Jones, disagreed:

> We have had a great success with the opening of our radio and television station . . . a major step in the direction of getting the warring parties to at least sit down and listen to radio stations that broadcast a message of reconciliation. We have five young people who have spent their time at the station, of course guarded by U.S. troops, but they've been able to put together a program that's on the air twenty-three hours per day. . . . We have had success in getting money from the central bank . . . up to Baqubah so that salaries could be paid to public servants. We've already set in place a process by which we can get fuel oil into the province. And we are working on a procedure to get food into the province. So this is an attempt by the PRT and our support brigade to assist the people of Diyala province in spite of all the violence.[12]

In Hillah in agricultural Babil province, a forty-five-person PRT, about half civilian and half military, replaced a regional embassy office in November 2005. By January 2007 team leader Chuck Hunter, a midlevel foreign service officer fluent in Arabic, could tell reporters:

> The local leaders are engaging with the idea of democracy. . . . We've now got a local council that has a radio call-in show and puts out its ideas through a newspaper. . . . In terms of provision of basic services, we've been able to do sector studies . . . to give [local officials] a base for their analyses to decide how to prioritize resources now that there's increasingly Iraqi government money that is coming their way. . . . My local staff also comes to work day in and day out, even though, for some of them, that presents a very real risk. One of my colleagues unfortunately had a close relative kidnapped and killed just a couple of weeks ago, and he feels that he's under observation. And yet they believe in this mission too.[13]

The PRT in Saddam Hussein's native town of Tikrit, in Salah ad Din province, opened in May 2006 just north of the city on an old Iraqi air force base that is now Camp Speicher, headquarters for the 101st Airborne Division. The first team leader, Stephanie Miley, was a foreign service officer who did not speak Arabic. She headed a group of about forty, including civilians from the departments of State, Agriculture, and Justice, USAID officials and contractors, and military personnel, mostly reservists, with a range of civil-affairs and technical specialties. Miley told reporters in January 2007 that the PRT had persuaded the local provincial council to publish minutes and bring media into their meetings; had improved fiscal management by showing officials how to use "simple but usable" Microsoft Excel spreadsheets and graphs to track the flow of resources; and had strengthened the rule of law by hosting meetings that led to Iraqi decisions to have investigative judges teach police officers about preserving evidence and building a case.

Security problems limited travel off base by team members to five or six trips a week, for fairly short meetings with local officials. Miley's successor, foreign service officer and Arabic speaker Steven Buckler, called the security requirements "extremely inconvenient" and said "we are always keenly aware that we're putting the young soldiers at risk who are operating the convoys that transport us in and out of the city. [Even so,] I've worked in embassies for several decades now and I have never seen an embassy as actively engaged on a daily basis in a personal way as I have our office in Tikrit. The military unit that helps us with security is very, very, responsive."[14] Buckler's brigade combat team commander, Colonel Michael McBride, pointed out that "the most effective work happens in places that are the least secure." The State, USAID, and other civilian members of the PRT, he said, "have never backed down from going into some of the most tenuous places that we have in this province, because that is where the most good is going to be done."[15]

Impact on the Service

The evidence shows that the foreign service was willing, but not ready or able, to meet the demands that Iraq placed upon it. Steps to correct the obvious deficiencies have been weak and halting.

Readiness, in terms of professional preparation and training, was inadequate. Arabic speakers were and are in notoriously short supply. Among the more than one thousand U.S. government employees at the Baghdad embassy in June 2007 were more than three hundred members of the foreign service, of whom only 5 percent—fifteen people—spoke Arabic at a level of professional utility (the S-3 level—see table 7.1). In the service as a whole, only 1 percent (112 out of 11,467) spoke Arabic at that level, and of that 1 percent almost half had already served in postinvasion Iraq for six months or more [16]

Iraq is not the only place where diplomacy requires fluency in Arabic. In mid-2007 there were 219 positions around the world that, according to the Department of State, required staffing with foreign service officers who speak Arabic (some of those positions are designated at the S-2 level). If every foreign service officer qualified in Arabic were to spend 40 percent of his or her career in Arabic language-designated positions, the service would need 547 Arabic speakers to keep 219 positions staffed. Training from scratch to professional utility in Arabic normally takes two years of full-time study, time away from other duties that need to be performed.[17] In 2007, four years after the start of the war, the department announced that it would immediately break any assignment to redirect into Arabic language training any foreign service officer or specialist who volunteered for it, regardless of the staffing gaps that might result.[18] That was a policy decision that may have shown sound priorities, but it also certainly showed poor planning.

Lack of readiness extended beyond language. In February 2007 the Department of State had to turn to the Department of Defense to fill 129 civilian positions in Iraq, because State had neither the personnel nor the wherewithal to hire or contract personnel with necessary skills in areas like civil engineering, veterinary medicine, and public sanitation. Secretary of Defense Gates, testifying before the Senate Armed Service Committee, was publicly irritated with the request.[19] Foreign service personnel assigned to Iraq or Afghanistan typically received no more than two weeks of training to cover language, civil affairs and reconstruction, and how to conduct oneself as an unarmed civilian working in a combat zone. Forty years ago foreign service officers assigned to Vietnam routinely received four months or more of training, and many spent twenty-two weeks in full-time Vietnamese language study.

If the service had not prepared its members for Iraq, neither was it able to fill the positions required. The replenishment of the ranks under the Diplomatic Readiness Initiative of 2001 through 2004 proved inadequate. Even before the expansion of PRTs in 2007, Iraq and Afghanistan had absorbed all of the float (personnel available for training or in transit) that the DRI had constructed.

The service took a number of steps to stretch its resources. It moved three hundred positions from low-priority areas, chiefly in Europe, to high-priority regions in the Middle East, China, India, and Africa. Sacrificing the important to the urgent, it curtailed long-term training, defined as training lasting four months or more. It banned extensions of tours in nonhardship posts, making personnel in those positions available for assignment to less comfortable places, and making their positions available to people coming out of places like Iraq. It determined to make assignments in a particular order: Positions in Iraq, Afghanistan, and other posts where minor dependents are not allowed were filled first, followed by other high-hardship and high-danger posts, posts with critical needs, and posts that historically are hard to staff[20] (see chapter 9 for more information on how assignments are made).

Even so, unplanned gaps and vacancies began to appear in posts around the world, as personnel departed with no replacements in sight. The Government Accountability Office reported in May 2006 that 15 percent of State's worldwide public diplomacy positions were vacant. A year later, despite the high visibility and high priority assigned to public diplomacy, that number had risen to 22 percent.[21] Other areas were similarly shortchanged. In November 2007, 21 percent of foreign service positions, overseas and in the State Department, had no one in them.[22]

In December 2007 the service finally admitted the obvious: that it could not fill its own positions. The admission led to a policy whereby vacancies are planned, rather than randomly occurring. Director General Harry Thomas ordered each regional bureau to identify the least critical 10 percent of positions—consular positions excepted—which will stay empty at least in 2008.[23] Vacancies above the 10 percent rate remain haphazard.

The difficulty in staffing positions called into question the performance and willingness of the foreign service and the State Department in Iraq. The increase in staffing demanded by the expansion of the PRTs in 2007 and the practice of one-year rotations meant that about 250 foreign service positions would have to be filled in Iraq in 2008. By October 2007 the service had identified only two hundred volunteers. The director general has the authority to direct employees to assignments they are unwilling to take, but no one is eager to see it used. The concern is not so much that large numbers of people will quit—retention rates in the foreign service are much higher than in the private sector, and higher than in most of government—but that people in a place they do not want to be will perform badly.[24] Nevertheless, Director General Harry Thomas announced that the department was prepared to order people to go. Reuters quoted Thomas: "If someone decides they do not want to go, then we would then consider appropriate action. We have many options, including dismissal from the foreign service."[25]

Thomas held an open meeting on the new policy on October 31, 2007. The event was a public relations debacle during which one officer reportedly called assignment to Iraq "a potential death sentence." John Naland, president of the American Foreign Service Association, reportedly said that there were "only about thirty spaces left" on the plaque in the State Department lobby that honors members of the service who died on duty (see chapter 3). He also told Thomas that an AFSA poll indicated that only 12 percent of foreign service members believed that Secretary Rice is fighting in their interests. Less melodramatically, others at the meeting chastised the department for its failure to provide treatment for employees affected by posttraumatic stress disorders. [26]

Critics for months had accused the foreign service and the State Department of weakness, especially in Iraq—and especially in contrast with the military. Ralph Peters of the *New York Post* in December 2006 had attacked "our self-adoring diplomats" and identified State as the source of "the worst failure" in Iraq: "State couldn't get enough volunteers even for its 90-day stints in Iraq—*every* major program that it insisted on running failed."[27] Two months later, Admiral Edmund Giambastiani, vice chairman of the joint chiefs of staff, contrasted the foreign service and the military: "We send out orders, we execute orders, we deploy our military, and guess what happens? They turn up and do their job."[28]

The shortage of volunteers and the tone of the October open meeting reinforced that line of thinking. Max Boot of the Council on Foreign Relations suggested that "diplomats aren't pulling their weight in Iraq and Afghanistan"[29] The State Department's newly launched weblog, Dipnote, posted some two hundred messages on the topic, many of them easily located with an Internet search linking the terms *diplomat* and *weenie*.[30]

Less attention was paid to the outcome of the affair. Perhaps in reaction to the media coverage, the department redoubled its efforts to find volunteers, and members of the service came forward. Assignments were completed for all Iraq vacancies in January 2008, without the need to order unwilling diplomats to go.

The willingness of the foreign service, despite its lack of readiness and the shortage of personnel, is the untold story. By November 2007 more than fifteen hundred foreign service personnel, about 13 percent of the total workforce of officers and specialists, had already served in postinvasion Iraq.[31] All of these volunteered for their assignments.[32] In the 2008 assignment cycle, about seven percent of all postings (252 out of 3,577) have been in Iraq, and all have been filled by volunteers. To encourage volunteers, the department offered incentives, including hardship pay and unenforceable promises of rapid promotion and opportunity to choose future assignments. (Government-backed life insurance, however, is a benefit available to the military only.) Some of the most effective incentives involved nothing more than administrative flexibility. One especially welcome innovation allowed the dependents of an officer or specialist transferred from an overseas post to Iraq to remain at their overseas post, rather than be shipped back to Washington with the prospect of moving again in a year's time.

But most foreign service volunteers in Iraq are surely not there for the money. Andy Passen, a fifty-year-old senior foreign service officer who headed the Baghdad PRT, described his motivation:

> *Like many of us, I questioned, back in 2003, whether it was the right decision for our country to go to war. But it's no longer March 2003; it's late in 2007, and our involvement in Iraq is unquestionably the single most important foreign policy issue of our generation. . . . Now, as a senior officer, I can make a contribution to this new foreign policy priority. I can respond to our secretary's call for volunteers, and use my talents and skills to engage with Iraqi leaders, to build capacity in provincial governance, to help Iraqis to rebuild and reconstruct their country and their government. There is no doubt that service on a PRT is among the most dangerous assignments in the Foreign Service. But I look at the thousands of young soldiers patrolling Baghdad's streets—some of them on their second deployment—every day serving as some of our most effective street-level diplomats, and I am honored to put on my body armor and move out beside them.[33]*

Increasing the size of the service is essential. The most eloquent argument on behalf of this proposition came from an unexpected source, Secretary of Defense Robert Gates. "My message," he said, "is not about the defense budget or the military power. My message is that if we are to meet the myriad challenges around the world in the coming decades, the country must strengthen other important elements of national power both institutionally and financially." Thus he called for "a dramatic increase in spending on the civilian instruments of national security—diplomacy, strategic communications, foreign assistance, civic action, economic reconstruction and development." He lamented the loss of USIA and the depletion of USAID but called for "new institutions." He contrasted the Defense Department's $500 billion budget (not counting operations in Iraq and Afghanistan) with the Department of State's $36 billion budget. "Despite new hires," he said, "there are only about 6,600 professional Foreign Service officers—less than the manning for one aircraft carrier strike group."[34]

Gates did not comment on the State Department's budget request for fiscal year 2008. The department asked for 254 new positions to support transformational diplomacy, including 104 positions for training enhancement.[35]

This request was the first of three then-planned annual increases that would have increased the authorized size of the foreign service by about 550, or 5 percent. Congress rejected the request as this book went to press.

The modesty of the request stands in contrasts to the grandeur of the mission. The chairman of the Senate appropriations subcommittee with jurisdiction over the State-AID budget, Patrick Leahy, told Secretary Rice: "'Transformational diplomacy' is a lofty slogan for what amounts to adding new positions at posts that have been understaffed for years. I welcome it. But beyond that, your 2008 budget offers little confidence that this Administration is prepared to devote the resources necessary to successfully exert America's influence in such a complex and dangerous world."[36] Former House Speaker Newt Gingrich, a harsh and frequent critic of the Department of State and the foreign service, believes that the service needs another four thousand members—"a Foreign Service that is at least 40 percent larger"—to do its job.[37]

That kind of expansion is improbable, at least in the near term. Where the department can act on the cheap, however, action is more likely. Promotions are cheaper than positions, and they can be used to shape the service within the limits of its current size. Management has instructed promotion boards to give due weight to creditable performance in Iraq, Afghanistan, and other posts where service entails hardship and danger, and the mission requires leadership, imagination, and diplomatic skill. Some members of the foreign service object. An anonymous officer told the *Foreign Service Journal*: "The general perception is that service in Iraq equates to instant promotions and/ or preferred onward assignments. Those of us serving elsewhere often feel that no matter how hard we work or how deserving [we are], we'll be overlooked for someone who has 'done time' in Iraq."[38]

The military and, it is said, Secretary Rice, have little patience with this kind of complaining. One Navy veteran, a senior officer in personnel, put it this way: "We call what we do 'orders.' When volunteers are insufficient, we direct. . . . The key, in the long term, is to ensure that when the system requires hard service, those who perform it will find career reward. Sooner or later it will dawn on folks that the way to success is to serve. State may be coming around to that."[39]

Just so. If the department's leadership is right about the kind of diplomacy the world demands now, then foreign service officers and specialists who can perform with distinction in anarchic environments of conflict and change will be the elite of the service in the years ahead.

6

•

Politics and Professionalism

Tension between the professional foreign service and its political masters is inevitable. It can be invigorating or corrosive. The professionals are proud of their knowledge, skill, and experience, but it's the elected officials and those they appoint who set the policies and vote the taxes and budgets to carry them out. Foreign service professionals must give effect to the policies of the administration and the laws of the land, even as policies change and laws are revised. To maintain the flexibility they need, many professionals try to hold themselves above politics. If they succeed, they succeed just barely, for try as they may they are in politics up to their eyeballs.

There is no way around it. As members of the foreign service advance in their careers, they take on jobs of increasing responsibility and public presence. Whatever their position in internal foreign service debates, when ambassadors, their deputies, their press officers, and their senior aides deal with foreign officials or the public, they have to follow the official line and defend it vigorously. So do assistant secretaries, their deputies, and their office directors. All foreign service officers are commissioned by the president and, at least notionally, serve at his pleasure. They speak not only for their country, but also for their government, which means for the administration in power.

Once upon a time, politics stopped at the water's edge. So said Senator Arthur Vandenberg, the Republican chairman of the foreign relations committee who abandoned isolationism to support the Marshall Plan and the United Nations during Truman's presidency. But bipartisanship in foreign policy was a bit of a myth even during Senator Vandenberg's ascendancy (he died in 1951), and in recent years it has been rarer than the unicorn.

One reason surely is that foreign policy is no longer foreign. Ambassador L. Craig Johnstone wrote in 1997: "Almost every international issue has a domestic consequent, more visible and direct than ever before. Almost every major domestic issue has an international component. The distinctions between domestic and foreign are gone."[1]

The past decade has proved him right. How we respond to international terrorism affects our civil liberties, and how we define our liberties affects our response to terrorism. Budget decisions made in the U.S. Congress affect the value of the trillion dollars of U.S. bonds held by the Bank of China, and what China does with its holdings affects U.S. economic welfare. How we deal with global warming affects spending by domestic businesses, and vice versa. Political differences over privacy, taxes, and regulation—and over almost any other domestic issue—are differences over foreign policy as well.

Political clashes over foreign policy pose two questions for the foreign service. First, how does the foreign service remain professional while carrying out policies that may change radically with each election? Second, how can each new political leadership comfortably entrust its policies to a foreign service that worked hard and effectively for the policies of its predecessor?

Staying Professional

The first question is less difficult than it seems. Diplomats represent their countries the way lawyers represent their clients. They do not speak for themselves. The placard on the green baize table says "United States," not "Ambassador Patterson" or "Ms. Woods." A foreign service officer conducting official business always says "my government believes" or "the position of my government is." An officer's personal views are of no consequence and should never enter an official discussion.

The result of this self-effacement is that when policies change, the foreign service—both as a whole and as individuals—can remain a zealous advocate. It is still "my government believes" and "the position of my government is." A foreign service officer below the rank of ambassador or assistant secretary who becomes personally identified with a policy has probably let ego interfere with professional detachment.

Frequent and radical changes in foreign policy may pose problems for the country's international credibility and influence, but foreign service personnel have to cope as best they can. Henry Kissinger wrote that "frequent gyrations in our national direction demoralize the Foreign Service, as they do foreign nations."[2] However, Tony Motley, a political ambassador and assistant secretary of state in the Reagan administration, says partisan differences over foreign policy should not be an issue for the foreign service. "It's not the job of foreign service officers to figure out what America really thinks. Their job is to defend the policy, and they shouldn't complain when a policy is unpopular at home or under attack in Washington."

How the Secretary Sees the Service

The second question—how to create trust between the political leadership and the foreign service professionals—is more problematic. How bad can things get? Former House Speaker Newt Gingrich in 2003 called the State Department "ineffective and incoherent," engaged in "a deliberate and systematic effort to undermine the President's policies."[3] When such corrosive attitudes prevail, they ensure that the White House and the National Security Council staff will keep the State Department and the foreign service in the dark and on the margins—a recipe for a diplomacy that is ineffective and incoherent after all.

As Henry Kissinger observed, the foreign service has little influence through any formal role; its ability to shape policy depends on an "intangible bond" between the secretary of state and the president.[4] When that bond is lacking—as was arguably the case between President Nixon and his first secretary of state, William P. Rogers, between President Carter and Cyrus Vance, between President Clinton and Warren Christopher, and between George W. Bush and Colin Powell—the foreign service will be generally ignored in policymaking and often left uninformed about decisions and actions taken.

But even a secretary of state who is close to the president may not fully trust the professional foreign service. Dean Acheson was infuriated by foreign service officers who believed the career service should control the formation of foreign policy.[5] James P. Baker III, secretary of state under President George H. W. Bush (1989–92), deliberately put the professionals on the sidelines:

> *I thought the institutional rigidity of the Foreign Service, with its separate rules, mores, and bureaucratic hierarchy, precluded a reliance solely on it in order to meet the challenges at hand. Most FSOs are talented and loyal public servants, and any Secretary would be foolish not to harness their strengths. I did so, and was served very ably by many of them. But as with any large group, some of them tend to avoid risk taking or creative thinking. . . . Primarily for these reasons, I preferred to centralize policy authority in a small team of talented, loyal aides, and build outward from them. This approach has been a hallmark of my government career.[6]*

Baker is not alone in finding the foreign service bureaucratic and excessively cautious. Alexander Haig, Ronald Reagan's first secretary of state (1981–82), and Henry Kissinger both thought the service had been traumatized by past attacks. Haig said "the recriminations of the McCarthy era" led to "intellectual timidity" and "professional diffidence" and taught the service that "it is prudent to equivocate."[7] Henry Kissinger wrote that "the permanent career service has endured so much abuse that its sense of beleaguerment is accompanied by an acute consciousness of bureaucratic prerogative." The appointment of amateurs to top policy jobs compounds the problem: "Leadership clearly incapable of grasping the complexity of the office or in constant need of briefing on the most elementary issues elicits the most self-willed assertions of Foreign Service parochialism."[8]

Haig and Kissinger both fretted about how difficult it is to harness the talents of the service. Their accounts hold lessons for the foreign service and for its leadership today.

Kissinger argued that the secretary needs to ride close herd on the service, lest the service follow its own lead instead of the secretary of state's:

> On one level, gaining control of the machinery of the Department of State is relatively easy. The Secretary's unambiguous orders are scrupulously carried out, at least at the outset, because the Foreign Service begins with the presumption that the Secretary deserves its support—until it has tested the limits of his tolerance. . . . In the hands of a determined Secretary, the Foreign Service can be a splendid instrument, staffed by knowledgeable, discreet, and energetic individuals. They do require constant vigilance lest the convictions that led them into a penurious career tempt them to preempt decision-making.[9]

Haig called the foreign service "a remarkable group of men and women, scholarly and sober and versed in foreign languages and the nuances of foreign culture and politics." He wanted "a strong ring of professionals" around him: "I needed their experience and their competence. The Foreign Service . . . helps to preserve political appointees who temporarily reign over the department from error." Like Kissinger, though, Haig found the service difficult to manage: "It is like an asteroid, spinning in an eccentric orbit, captured by the gravity of its procedures and its self-interest, deeply suspicious of politicians who threaten its stability by changing its work habits." Haig also remarked on the special difficulty of getting the foreign service to sign on to the policies of a Republican administration: "The Foreign Service . . . is not infected by Republican sentiment."[10]

To strengthen political control over this unruly bureaucracy, the department during Haig's tenure instituted the practice of assigning every assistant secretary of state in charge of a bureau at least one deputy who was a political appointee. In subsequent administrations, some especially sensitive bureaus also acquired special advisers—that is, political appointees named under Schedule C of the civil service rules.[11] With few exceptions, these practices have continued to the present day.

Despite their doubts, Kissinger and Haig became strong supporters of the foreign service, and the service became a strong source of support for their stewardships of the Department of State. Kissinger issued a warning to those who think America's diplomats should be sacked or relegated to menial chores:

> *In American folklore, our professional diplomats tend to be maligned as a collection of striped-pants fuddy-duddies, excessively internationalist in outlook, soft in defense of the national interest, as often a contributory cause of our difficulties abroad as agents of their resolution. The need to "clean out" the State Department has become a staple of our political oratory. Several Secretaries have begun their tours of office with that expressed determination. I know of none that has left office without having come to admire the dedicated men and women who supply the continuity and expertise of our foreign policy. I entered the State Department a skeptic, I left a convert.[12]*

Dissent

Dedication and loyalty do not imply servility. On the contrary, a member of the foreign service owes his political superiors his honest opinion and best judgment, even (or especially) when they conflict with the current line of policy. Sometimes, though, conflicts between the policies adopted by the administration and those favored by the individual member of the foreign service are more than differences of opinion. They may be differences of values, or of conscience.

How does a member of the foreign service remain true to his profession, his country, and his conscience, when each may pull in a different direction? What military historian S. L. A. Marshall wrote of the military officer applies to the foreign service officer and specialist as well: "His ultimate commanding loyalty at all times is to his country, and not to his service or his superior. He owes it to his country to speak the truth as he sees it. This implies a steadying judgment as to when it should be spoken, and to whom it should be addressed."[13] Marshall's answer starts with clarity but ends in ambiguity. If there is a better answer, it has not been revealed.

Tony Motley, who taught a State Department seminar for new ambassadors from 1986 to 2001, has straightforward advice for dissenters: "When you don't like a policy, admit it." A professional member of the foreign service should be enough of a diplomat to figure out how to tell his boss what he thinks without committing sabotage, and how to be loyal without pandering. "It's more art than science," says Motley. "Some people are just better at it than others."[14]

Of course, supervisors, whether political or professional, need to be able to tell the difference between frank advice on the one hand and disloyalty or flattery on the other. Ambassador Chas Freeman wrote: "Governments that condone candor will get it; those that don't, won't. . . . The candor of diplomatic reporting depends on the integrity of the reporting diplomat, which in turn reflects the degree of official tolerance for the confidential expression of unconventional, nonconforming, or dissenting views."[15]

Many foreign service officers—no telling how many, but more than a few—believe that the top levels of the Department of State have a low tolerance for candor, even privately expressed. "This [George W. Bush] administration poses every question in terms of loyalty," said a political officer with twenty years of service. "In the past, professionals were chosen for senior positions so that policymakers could draw on their knowledge and experience. Now they're yes-men. You don't have people who will stand up and say, 'Madam Secretary, what you propose won't work in my region of the world, which I know intimately.' There is no discussion of policy or policy implementation, at least none that involves the foreign service."[16] Another officer, quoted in the *Washington Post*, said: "I've heard about low morale and a number of people seeking to leave because they don't find the atmosphere so rewarding as it had been when it was not so politicized."[17]

Ambassador Craig Kelly, a career officer who served as executive assistant to Secretary of State Colin Powell, said, "Powell and his top aides—Deputy Secretary Armitage and Undersecretary for Political Affairs Marc Grossman—were always willing to listen to people who walked into their offices with divergent views. They often pushed back, but their minds were open. Meetings on policy issues were free-wheeling, with no punishment for contrary views."[18] Foreign service officers don't seem to have the same feelings about Secretary Rice.

The State Department's leadership recognized years ago that employees who are afraid to say what they think may become unhappy and unproductive.

However, the results of the department's efforts to protect the expression of views that challenge the official line have been mixed. In 1971, during the Vietnam War, the department created a dissent channel to allow foreign service personnel to express their opinions on important policy issues in writing directly and confidentially to the department's most senior officials. The channel has had a checkered history. Use of the channel declined from a high of thirty-two messages in 1977 to fewer than five in 2005.[19] The department's regulations prohibit reprisals against dissenters, and no formal complaint of reprisal has ever been lodged, but off the record some officers believe that dissenters are often punished with poor assignments and slow promotions. Is this cynicism justified? Craig Kelly, writing about his time as executive assistant to Secretary Powell, says that "dissent channel messages were read by the very top people. They got very careful replies. I always felt that [dissent messages] were not used more because people felt they could weigh in through more normal channels."[20]

It may also be true that would-be dissenters stay silent because their messages rarely if ever carry the day. Dissenters are often speaking for the losing side of a policy debate that has already taken place. The arguments they raise may have been considered and rejected or discounted before the decision was taken.

In recent years the dissent channel has been used more for management than policy issues. The American Foreign Service Association gives four annual awards for constructive dissent. The issues addressed by recipients of the 2006 awards included an employment dispute involving a foreign service national, procedures for issuance of visas to skilled workers, screening procedures for certain Muslim travelers, and parity in benefits and training between spouses and unmarried partners of foreign service personnel. Yet the 2007 awards show that the channel may be regaining the purpose its designers intended. Awards went to one officer who warned that a covert operation in support of Somali warlords opposing Islamist forces would backfire (it did), and to another officer who argued that much greater U.S. engagement in Sudan would be needed to end what the U.S. government called genocide in Darfur. At the ceremony, former Secretary of State Lawrence Eagleburger urged foreign service officers to take constructive dissent seriously. "Maybe if there were more of that," he said, "we wouldn't be in the mess we are in."[21]

What should members of the foreign service do when they disagree with a policy or course of conduct that as a matter of professional duty they must publicly support? The Department of State puts a weaselly answer on its website: "As public servants, Foreign Service [specialists and officers] must publicly defend U.S. government policy, despite personal reservations. There is an internal channel through which an employee may present dissenting views on specific foreign policy issues. If a [specialist or officer] cannot publicly defend official U.S. policy, he or she has the option to resign."[22]

Are there other options? The department does not say, but one senior officer laid it out this way: "In the beginning we were told that if you didn't agree with a policy you could, one—shut up, two—move and work on something else, or—three—tackle the issue and seek to change it. I think I have done all three. In some cases I argued for change, sometimes successfully, sometimes not, with no consequences to my career. In some cases I've said nothing, where the ball is already rolling. In some cases I've managed just to stay away from an issue and not work on it."[23] Another said, "For the most part we manage to put our views and our politics aside. There are times when that's hard to do, but I've usually found that there are at least some rational policy grounds on the other side of the argument, so I can say there are good reasons behind this, and I can live with that."[24]

Most members of the foreign service have had serious reservations about some U.S. policy at some point in their careers, but in fact very few people resign over policy. Attrition rates in general are low compared to the private sector, and they have not changed significantly in over twenty years, despite policy shifts and ups and downs in the general morale of the service. However disgruntled some members of the service may be, they are rarely unhappy enough to quit, and it is news when they do. In recent years, three foreign service officers have resigned over Balkan policy, and three over Iraq.[25]

Family obligations are one undeniable reason why some dissenters stay on the job. It is hard to quit your job when your skills are esoteric, your kids are growing up, and your benefits, including your pension, are not portable. Some dissenters may also be too cynical to take an action based purely on principle. A more important reason, though, may be that most members of the foreign service, especially those who have spent long years abroad, are deeply if quietly patriotic and passionate about their work. They believe that what they do will over time make America a better, safer country, and even if they believe current policies are profoundly wrong, they will not abandon their profession.

Congress

Congress looks to members of the foreign service, and to civil servants in the foreign affairs agencies, to provide prompt, accurate information untainted by partisanship. At the same time, Congress and the administration expect members of the service to transmit and defend the administration's views. Performing at a high level in both capacities requires skill, practice, time, and effort. That said, abroad or at home, professional diplomats should be able to carry a politically colored message without discarding their professional status.

The executive branch has the lead in foreign policy. As many presidents have learned, however, Congress has the tools to block almost any presidential initiative. Keeping key members of Congress informed of the administration's strategy, plans, and activities does not prevent clashes between the executive and the legislature. However, it does reduce their number and make debate more constructive. Members of Congress challenge the administration every day over foreign policy, often in dramatic ways, but for every headline there are literally thousands of cooperative transactions.

In Washington, the foreign service deals with Congress in four areas: policy, oversight, personnel, and resources. A glance at the list of testimony given before Congress shows that policy presentations to the House Foreign Affairs Committee and the Senate Committee on Foreign Relations receive the most attention, followed closely by budget presentations to the appropriations committees.[26]

Most personnel matters are internal to the foreign service agencies, but because foreign service officers—whether at State, USAID, Commerce, or Agriculture—are commissioned, their inductions and promotions, like those of the armed services, must be approved by the Senate. Promotion lists are almost always approved without controversy and by voice vote or unanimous consent, but almost always is not always. Ambassadors and policy-level officials (roughly assistant secretary and above) also require Senate confirmation.[27] AFSA, the collective bargaining agent for foreign service members in all four foreign service agencies, maintains active contact with congressional staff and key members of the foreign affairs committees on issues of pay and working conditions.

Congress also exercises oversight responsibilities, reviewing the way in which the executive branch carries out the laws that Congress has enacted. For the foreign service, oversight is especially intense where the service bears direct responsibility for execution of the law, for example, in issuing visas pursuant to the Immigration and Nationality Act or licensing weapons sales under the Arms Export Control Act. Oversight hearings are generally conducted by the committees with primary jurisdiction over the legislation, but other committees with an interest may also become involved.

Foreign policy is not a congressional preoccupation. The House Foreign Affairs Committee, said a member, "is not an A committee. It's not linked to any interest groups" that are willing and able to finance campaigns.[28] A serious interest in foreign relations can be an electoral millstone for a representative or senator, taking time away from matters of greater or more immediate interest to important constituents. Under these circumstances, it is remarkable how many members have taken risks to perform great service in foreign affairs, through legislation and sometimes through direct diplomacy. The list is long, distinguished, and bipartisan.

Much of the liaison work with Congress falls to the State Department's Bureau of Legislative Affairs, called H for Hill, and to USAID's Bureau of Legislative and Public Affairs. There is no lack of contact: The H bureau says on its website that each year it handles fifteen hundred pieces of legislation, eight thousand pieces of correspondence, eighteen thousand congressional inquiries, and three hundred hearings, and that it sends the Hill more than five hundred mandated reports and notifications.[29] The website doesn't count them, but the bureau also arranges scores of briefings for staff and members.

The department has struggled, however, to make its liaison effective, and congressional staffers often feel frustration at the tight control they believe the H bureau exercises over the flow of information. A 2002 study prepared for the Una Chapman Cox Foundation documented some serious problems. One Senate aide said: "We have a devil of a time just getting State Department folks to come up and talk off the record. And then when we do get them, we have this legislative shop person in the middle, making sure they don't say anything out of the box." A House staffer said of H: "I swear if they could they would come up to the Hill with their foreign service officers with ankle shocks and a remote control to make them shut up and say what they want." The usual view from the Hill is that foreign service officers are intelligent, dedicated to public service, professional, and nonpartisan, but also aloof and cautious to a fault.[30]

Maybe times have changed. Jennifer Butte-Dahl, a civil servant who handles Near East Asian affairs for the H bureau, said: "I know that study, and it's out of date. Secretary Powell and Deputy Secretary Armitage did a lot to change the system. They encouraged direct contacts between the desks [the offices with regional responsibilities] and the Hill."

For people in H, she claimed,

> it matters whether you are just a pass-through for the [regional] bureau or whether you actually add value. There's a sense inside the State Department that H doesn't really help. I think most people in the building don't know what H does. If they realized the ability we have, based on personal relationships, to change the course of events on the Hill—for example, to tweak bill language, kill a damaging amendment, or negotiate budget allocations—they'd be a lot more appreciative. At the end of the day, however, appreciation doesn't really

matter. H supports the Secretary's priorities on the Hill—full stop. We'll never be able to make everybody happy.[31]

At least some on Capitol Hill are appreciative. Senator Patrick Leahy, chairman of the subcommittee that handles appropriations for the Department of State, told Secretary Rice during an otherwise confrontational hearing: "We may have our disagreements, but you, Madam Secretary, and your staff, have always been accessible and willing to discuss ways that we can work together."[32]

The H bureau is off the beaten career track for most foreign service officers. Unlike most of the State Department, where foreign service and civil service personnel work under a fairly thin layer of political leadership, the H bureau is about evenly divided among the three groups: one-third foreign service, one-third civil service, and one-third political appointees. In the regional bureaus, foreign service officers come and go, but when they go, they often go to jobs in the region and remain closely connected to the bureau in Washington. In H, when foreign service officers go, they don't go to the Hill, they just move on. It is the civil service personnel who provide the bureau's institutional memory; but even though many have been in the bureau for ten years or more, they have trouble matching the longevity of members and staff on Capitol Hill.[33]

Overseas, members of the foreign service work with senators, representatives, and staff traveling on official congressional delegations, or codels, of which in 2005 there were about 650 involving more than 2,000 travelers. Codels are not the only type of congressional travel: State Department lingo includes staffdels (congressional staff traveling on official business but without members) and nodels (members of congress traveling unofficially). Some codels are ugly junkets, but most are serious business. Embassies take all of them seriously.

Codels give embassies a chance to take policy out of the briefing paper and put it on the street, a chance to show, not just tell, the legislative branch how resources are being used and what is being accomplished. To host-government officials, members of Congress are outside voices that can reinforce, or undercut, the U.S. government's message.

Of course, codels can also be used to make a political point. In 2007 several leading congressional Democrats, including new House Speaker Nancy Pelosi, traveled to Damascus in defiance of the administration's long-standing policy of refusing to engage the government of Syria in high-level meetings. This codel placed the ambassador and the embassy in a difficult position, one that called for—what else—some delicate diplomacy.

Embassies catch the brunt of congressional travel. The H bureau has a travel unit to handle codel logistics, and the regional bureaus handle substantive issues, but the main effort takes place overseas. Although many elements of an embassy, and very large numbers of hours, are involved in even a small codel, the ambassador or his deputy usually assigns one person, called the control officer, to take responsibility for all elements of the visit: arrival and clearance through customs and immigration, accommodations, all ground transportation, and substantive, social, and recreational schedules for all members of the party. Control officers, usually junior or midlevel officers, are thrown into close contact with staff and members of Congress under circumstances that are often less than ideal on both sides—lost luggage, failed appointments, missed flights, sudden illness, bad food, bad press.

"In Moscow," said a midlevel officer, "the foreign service nationals in the embassy's visitor's unit knew the routine, and we would have everything lined up when the delegation arrived. Then the plans go out the window, and you have to react to the situation. It was hard to get high-level meetings. President Putin would only meet with the president or secretary of state. Some staff understood and were gracious, but others said, 'What good are you?' Being control officer is what you call a learning experience."[34]

Members of the foreign service who deal with the Congress need to understand the institution and the motivations of its members as well or better than they do foreign governments and parliaments. Fortunately, foreign service work offers many opportunities beyond codels for members of the service to develop personal relationships with members of Congress and congressional staff. Unfortunately, neither State nor USAID seems to know how to build on those relationships as part of career development. For example, six or eight foreign service officers are assigned each year to a one-year tour on detail to a congressional office under a program started by Senator James B. Pearson of Kansas in the 1970s.[35] The number of Pearson fellows in the service is now quite large. However, there is no systematic effort to assign Pearson alumni to jobs where the knowledge and relationships they acquired on the Hill will be especially useful. Nor is there any special effort to identify, much less cultivate, the many former foreign service officers who work on the Hill.

Budgets

The relationship between Congress and the foreign service faces a test each year at budget time, though the budget yields only a murky picture of congressional satisfaction with the service's past performance or its expectations for the future. That is because in the vast federal budget, there is no line or box marked *foreign service*. The funds for America's diplomats are scattered throughout the budget and hard to find. Foreign service people watching the progress of the budget through the Congress are often confused or disheartened, because the process itself is confusing and often discouraging.

One source of confusion is the difference between legislation that authorizes programs and legislation that appropriates funds. Authorizing laws establish or modify federal programs but do not necessarily provide the money to run them.[36] Authorizing legislation often indicates a dollar amount for a program, but authorizers cannot require appropriators to provide it. Appropriators, however, can effectively kill an authorized program by failing to fund it. They can also use appropriations to fund a program that has not been authorized.

The authorizing committees for most international activities are the Foreign Affairs Committee in the House and the Foreign Relations Committee in the Senate. These are responsible for oversight—for making sure that the executive branch faithfully carries out congressional intent. A strong committee or subcommittee chairman can use oversight hearings to influence policy, but in recent years the budgetary role of the authorizing committees has largely broken down. To the deep frustration and occasional anger of the authorizers, the appropriations committees and subcommittees are in control.

A second source of confusion is the calendar. Budgeteers juggle three or four or more budgets at once: the budget under which the agency is currently operating, the budget pending before the Congress, the budget being drawn up for the following year, and any relevant supplemental or emergency funding. Supplemental budgets related to funding the wars in Iraq and Afghanistan have been part of the appropriations for State and USAID in each fiscal year since 2003.

Money available for an activity or program in one period may not be available in another. Nor is money appropriated for one activity available to be spent on another, though sometimes adjustments can be made with notification to Congress. Students in Economics 101 learn that money is fungible; students in Budgets 101 learn that it isn't.

The meat and potatoes for the foreign service—salaries, allowances, positions, and so forth—are in the State Department's budget for administration of foreign affairs and AID's budget for operating expenses. Beginning with the 110th Congress (2007) and with the budget for fiscal year 2008, State and AID received their funds in the same appropriations bill, handled in the appropriations committees of both the House and the Senate by subcommittees on State, foreign operations, and related programs.[37] The U.S. Commercial Service is in the Commerce Department's budget, under the jurisdiction of the House and Senate subcommittees on commerce, justice, science, and related agencies. Funds for the Foreign Agricultural Service are bundled in the Agriculture, Rural Development, Food and Drug Administration, and Related Agencies Appropriations Act, which covers nearly all of the Department of Agriculture and comes under the jurisdiction of the subcommittees of the same name in the House and Senate.

The budgets that directly affect the foreign service are small portions of the bills in which they appear. In fiscal year 2006, when the State and USAID budgets were funded in different appropriations bills, the operating expenses for State, AID, the FCS, and the FAS were around 8 percent, 3 percent, 0.8 percent, and less than 0.1 percent of the total appropriations in the bills in which those funds were included. "That can be a problem," said Jim Morhard, staff director of the Senate Appropriations Committee. "It's hard to hold members' attention on budget issues that don't have much impact on the bottom line."[38]

It's not just the Congress that sees the budget with a short attention span. Foreign service officers also tend to neglect the budget, for several reasons. The budget is Washington work, which most foreign service people find less appealing than work overseas. It is a matter of numbers, which many foreign service people regard with fear and boredom. And it can be astonishingly complex. Foreign service people, with their three-year rotations, barely have the time to learn the intricacies of the budget process and to build necessary negotiating relationships before they are off to another assignment. They are at a disadvantage.

But Steve Dietz, a member of the civil service who handles State's budget in the department's Bureau of Resource Management, wants to attract more foreign service officers and specialists to the Office of State Programs, Operations, and Budget. "They understand the real impact of funding reductions on posts overseas. And when they finish a tour here, they go back to the field and educate others about the budget process and budget pressures. That leads to stronger input from the posts and bureaus and makes the justifications that we send to Congress more informative and persuasive."[39]

Long before the budget gets to the Congress, it is thrashed out inside the administration. The first step is presidential guidance on fiscal policy, which depends in part on forecasts of how the country's economy will perform two and three years in the future. With that guidance in hand, the Office of Management and Budget (OMB) sends its initial targets to the agencies funded by the budget, usually in the spring, and at least eighteen months before the fiscal year begins. (The government's fiscal year begins October 1 and ends September 30. OMB sent agencies guidance for FY 2010, ending September 30, 2010, in March 2008.) This is the point at which budget officers all over Washington know whether they are facing a lean or a fat year. Agencies have about six months to put their detailed budget requests together and get them to OMB in the fall, a year before the start of the fiscal year. Negotiations inside the administration last another six months or so, but by law and custom the president must send his budget proposal to the Congress on the first Monday in February, eight months before the fiscal year begins.

The budgets from State and USAID that go to OMB don't look like the budgets that will go to Congress. The Congress carves the pie of federal spending into thirteen appropriations bills, but OMB slices the same pastry into nineteen areas or functions of government (agriculture, defense, income security, and so forth). Each function is typically carried out in more than one agency, and each agency is typically engaged in more than one function. For the foreign service, the key budget is Function 150, international affairs. A summary of the president's budget request for Function 150 for FY 2009 (the year that ends on September 30, 2009) appears in table 6.1.[40]

The Department of State and USAID receive nearly all their appropriated funds through the 150 account, as do more than a dozen other government agencies and a few nongovernmental organizations that depend on government funds. Bits of the 150 account also go to agencies principally funded elsewhere. The State Department assembles the Function 150 request and leads the negotiations with OMB, which effectively decides who gets what in the president's budget.[41]

This is where the embassies weigh in. In every post overseas, and in every bureau, State and AID submit a joint budget request called a strategic plan. Plans from overseas missions go up through the regional bureaus. Mission and bureau strategic plans (MSPs and BSPs) identify the objectives they are supposed to achieve and connect them with the resources—not just money but people, counted as full-time and part-time positions or contract employees—they need to achieve them. The objectives often come from the top, from the president and the secretary of state, but bureaus and missions have latitude to devise the programs and estimate the resources needed to accomplish the objectives in the local arena.

Ambassador Craig Johnstone led resource planning in the State Department for Secretaries Christopher and Albright. "The biggest problem State has," Johnstone explained, "is aligning resources and objectives. If you have a clear objective and a clear strategy, and you have a plausible argument and avoid political minefields, you have a good chance in the Congress. For State and AID, the performance plans define what it is you're trying to get done in the country. They affect thinking in the regional bureaus. Only State and AID do this kind of regional planning."[42]

Steve Dietz explained how the FY 2009 budget request came together:

> *We start with the current level of services. How much will it cost in 2009 to do what we are doing in 2008? We have to make assumptions here about inflation and exchange rates. Then we take out expenditures for what we did in 2008 that we won't do or don't plan to do in 2009. Then we add what we have to do in 2009 that we didn't do in 2008—mandatory pay raises go here, for example. Finally we add what we want to do in 2009 that we are not doing in 2008, discretionary spending. The MSPs and BSPs are essential to this process.*[43]

The budget process is competitive, especially in lean years when resources are static or shrinking. Posts compete within a mission: In South Africa, the U.S. consulates in Johannesburg, Cape Town, and Durban compete with each other and with the embassy in Pretoria to press their claims, and the ambassador resolves disputes. Within a bureau the missions compete: More money for South Africa may mean less for Nigeria; adding an HIV/AIDS officer in Botswana could mean cutting a press officer in Nairobi. At the next level up, the bureaus compete: Africa against Latin America against East Asia, refugee affairs against counterterrorism against public diplomacy. The agencies and programs funded in Function 150 compete: USAID against State, bilateral assistance against money for international organizations. In OMB, Function 150 competes with the other eighteen functions in the federal budget. The ultimate arbiter is the U.S. Congress.

Foreign service officers, especially those in the field, see themselves as budget takers, not budget makers. For the most part they are right. They are too distant in time and place from budget decisions to have much impact on them. They are poorly placed to weigh competing claims for scarce resources. But foreign service officers, and especially ambassadors, should not underestimate the importance of the mission and bureau strategic plans, which build toward the State-AID joint strategic plan that is submitted to Congress with the budget. A U.S. ambassador in Africa remarked, "Initially I thought the mission plan was a waste of time, but over ten years it's evolved into a useful tool. You have control over your priorities, and to some extent over your budget."[44]

Table 6.1. FY 2009 International Affairs Request ($ in thousands)

	FY 2007 Total	FY 2008 Total Est.	FY 2009 Request
INTERNATIONAL AFFAIRS	38,671,802	36,399,395	39,498,234
FOREIGN OPERATIONS	26,384,038	23,995,766	26,141,318
Export & Investment Assistance	(103,568)	(114,016)	(157,700)
Bilateral Economic Assistance	19,545,572	17,618,553	18,801,113
U.S. Agency for International Development Child Survival & Health Programs Fund (CSH)	1,901,425	[1,829,152]	1,577,830
Other Bilateral Economic Assistance			
Economic Support Fund (ESF)	5,117,675	2,989,838	3,153,743
Assistance for Eastern Europe and the Baltic States (AEEB)	462,900	293,553	275,625
Assistance for the Independent States of the Former Soviet Union (FSA)	452,000	396,497	346,108
Independent Agencies			
Peace Corps	319,700	330,799	343,500
Inter-American Foundation	19,347	20,830	20,000
African Development Foundation	22,800	29,757	30,000
Millennium Challenge Corporation	1,752,300	1,544,388	2,225,000
Department of State			
Global Health and Child Survival (Includes GHAI and CSH in FY 2008)		6,491,082	-
Global HIV/AIDS Initiative (GHAI)	3,246,520	[4,661,930]	4,779,000
Global Fund to Fight AIDS, Tuberculosis & Malaria	[377,500]	[198,000]	[200,000]
Democracy Fund	354,050	162,672	-
International Narcotics Control and Law Enforcement (INCLE)	724,616	556,405	1,202,061
Andean Counterdrug Program (ACP)	721,500	319,848	406,757
U.S. Emergency Refugee & Migration Assistance (ERMA)	110,000	44,636	45,000
Nonproliferation, Anti-Terrorism, Demining (NADR)	463,499	483,055	499,000
Migration and Refugee Assistance (MRA)	963,533	1,023,178	764,000
Department of Treasury	**86,900**	**50,288**	**170,000**
Treasury Technical Assistance	20,234	20,234	29,000
Debt Restructuring	64,350	30,054	141,000
Military Assistance	**5,364,927**	**4,897,044**	**5,149,700**
Multilateral Economic Assistance			
International Financial Institutions (IFIs)	**1,273,219**	**1,277,289**	**2,071,305**
International Organizations & Programs (IO&P)	**303,888**	**316,897**	**276,900**

Table 6.1. *cont.*

	FY 2007 Total	FY 2008 Total Est.	FY 2009 Request
STATE OPERATIONS &			
RELATED ACCOUNTS			
DEPARTMENT OF STATE	**10,023,759**	**10,474,657**	**11,223,104**
Administration of Foreign Affairs	**7,295,706**	**7,404,259**	**8,094,954**
Diplomatic & Consular			
Programs (D&CP)	5,201,613	5,326,686	5,364,269
Capital Investment Fund	58,143	59,575	71,000
Embassy Security, Construction			
& Maintenance	1,490,852	1,425,574	1,789,734
Civilian Stabilization Initiative	-	-	248,631
Office of Inspector General	31,414	33,733	35,508
Educational & Cultural			
Exchange Programs	465,671	501,347	522,444
Representation Allowances	8,175	8,109	8,175
Protection of Foreign Missions & Officials	9,270	22,814	18,000
Emergencies in the Diplomatic &			
Consular Service	13,440	8,927	19,000
Repatriation Loans Program Account	1,302	1,275	1,353
Payment to the American Institute			
in Taiwan	15,826	16,219	16,840
Foreign Service Retirement and			
Disability Fund [Mandatory]	[126,400]	[122,500]	[122,500]
International Organizations	**2,619,592**	**3,033,946**	**3,026,400**
Related Appropriations	**108,461**	**36,452**	**101,750**
BROADCASTING BOARD			
OF GOVERNORS	**656,750**	**682,004**	**699,489**
OTHER PROGRAMS	**87,894**	**94,804**	**108,423**
DEPARTMENT OF AGRICULTURE	**1,763,711**	**1,310,164**	**1,325,900**
P.L. 480 Title II (Agriculture Bill)	1,664,711	1,210,864	1,225,900
McGovern-Dole International			
Food for Education	99,000	99,300	100,000
RESCISSION OF PRIOR			
YEAR'S BALANCES	**(244,350)**	**(158,000)**	

The FY 2007 Total and FY 2008 Total Estimates include supplemental and emergency funding, but the FY 2009 Request does not.

This table is a condensed version of the table that appears in Department of State, *Summary and Highlights, International Affairs Function 150, Fiscal Year 2009 Budget Request*, 1-4, available at http://www.state.gov/documents/organization/100014.pdf. The request was submitted to Congress February 5, 2008, with the note that the administration will request supplemental funding for FY 2009 when needs for foreign operations in Iraq and Afghanistan are better known.

Interagency Conflict and Coordination

The competition for budgetary resources—money and people—is part of a broader contest over who shapes policy and controls its execution. Most of these struggles take place in Washington, not overseas. The foreign service as an institution rarely takes part in these struggles, because the service itself rarely has reason to favor any particular policy. But, as the Washington adage puts it, "Where you stand is where you sit." The positions advanced by individual members of the service depend on where they are in the foreign affairs bureaucracy. In Washington, members of the foreign service, like their civil service colleagues, spend many hours in inter- and intra-agency wrangles, advancing the point of view of the bureaucratic unit to which they are assigned. For nine out of ten members of the foreign service, that unit is somewhere in the Department of State.

Thrashing out positions within and between government agencies is time-consuming and often frustrating. George Shultz, who may have headed as many large bureaucracies as anyone in the history of American government, wrote that "in government, if [a] decision is going to stick, the divergent and divisive constituencies with a stake in the decision have to be persuaded—or if not fully persuaded, at least consulted—so they feel that their views were considered. Even then," he added, "they can give you plenty of grief."[45] Business executives and others from outside government who take on cabinet and subcabinet positions are almost always astonished by the amount of effort and the degree of compromise required to move a proposal or project through the system. "Don't we all work for the same president?" they lament. "Aren't we all on the same team?"

In fact, the team must be built anew for each issue. No agency has a full grasp of all the considerations that bear on a negotiation. Finding an efficient way to tap the government's expertise across agencies is a central task of management—and one not always carried out successfully. In foreign affairs, interagency coordination aims first at developing positions that fairly reflect the full range of U.S. interests, and second at maintaining discipline in negotiations and in the execution of policy. The formal mechanisms for accomplishing these aims are, for the first, the interagency group and, for the second, the widely hated clearance process. But the informal machinery of government, the networks of professionals who know and respect each other, is at least as important.

Interagency groups have been around since George Washington's cabinet met in Philadelphia, but in the areas of security and foreign affairs the current system begins with the 1947 National Security Act, which established the National Security Council (NSC). The NSC today includes the president, the vice president, the secretaries of state, treasury, and defense, and the assistant to the president for national security affairs (the national security adviser, who heads the NSC staff), with attendance from the chairman of the joint chiefs of staff, the director of national intelligence, and others as appropriate. An NSC principals committee (cabinet level) and an NSC deputies committee (subcabinet level) oversee the work of dozens of policy coordination committees and working groups, organized along regional lines that mirror the regional bureaus of the Department of State. The NSC staff, part of the executive office of the president, provides executive secretaries for each of these committees and manages their work. [46] In areas outside of national security, similar pyramids of interagency committees and working groups derive their authority from other statutes or from executive orders.

Positions are debated through the hierarchy of committees, usually from the bottom up. Differences that cannot be resolved among office directors move up to deputy assistant secretaries, and then to assistant secretaries, undersecretaries, and heads of department. When disagreements persist, events may overtake the debate. The pressure of time, as well as the desire for unconstrained action, often leads one agency or another to ignore the process, which it can do so long as it retains the president's confidence. No amount of fiddling with organizational structures can force consensus.

Clearance

No bureaucratic battle is ever really over. A policy once decided must still be carried out. Any instruction to an overseas post requires approval from all of the offices and agencies involved with the issue, and losers in the policy debate may use this clearance process to win back ground. The clearance system, intended to maintain discipline, often serves only to push instructions for action to a lowest common denominator, or to delay action until events make the matter moot. Small wonder that the system often breaks down and back channels—unofficial communications—proliferate.

Aggressive embassies can use these Washington logjams to make policy by default. When instructions are late or inadequate, an ambassador can write his own, telling Washington (usually, the State Department officer in charge of the issue) that "unless otherwise directed, I intend to carry out the following actions," setting a short deadline for response. This device—known as *you know, dear,* for UNless Otherwise DIRected—is bureaucratic jiujitsu that flips the inertia of the clearance process around, making action as difficult to stop as it had been to initiate. A slightly less confrontational approach is using e-mail to achieve the same purpose.

Foreign service officers assigned to Washington quickly become familiar with interagency work, and they learn to recognize the downside of agency or ambassadorial freelancing. The State Department is a relatively small agency with a relatively small budget. It cannot carry out its mission without the political support and often the resources of other agencies. Other agencies, of course, have international interests but not the mandate or, in most cases, the global reach of State. Without coordination, either nothing gets done, or what does get done is done badly.

Ambassador Owens-Kirkpatrick, recalling her time as the State Department's officer overseeing U.S. representation at NATO, said:

> *I can't emphasize enough the importance of understanding interagency coordination. You have to learn how to be a constructive player. Collegial relationships with people in the Department of Defense, the White House, and other agencies, are critical to success. You need to deal, to negotiate, to horse trade. It's a lot of fun and you can become very good at it. Sometimes the need to coordinate would hold up instructions until the early morning hours, which is frustrating, but in the end you reach a higher quality outcome.*[47]

The presence of active and former foreign service officers in agencies outside State can make coordination a bit easier. The trust and confidence needed for effective cooperation are more quickly established between people who know each other, or who at least share common experiences, than between strangers. Foreign service officers, especially in midcareer, can benefit from the new perspective that an out-of-agency tour provides.

Numbers vary widely from year to year, but there are often as many as fifteen or twenty foreign service officers serving temporarily in White House agencies, mainly the National Security Council staff and the U.S. Trade Representative's office. These assignments can be heady stuff. Hugo Llorens was director of Andean affairs on the NSC staff when Lucio Gutierrez won election as Ecuador's president in 2002.

> *At seven thirty in the morning I got the call to brief the president for a nine o'clock congratulatory call. I got six or seven minutes to be alone with and brief the president, then I had the opportunity to listen in on the call.... But you do have to be careful. I always knew that I had to go back to the Department of State. Sometimes I had to pass a message, to tell a more senior*

State Department official, "Look, that's not the way the White House wants it done." I wasn't the FSO at the NSC, I was part of the NSC team.[48]

On the Southern Border

Coordination is especially challenging where relations are deep as well as broad, and where U.S. government agencies communicate easily and frequently with their foreign counterparts—places like Mexico, and especially with regard to the Mexican border. Amid the range of cross-border issues— trade, crime, pollution, transportation—the most sensitive and important is immigration.

Travel across the border is vital to commerce and family life. In 2005, about thirteen million Mexicans visited the United States, and twenty-one million Americans went to Mexico, accounting for over a million legal border crossings per day. The U.S. embassy in Mexico City calculates that twelve million people live in the counties and *municípios* adjacent to the border. The Mexican-born population of the United States numbers well over ten million. But though U.S. efforts to control the border certainly affect U.S. foreign relations, they are not really part of American foreign policy.

Ambassador James Derham, a career foreign service officer who was the U.S. ambassador's deputy in Mexico from 1998 to 2002, remarked: "Humane, orderly, legal immigration. That's the goal and the policy as they come down to us from Congress and the White House, and we reinforce that message with Mexico at every opportunity. But immigration is essentially a U.S. domestic issue. Mexico has a role, of course, and the Mexicans can be helpful or harmful by their actions, but immigration policy is not like trade policy. There are no international negotiations."[49]

So what is the role of the foreign service? Derham explained:

> *The foreign service has no direct role in setting immigration policy, but we do want to make sure that the domestic debate is an informed debate, that the realities from the Mexican side are understood. It's important that we understand how Mexico thinks about immigration and that we explain to Washington what effect it has on other areas of our relationship. It's our job, the job of the foreign service, to place enforcement work, including our own visa work, in the context of all U.S. interests in Mexico, and to maintain consistency between our policies and our actions.*

Consistency is hard to achieve. Most of the federal, state, and local agencies involved in border control see their work in purely domestic terms. Three bureaus of the Department of Homeland Security—Citizenship and Immigration Services, Immigration and Customs Enforcement, and Customs and Border Protection (including the Border Patrol)—strike a balance as best they can between maintaining security and promoting commerce. The Department of Justice is also heavily involved along the border, through the Bureau of Alcohol, Tobacco and Firearms, the U.S. Marshals Service, the Federal Bureau of Investigation, and the Drug Enforcement Administration.

They don't always cooperate. "All these agencies have their jobs to do," said Derham. "They don't spend a lot of time thinking broadly about Mexico or even about each other, but they understand precisely what they're doing." A former U.S. consul at a border post added, "Law enforcement agencies don't do foreign policy, they do law enforcement. They don't like to share information, even with each other. We talk about 'humane, orderly, legal,' immigration but there's a gap between policy and what happens on the border. And the border region has its own culture. Local officials on both sides have a big say in everything that happens, including law enforcement, and they don't necessarily respond to their capitals. People along the border like to do things their own way."[50]

Working on the border or with border issues means constant negotiation, not all of it with Mexico. The State Department calls its officer in charge of border affairs a coordinator, not a director, and for good reason. "Before we can deal with the Mexicans," said John Ritchie, who formerly held that job, "we have to negotiate among ourselves. For example, if someone wants to open or close or modify a border crossing, we issue the licenses for construction. At a minimum we have to clear our decisions with twelve federal agencies, plus the affected states. We're long on responsibility but short on resources. We have to be very good at dealing with people in our own society and government."[51] Without that coordination, U.S.–Mexican relations will deteriorate and cooperation on the border will break down.

In some ways that has already occurred. "The flow across the border, legal or illegal, is so massive," John Ritchie said, "a million legal crossings every day, maybe half a million or a million illegal crossings every year. In the past few years Mexican migration has spread way beyond the border states. It's transforming the United States."

"The border is a great example of 'you can't fix just one thing,'" said Jim Derham. "You need a coherent approach, one that looks at the incentives and disincentives, the economic differentials, the lack of employer sanctions, enforcement at the border, and everything else that's going on. If you focus just on one part of the problem, you will have consequences throughout the system that you failed to predict, with results that may not be at all what you wanted."

No policy, however, has any meaning unless it is enforced. The Department of Homeland Security establishes visa policies and frames its regulations and enforces policies on the U.S. side of the border. The foreign service, through its consuls and vice consuls, carries out U.S. immigration policy on the Mexican side of the border.

The Mexican border is where many members of the foreign service start their careers. Entrants typically spend at least a portion of their first overseas tours in consular work, and especially in visas. The United States issues visas and similar official travel documents at ten posts in Mexico, including seven along the border.

Visa work is hard, tedious, and challenging. It entails long hours in front of a line of nervous applicants, trying to separate legitimate travelers from potential illegal immigrants and security threats in interviews that last little more than a minute. A new officer may conduct one hundred interviews in a day; an experienced officer may conduct two hundred or more each day, and as many as one thousand in a week. There is no time for a lot of analysis. An experienced visa officer comes to rely on visual clues, an applicant's manner and air of confidence, as much as on answers to questions: "A good consular officer can make good decisions about 90 percent of the time as the applicant walks up to the window."[52]

A year on the visa line, one former visa officer said, "is absolutely the best way to learn about a society—what people do, how much they earn, how they live and how they would like to live, how their families are put together, how they relate to the United States."[53] Visa work tests stamina, language skills, and the willingness to say "no" to people who are desperate for "yes." It is daily instruction in making quick decisions, and daily proof that sensitivity to a foreign culture does not mean softness.

Role of the Ambassador and the Country Team

Interagency conflicts are more acute in Washington than in posts overseas. The opportunity for conflict certainly exists—some forty U.S. agencies are represented abroad, and in the typical embassy less than a third of the American staff gets its paycheck from the Department of State. But the opportunity for strife is rarely seized. There are many reasons why this is so. Here are a few of them:

1. Embassies are policytakers, not policymakers. There are fewer fights because there is less to fight about.
2. Small is beautiful. In all but the largest posts, everyone knows everyone else. Relationships are more personal, less bureaucratic. There are few or no layers of staff. Decisions can be quickly and cleanly taken.
3. We're in this together. In a foreign clime and culture, agency identification fades and national identity takes over. And the more difficult the circumstances, the closer the embassy staff becomes. Morale tends to be high in hardship posts.
4. The boss is nigh. In Washington the president is distant, his wishes made known through surrogates and artifacts— an initial on a memo, an ambiguous speech. Like Russian peasants thinking of the tsar, even high-level officials may believe against the evidence that the president really sides with them. But overseas, the president's representative, the ambassador, is right there, face to face. There should be no doubt about what the boss thinks or what the boss wants.

The idea that the ambassador is fully in charge of the embassy and all subordinate posts in the country seems an ancient notion, dating to the Greeks perhaps. But in U.S. practice it dates to the postwar period, and particularly to the administration of John F. Kennedy and the idea of the country team. Since 1961 the president has provided each chief of mission with a letter that charges him or her with responsibility for the conduct of foreign affairs in his or her country of assignment, and gives him or her authority over all executive branch personnel in the country, except those under the command of a U.S. area military commander, those seconded to an international organization, or those serving under another chief of mission. (For example, the U.S. ambassador to Belgium has no authority over the U.S. missions to the European Union or to NATO, which are also in Brussels.) Ambassadorial responsibility was placed in law in the Foreign Service Act of 1980.[54]

The terms *chief of mission* and *ambassador* are often used interchangeably, but chiefs of mission are not always ambassadors, and vice versa. A chief of mission (COM) is the principal officer in charge of a diplomatic mission of the United States. A COM is usually an ambassador—indeed, an ambassador extraordinary and plenipotentiary, or AEP—but may be a chargé d'affaires. He or she usually heads an embassy, which may have subordinate posts, typically consulates and consulates general. The heads of subordinate posts are also called principal officers, but they are not chiefs of mission.

Some ambassadors are not chiefs of mission. Ambassadors at large, like the ambassador at large for war crimes issues or the ambassador at large for international religious freedom, both established by acts of Congress, have no missions; others, like the U.S. global AIDS coordinator, are confirmed by the Senate with the personal rank of ambassador. A few individuals, appointed by the president for no more than six months, may be given the title of ambassador without Senate confirmation. By custom, once an ambassador, always an ambassador: If you ever hold the title, you may use it for the rest of your life.

An area commander does not command all forces in the area. Excluded are service attachés, military advisory groups or liaison offices, marine security guards, or other military elements that are part of the diplomatic mission and are under the COM's authority.

The chief of mission carries out his responsibility through the country team, which is made up of members of the staff he chooses to advise him and on whom he relies to see that policy is carried out. The chief of mission has a free hand in choosing the country team. Some ambassadors prefer a large group, with representatives of every element in the embassy. Others want a smaller group, focused on the most important areas of the ambassador's concern. A typical country team is shown in figure 6.1.

An ambassador's responsibilities have grown over the years. The State Department's *Foreign Affairs Manual* lists them in nineteen numbered paragraphs: opening markets for U.S. exports, halting arms proliferation, preventing conflict, countering terrorism, upholding human rights, promoting international cooperation on environmental issues, suppression of narcotics, and assisting refugees—and these are just in paragraph one. Eighteen others follow.[55] Every ambassador has to be concerned about whether his authority, which depends largely on his leadership and his support in Washington, is commensurate with these responsibilities.

A chief of mission has several tools that he can use to maintain his mission as an integrated structure. One is country clearance. Any government employee not already stationed in the country must have the approval of the chief of mission before entering the country on official business. Is a delegation from the Department of Energy planning a visit to promote an exchange of research with an institute that, according to intelligence sources, is mixed up in illegal transfers of nuclear technology? The chief of mission can say no.

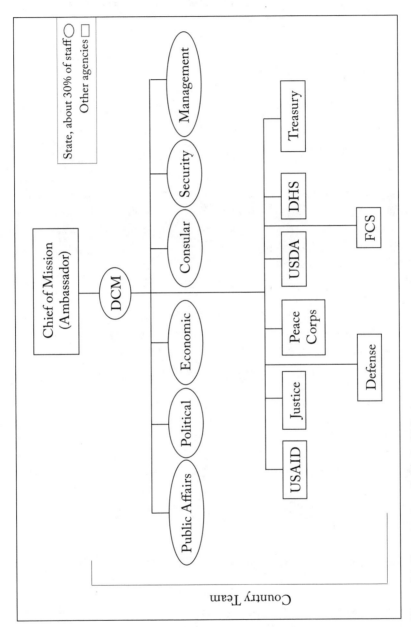

Figure 6.1 Organization of a Typical Mission

Is an FBI team coming to investigate a kidnapping just as negotiations on an agreement on child custody cases approach a conclusion? The chief of mission can put the FBI on hold. An ambassador may refuse clearance, or place restrictions or conditions on official travelers, as he considers necessary.[56]

A chief of mission also has limited control over the structure and staffing of the embassy and its subordinate posts. The COM cannot increase staff without Washington's approval, including budgetary authority, but he can often block attempts by Washington agencies to send staff he does not want—at least if the Department of State backs him up.[57] The ambassador is, by law, accountable for the security of his mission and all U.S. government personnel and their dependents in the country. If AID wants to put additional personnel in the field, but the COM sees an unacceptable security risk, the COM will likely prevail. He can reorganize State Department staff (combine the political and economic sections, for example, or establish separate sections for immigrant and nonimmigrant visas), but he cannot do much with the staff of other agencies without their approval.[58] He can, however, terminate the assignment and send home anyone under his authority whose behavior or performance is seriously unsatisfactory.

Of course, the wise ambassador picks no unnecessary fights and keeps Washington well informed of his thinking. All foreign service personnel should remember this: If you want the State Department to watch your back, make sure they know which way you're facing.

The State Department helps the ambassador out by negotiating some of the toughest interagency issues—who provides security, who controls communications, who pays for what, whose writ runs how far—in memoranda of understanding (MOU) signed in Washington, not at post. Some MOUs have been contentious—State has negotiated at least four with the FBI—but all of them tend to reinforce the ambassador's authority in the embassy and across the host country. Agreements between the chief of mission and the local agency, or—most important—between the chief of mission and the area combatant commander, can supplement agency-to-agency understandings.

Nearly every embassy has a military component. The highest-ranking military officer inside a U.S. embassy is ordinarily the defense attaché, a member of the worldwide defense attaché system run by the Defense Intelligence Agency (DIA). The defense attaché, typically an O-6 (full colonel or navy captain), may be from any of the services, and DIA often rotates the assignment from service to service. The defense attaché is principal military advisor to the ambassador and operates under the ambassador's authority. He is a member of the country team. His office carries out traditional responsibilities:

liaison with the forces of the host country, including sharing of intelligence; weapons sales programs like foreign military sales (FMS) and foreign military financing (FMF); military-to-military exchanges, like IMET (International Military Education and Training, which brings foreign forces to the United States); and management of programs like the GPOI (Global Peace Operations Initiative, which provides U.S. training and equipment for host-government forces engaged in international peacekeeping). GPOI and the FMS, FMF, and IMET programs are all funded through the Department of State.

In some embassies, a separate security assistance component, which may be called military liaison office, military group, office of defense cooperation, or any similar name that is acceptable to the host government, handles weapons sales. The officer in charge of this unit may outrank the defense attaché, but even if he does not, his chain of command runs to the Pentagon, not to the defense attaché. He is, however, subject to the authority of the ambassador. Most ambassadors will include the head of security assistance in the country team, along with the defense attaché.

Much of the military's growing nontraditional engagement abroad is in the area combatant commands, which lie outside ambassadorial authority. In Iraq, and to a large extent also in Afghanistan, the U.S. military has deployed civil affairs teams to carry out reconstruction and humanitarian assistance in areas where the absence of security prevented State, USAID, and nongovernmental organizations from operating. A report by staff of the Senate Foreign Relations Committee says that the Defense Department built on this experience to carry out similar projects in other countries where the United States conducts military operations, using funds available to combatant commanders.[59] Also outside ambassadorial authority are the area commands' public-diplomacy efforts—in 2007 the Joint Forces Command ordered up a $400,000 RAND study, *Enlisting Madison Avenue: The Marketing Approach to Earning Popular Support in Theaters of Operation*—that may or may not run parallel with the efforts of the embassy or the Department of State.[60] And in the gray area between area combatant commands and defense personnel subject to ambassadorial authority are military personnel under the Special Operations Command (SOCOM), who provide military-to-military counterterrorism training.

The Senate Foreign Relations Committee staff found that "the number of military personnel and Defense Department activities in non-combat countries is increasing significantly" and warned that "the increases of funding streams, self-assigned missions, and realigned authorities for the Secretary of Defense and the combatant commanders are placing new stresses on in-ter-agency coordination in the field."[61] An ambassador needs to develop and maintain solid working relationships with the area combatant commands and with other relevant military centers, whose activities may affect local percep-tions and bilateral relations as much as or more than anything the embassy itself may be doing. Also, in the absence of clear direction from Washing-ton, an ambassador needs to adjudicate disputes between Defense and other agencies and prevent interagency conflicts from weakening American foreign policy.

An embassy of any size is always at risk of breaking down into a collec-tion of agency staffs, each pursuing its own goals. Ambassadorial authority is not enough to hold things together—that takes ambassadorial leadership. The ambassador who understands his mission's mission, and who articulates an integrated set of objectives for the people and resources under his control, will meet with a strong and positive response. Foreign service, civil service, armed service—everyone who is part of the mission wants to feel the pride of working together for the good of the country. The ambassador who provides that feeling will be rewarded with effort, loyalty, and success.

The Foreign Service and the Military

The relationship between the foreign service and the military deserves spe-cial attention. It is close and essential yet filled with tension, like the rela-tionship between diplomacy and force.

Since World War II three military men have led the Department of State (General Marshall from 1947 to 1949, General Haig from 1981 to 1982, and General Powell from 2001 to 2005), and one foreign service officer has headed the Department of Defense (Frank Carlucci, from 1987 to 1989). The two departments, however, are as much competitors as collaborators. They are inevitably involved in each other's business.

The military's growing involvement in what had been civilian diplo-matic activities is clear. Between 1990 and 2000, while international affairs budgets were shrinking and the foreign service was growing smaller by the year, the budgets of the military regional commands grew rapidly. Each of the five area combat commands—Northern (NORTHCOM), Southern (SOUTHCOM), European (EUCOM), Central (CENTCOM), and Pacific (PACOM)—saw budget increases of at least 35 percent.[62] The commands, headed by area military commanders who are exempt from ambassadorial authority, put those resources to work in nontraditional ways, expanding their roles in peacekeeping, civil reconstruction, suppression of narcotics trafficking, de-mining, and disaster relief. Their purpose was and is to forestall the anarchy that provides cover for terrorism and transnational crime by creating or shoring up governments that function with the consent of the governed. Now, with the new emphasis in State and USAID on transformational diplomacy, the foreign service is devoting even more attention to assignments of this sort. This kind of work, which used to be called nation-building, is not new to either the foreign service or the military, but neither is entirely comfortable with its current role.

A growing share of the foreign assistance budget goes to security assistance, where military involvement is of course greatest. In 2006, for the first time, the administration sought and Congress granted approval for foreign aid programs directly under the Department of Defense—not under State or USAID. They were relatively small programs ($300 million authorized in FY 2006), but their bureaucratic novelty and the trend they suggested attracted attention.[63] The trend seemed validated when the administration followed up by asking Congress in 2007 for separate legislation to authorize the Defense Department to spend $750 million on programs to "combat terrorism and enhance stability."[64] Secretary Rice, in a written reply to a question from Senator Lugar, reacted with testy gobbledygook:

> *Select new DOD authorities offer an essential means of addressing rapidly evolving security challenges posed by, among other things, the GWOT [global war on terrorism]. . . . I support such authorities in many cases, contingent upon the explicit preservation of my aforementioned statutory role with respect to foreign assistance, through their exercise 'with the concurrence of the Secretary of State,' and in some cases through joint development procedures.*[65]

Military attitudes toward these nontraditional missions are decidedly mixed. At the level of doctrine, the military would just as soon get out of the nation-building business. *Counterinsurgency*, an army and Marine Corps field manual published in 2006, states: "In COIN [counterinsurgency] it is always preferred for civilians to perform civilian tasks." But what is preferred is not always possible: "The more violent the insurgency, the more unrealistic is this division of labor."[66] The manual quotes counterinsurgency expert David Galula: "To confine soldiers to purely military functions while urgent and vital tasks have to be done, and nobody else is available to undertake them, would be senseless. The soldier must then be prepared to become . . . a social worker, a civil engineer, a schoolteacher, a nurse, a boy scout. But only so long as he cannot be replaced, for it is always better to entrust civilian tasks to civilians."[67]

The decision to give the Department of Defense, and especially the armed services, broader responsibilities in foreign relations is in part a natural consequence of wartime. But it also flows from the great respect that policymakers have for the military's competence and energy. There is a sentiment, not always unspoken, that associates the U.S. military with decisiveness, a grasp of core issues, and a single-minded focus on U.S. interests, and that associates U.S. diplomacy with hesitation, infatuation with complexity, and a too-tender regard for the opinion of foreigners.

Barry Blechman, a member of both the Defense Policy Board and the secretary of state's Advisory Committee on Transformational Diplomacy, believes that even in times of armed conflict diplomats should be heeded. "If you look back historically, the most successful American interventions have been those where there was a real partnership between the military commander and the diplomats on the scene." Blechman recognizes, however, that foreign service officers and military officers approach problems in different ways, often leaving the diplomats at a disadvantage. People in the military, he says, "are trained to take a problem, break it down into subparts, think about the solution to each subpart, organize it into specific tasks, and get each task done." At the same time, most foreign service officers are "oriented to be observers, analysts, reporters. Naturally they are not so operational."[68]

Military officers also gain command responsibility at a much earlier stage in their careers. "As a twenty-four-year-old army lieutenant I was responsible for thirty men," said Richard Miles, who joined the foreign service in 1993 after four years in uniform. "The foreign service can't offer that. I probably won't have that level of responsibility until I make deputy chief of mission," after about twenty years of service. Miles also sees the foreign service as a bit loose in discipline. "If the division or brigade commander says, 'This is going to happen,' and it doesn't happen, someone pays a price. But if the ambassador says, 'This is going to happen,' and it doesn't happen, there may be no consequences."[69]

The flip side of having fewer troops to command is having fewer chiefs to report to. "It's amazing how close you are to the top," said Steve Dietz, a State Department civil servant and Naval Academy graduate who spent twenty years as a submarine officer. "I talk to assistant secretaries every day. I brief the deputy secretary. That never happened in DOD."[70] Another State Department officer who served as an adviser to a military unit in the Middle East said that hierarchy is more rigid in the military than at State. "I was a civilian, a young woman, serving above my pay grade. The hardest thing was to break through the colonels into the inner circle around the commanding general."[71]

The differences between military and foreign service officers in background, training, mission, resources, and responsibilities almost guarantee tension and misunderstanding when the two work closely together, as they have had to do in Iraq. Each group has its own stereotype of the other: To the military, foreign service officers are smart but indecisive and can't get things done; to FSOs, military officers get things done but leave a huge political mess behind them (and spend more money before breakfast than the whole foreign service does in a year).

During his time in Iraq in 2005 and 2006, foreign service officer Vincent Campos saw "a lot of discomfort" among FSOs who lacked military backgrounds. "People seemed to have the notion that if the military would just leave economic and political affairs alone everyone would be better off," he said. Working together under pressure, though, changed attitudes. "Across the board where I worked, and talking with foreign service people embedded with military units, we had excellent working relationships—people became friends, socialized. We absolutely depended on each other."[72]

The military in the field sees events from a unique perspective. But the military in the Pentagon, and its civilian leadership as well, is also deeply engaged in the nation's foreign policy. On the civilian side, the office of undersecretary of defense for policy (OUSD(P)) includes assistant secretaries, deputy assistant secretaries, and office directors with geographic responsibilities like those of the regional bureaus of the Department of State. On the military side, in the office of the joint chiefs of staff the figure most directly engaged in politico-military affairs, international negotiations, and interagency coordination is the director of strategic plans and policy (J5), a three-star general with a two-star vice director and five one-star deputies.[73]

Cross-training and exchanges of personnel are one way to bridge the gap between military and diplomatic officers. Virtually every class of new foreign service officers and specialists includes former members of the armed forces, who are joining the foreign service in rising numbers. Foreign service officers and State Department civil servants serve in the office of the secretary of defense, mainly in OUSD(P), under a State-Defense officer exchange program. Military officers on loan to the State Department serve throughout the building, but especially in the office of the secretary and her undersecretaries and in the bureau of politico-military affairs. Each year more than twenty foreign service officers (class FO-1) attend the National War College and the

Industrial College of the Armed Forces, both part of the National Defense University at Fort McNair in Washington, where a senior foreign service officer serves as vice president. Other FSOs attend the Army War College in Carlisle, Pennsylvania, the Air Force War College at Maxwell Air Force Base in Alabama, the Naval War College in Newport, Rhode Island, the Naval Postgraduate School in Monterey, California, and the Joint Forces Staff College in Norfolk, Virginia. Military officers study at the Foreign Service Institute in Arlington, Virginia, both on the campus and through distance learning. Senior foreign service officers serve as political advisors (POLADs) to four-star officers at regional and joint commands.[74]

Ambassador Robert Loftis, a career foreign service officer deeply involved in political-military affairs, is a strong proponent of the POLAD system. "We're trying to expand our political-advisor program," Loftis said.

> *Traditionally, State has supplied a senior foreign service officer—a flag-rank officer—to work as political advisor to a four-star at a regional or joint command. Now we're trying to push that idea down to more subordinate commands and mid-grade officers. For example, we're assigning a POLAD, a specialist in the region, to train and deploy with the First Infantry Division in Iraq, an eighteen-month tour. We've got a foreign service POLAD at the air base in Baghram, Afghanistan. The POLAD provides political advice and is a link back to the State Department—sort of a mirror image of what a defense attaché does in an embassy. We're working on a virtual POLAD, who would sit in Washington and be available to his or her military unit for role-playing and informal advice, with travel as necessary.[75]*

The military also places a high value on the POLADs—less for their analytic abilities than for their operational impact. When the Defense Department announced its intention to create AFRICOM, an area combatant command for Africa, in 2007, a department official said that AFRICOM's commander wanted not just an adviser but a civilian deputy, "a Senior Foreign Service officer from the Department of State. This civilian deputy will be responsible for the planning and oversight of the majority of AFRICOM's security assistance work."[76]

The military's counterinsurgency field manual says that the position of political adviser "is not suitable for intelligence professionals" because "their task is to understand the environment," whereas the "political advisor's job is to help shape the environment." The manual notes that "the current force structure gives corps and division commanders a political advisor" and says that "a force optimized for COIN operations would have political and cultural advisors at company level."[77] A company has one hundred to two hundred soldiers.

Exchanges notwithstanding, Loftis is concerned about the expansion of the military's mission. "There's an unfortunate tendency in the United States right now to idealize the military uncritically," he said.

> *Anyone who says anything about the military has to preface it by saying, 'We have the best armed forces in the world,' which is true of course, but the military doesn't have a monopoly on wisdom. The military has a great can-do culture, but that doesn't mean it can or should do it all. There's a certain contradiction when a lieutenant colonel is trying to set up, for example, a microcredit facility somewhere in the field. And most military officers see the contradiction and are unhappy with it.*
>
> *The stereotype—see Robert Kaplan's* Imperial Grunts*—of the soldier in the field who knows what's really going on, while the diplomat is clueless and isolated in the capital, is false. Many soldiers in the field, smart as they are, are in one place for only a few weeks. They talk only to a small group of people. They don't have the same depth that someone a long time in the country can acquire. The idea that the military is always right, while the State Department only cares what foreigners think, is powerful, but it's just not true.*[78]

Loftis, who negotiates agreements on military bases and the status of U.S. forces all over the world, is an exemplar of diplomatic-military integration. His negotiating team typically includes the desk officer and a civilian lawyer from the Office of the Secretary of Defense, the desk officer and a military lawyer from the Joint Chiefs of Staff, and relevant experts from the regional command. His chief legal advisor in the State Department is a navy JAG on loan to the State Department, and his deputy is an air force colonel. But Loftis said that personnel exchanges, training, and the growing number of former military officers like Richard Miles coming into the foreign service will not end tensions between the foreign service and the military, or between State and Defense.

"Tension starts at the top and flows down," Loftis explained. "If there's a fundamental disagreement at the top, you can mitigate it with personal relations, but in the end you can't work around it. You have to resolve it."

The Foreign Service and the Intelligence Community

For a brief period after World War II, the Department of State was the center of U.S. intelligence. In 1945 President Truman disbanded the Office of

Strategic Services (OSS) and transferred many of its personnel and functions to the department. Truman was unhappy with the often conflicting reports he received each day from army intelligence, navy intelligence, the State Department, and other sources. He asked the secretary of state to "take the lead in developing a comprehensive and coordinated foreign intelligence program for all Federal agencies concerned with that type of activity."[79]

But senior officials of the department, including the distinguished career diplomat Loy Henderson, decried intelligence as a mere duplication of foreign service reporting. One assistant secretary, showing that reckless accusations of disloyalty were not limited to the department's enemies, denounced OSS personnel transferred to State as "collectivists and 'do-gooders.'" The Secretary of State, James F. Byrnes, ignored the president's instructions and allowed the intelligence function to languish. In the end, Truman created the Central Intelligence Agency in 1947 as his second-choice solution. Dean Acheson, then State's undersecretary, later wrote that the department lost control of the intelligence function through "gross stupidity" and an abdication of leadership.[80]

Sixty years later, however, relations between the foreign service and the intelligence community are generally good, and they are less contentious than the service's relations with the military. Foreign service work, practice, and culture are far closer to intelligence work than to military activity. Foreign service officers are producers, analysts, and informed consumers of intelligence, and often very skilled at their work. The first director of national intelligence (DNI) was a career foreign service officer, Ambassador John Negroponte, later named deputy secretary of state.

Overseas, it is an open secret that officers of the Central Intelligence Agency work in many U.S. embassies under diplomatic cover. In most cases the intelligence affiliation of these officers is declared to the intelligence service of the host government, with which they exchange information. Military attachés, who work in the open, are also engaged in intelligence, as are legal attachés (who are agents of the Federal Bureau of Investigation), officers of the Drug Enforcement Administration (DEA), and to some extent Treasury attachés. Foreign service officers and specialists generally work comfortably with these colleagues, all of whom are under the authority of the chief of mission. Deputy chiefs of mission, who are career foreign service officers, may prepare personnel evaluations on the senior officers at post from each of these agencies, and ambassadors review them. How heavily a DCM's opinion weighs in the promotion process at the FBI, the DEA, or any other agency is a separate question.

The opportunities for conflict that arise between personnel under the authority of the ambassador and personnel under the authority of an area military commander are reduced when agencies work within the same mission, under the same chief. Jim Pavitt, a former deputy director for operations (head of the clandestine service) at the Central Intelligence Agency, said: "The ambassador is the president's representative. Period, end of discussion. Any intelligence personnel abroad are the representatives of their organizations. They are members of the country team. The only time there are major problems is when someone thinks he's smarter than the system, and you have an intelligence operation that bypasses the ambassador, or an ambassador who compromises an intelligence operation by talking about it. Successful foreign service officers and successful intelligence officers have good, productive exchanges."[81]

Their work overlaps. Intelligence officers conduct diplomacy as well as espionage. "At the height of the cold war, intelligence officers were talking to the KGB," Pavitt said. "And at the height of the coldest war, we were talking to the Chinese. These were exchanges that diplomats could not have. A diplomat's ability to maneuver is encumbered by considerations that don't weigh on an intelligence officer. The main difference is secrecy."

Diplomats do not conduct covert operations, but they do collect and analyze intelligence. Foreign service reporting is one of several streams of information—along with signals intelligence, imaging, and reporting from clandestine sources—that flow into Washington's pool of analysts and policymakers. "Intelligence is about informing," said Pavitt, "and how intelligence is collected is less important than whether it informs accurately and effectively."

Foreign service officers rely on what people freely tell them, and on their own observations. "They are not stealing information," Pavitt continued. What foreign service officers hear, whether from official or unofficial sources, is information that is often passed to them for a reason. "You have to recognize that ministry officials sometimes say what they do because they are acting in their interest, not ours. That's when you want a clandestine source, who can steal the briefing book, the talking points." Of course the motives of a clandestine source—for instance, money, ideology, and revenge—are often more obscure than those of a government official.

David Newsom, a retired three-time ambassador and former undersecretary of state, observed some years ago that "some officials in Washington, particularly in the higher echelons, place a special value on clandestine reporting, believing that it may give a more accurate picture. . . than the more overt reporting of the regular embassy personnel."[82] That prejudice still exists. "What's unknown, what's secret, what's black, is sort of sexy," Pavitt acknowledged. "In the minds of the uninformed consumer, something marked 'secret' has to be more important." The sense among foreign service officers that reporting by the spooks, which few FSOs in an embassy ever see, may cause readers in Washington to disregard their own analyses can be a galling source of friction. But knowing whether the source of information was overt or covert by itself says nothing about the information's value and validity. Collectors of overt and covert intelligence form judgments about the reliability of their sources, but sorting fact from fiction, integrating the data, and making forecasts with varying levels of confidence in the end is the analyst's job.

In Washington the State Department participates in the intelligence community through its Bureau of Intelligence and Research (INR). *Intelligence community* is a defined term, identifying a group of sixteen government agencies:[83]

- the Central Intelligence Agency
- the Defense Intelligence Agency
- the National Security Agency, the National Reconnaissance Office, and the National Geospatial-Intelligence Agency, all part of the Department of Defense
- Army, Navy, Air Force and Marine Intelligence
- the Department of Homeland Security, through its Information Analysis and Infrastructure Protection Directorate
- the Coast Guard, which is part of DHS
- the FBI
- units within four more agencies, the Department of State (Bureau of Intelligence and Research), the Treasury Department (financial intelligence), the Department of Energy (for nuclear matters), and the Drug Enforcement Administration.

About 80 percent of the intelligence budget flows through the Department of Defense.

After events in Iraq proved that many of the judgments of the intelligence community were wrong—and sometimes disastrously so—some in the INR bureau and in the Department argued that INR, which had been generally more cautious and skeptical than other agencies, should have equal status with them. State's INR bureau is small, with about 170 analysts. The CIA has between two thousand and three thousand analysts, DIA perhaps six thousand. "These agencies cannot, should not be equal," said Pavitt. "They have different structures and different missions. If they have the same mission, that's a mistake." A senior INR official agreed. "INR's mission is to supply all-source intelligence to the secretary, her staff, and to posts abroad. We serve the secretary and the director of national intelligence (DNI), but if their priorities conflict, the secretary comes first."[84]

Differences among analysts from different agencies are supposed to be resolved at the National Intelligence Council, an interagency operation run by the DNI. Those differences should be fewer and narrower as intelligence agencies learn to switch from the pre-9/11 rule that limited information exchange to those with a need to know, to the post-9/11 rule of responsibility to share. Analysts working with similar information should reach similar conclusions.

Among the INR analysts, civil servants outnumber foreign service officers by roughly three to one. "We'd like the ratio to be sixty-forty or even fifty-fifty," said the senior INR official, a civil servant. But many foreign service officers avoid INR because it has no overseas outposts and looks like a siding, not a main career track. Even so, the analysts build close relationships with foreign service officers in the field. Unlike the CIA, DIA, or other intelligence agencies, which have their own personnel abroad, INR cannot send orders to embassies asking for particular kinds of reports or for the collection of particular kinds of intelligence. But INR analysts generally know who is doing what at posts in the countries they cover, and they use email exchanges for informal queries. "Maybe 60 or 70 percent of the political and economic officers going out on assignment stop by INR to be briefed and make introductions," the official explained. "There's no requirement that they do so. It's really up to the INR analysts to build and maintain a network of contacts" overseas, in the Department, in other agencies, and outside of government.

Intelligence analysts are not policymakers and should not be advocates for particular policies. "Analysts who become advocates lose their advantage, their uniqueness," the INR official pointed out. "In a room full of policy people, the analyst has a special position. If he becomes an advocate, he joins the crowd." Pavitt gave an example. "You take analysts and put them in a meeting with ambassadors X and Y, assistant secretaries P and Q, and you ask, 'What if [former Thai Prime Minister] Thaksin comes back in a countercoup? What's the effect on Asian markets?' and watch them take over the room. That's when analysis serves policy best."

Foreign service officers serving as analysts in INR must check their policy hats at the door, but when they go abroad the hat goes on again. Embassy reporting often does and should argue for or against particular policies and tactics, even strategies, and the embassy's point of view has weight. "The sense that comes from being in the place has great value, there's no other way to get it," the INR official said. "When the president gets his daily intelligence brief from the DNI, it's surprising how often he asks, 'What does the ambassador think?'" A good ambassador has absorbed the intelligence from all sources available to him and formed a sound, well-reasoned opinion.

Part III

·

The Career

7

•

Stability and Change

Ask a member of the foreign service about the work, and it won't be long before you hear something like this: "Where else can you reinvent yourself every two or three years? There's always a new job, boss, country, culture just ahead. You change posts, and you walk into the middle of a new, ongoing adventure."

Change is only part of the story. Foreign service people don't talk much about it, but most of them take comfort in the stable framework that surrounds and cushions the constant change of foreign service life. That framework is the structure of a foreign service career, with its hierarchies and formalities, its annual evaluations, periodic training, competitive promotions, regional and functional specialization, rotation through a variety of posts, and rising levels of responsibility, pay, and status. Retirement, which can come as early as age fifty with twenty years of service, is generous. So are health benefits. There are moving allowances, housing allowances, education allowances, hardship allowances, and other benefits, along with a reliable salary that keeps foreign service families comfortably in America's middle class. That, along with their diplomatic status and privileges, places them among the elites of most of the countries where they are assigned. Whether one serves in Afghanistan or Zimbabwe or Washington, D.C., there is the ever-present mixed blessing of the same warm bureaucratic embrace. It is the relative security of the career that lets foreign service people thrive on the risk, tumult, and rootlessness of foreign service life.

Rank, Title, Pay, Benefits: Overview

Foreign service ranks run backwards, like NASA countdowns. Classes nine, eight, and seven are noncommissioned classes. The classes from FS-06 to FS-01 are roughly equivalent to civil service grades GS-08 to GS-15, or to military ranks O-1 (second lieutenant, ensign) to O-6 (colonel, navy captain). Above FS-01 is the senior foreign service, where the ranks have names.

The lowest of the senior grades—the words *grade*, *rank*, and *class* are used interchangeably—is FE-OC (counselor), rising to FE-MC (minister-counselor), and FE-CM (career minister). FS designates foreign service, and FE mysteriously designates the senior or executive level. The senior grades are roughly equivalent to military flag ranks (general, admiral) or to the grades of the civil service's senior executive service.

Beyond these senior grades, the secretary of state may award the most distinguished members of the service the honorary personal rank of career ambassador. By custom, the number of career ambassadors on active duty is limited to five and rarely exceeds two or three. Some diplomatic ranks and titles, which are more or less standard across the diplomatic establishments of all countries, look like but are not related to the personal ranks used by the U.S. Senior Foreign Service (see chapter 4).

Base pay is established each year under a statutory formula that the president may decide not to follow. The pay schedules for 2008 are delineated in tables 7.1, 7.2, and 7.3. The base pay tables are misleading. Throughout the federal government, base pay is adjusted within the United States for locality. Because the general wage level in the nation's capital is above the national average, federal workers in the Washington, D.C., area, including members of the foreign service assigned to Washington jobs, receive an adjustment above their base pay that in 2006 amounted to about 17.5 percent. Foreign service employees up to class FS-01 lose this adjustment when assigned abroad, so that assignment to a post that pays a 15 percent hardship differential actually results in a pay cut of about 2.5 percent. The administration and the American Foreign Service Association support legislation that would allow foreign service employees abroad to be paid at Washington rates and make other changes that would tie pay more closely to performance.[1] The locality pay issue does not arise for members of the senior foreign service, whose pay is linked to performance.

In the State Department, the foreign service is divided into generalists and specialists, with different career structures for each. Generalists are officers who for the most part enter the foreign service as career candidates by passing written and oral examinations, followed by a medical exam and a security investigation. They hold presidential commissions, and their appointments and subsequent promotions must be approved by the Senate. They will spend up to five years as career candidates. If they are awarded tenure, they can look forward to about twenty years in midcareer. If they are especially successful, they may spend another five years or more in the senior foreign service, at the top of their profession. Rank at entry depends on educational background

Table 7.1. Foreign Service Pay Scale, 2008—Base Pay

Step	Class								
	1	2	3	4	5	6	7	8	9
1	95,390	77,294	62,631	50,749	41,122	36,762	32,864	29,379	26,264
2	98,252	79,613	64,510	52,271	42,356	37,865	33,850	30,260	27,052
3	101,199	82,001	66,445	53,840	43,626	39,001	34,865	31,168	27,863
4	104,235	84,461	68,439	55,455	44,935	40,171	35,911	32,103	28,699
5	107,362	86,995	70,492	57,118	46,283	41,376	36,989	33,066	29,560
6	110,583	89,605	72,606	58,832	47,672	42,617	38,098	34,058	30,447
7	113,901	92,293	74,785	60,597	49,102	43,896	39,241	35,080	31,361
8	117,318	95,062	77,028	62,415	50,575	45,213	40,419	36,132	32,301
9	120,837	97,914	79,339	64,287	52,092	46,569	41,631	37,216	33,270
10	124,010	100,851	81,719	66,216	53,655	47,966	42,880	38,333	34,269
11	124,010	103,877	84,171	68,202	55,265	49,405	44,166	39,483	35,297
12	124,010	106,993	86,696	70,248	56,922	50,887	45,491	40,667	36,356
13	124,010	110,203	89,297	72,356	58,630	52,414	46,856	41,887	37,446
14	124,010	113,509	91,976	74,527	60,389	53,986	48,262	43,144	38,570

Table 7.2. Senior Foreign Service Pay Scale, 2008—Base Pay (Linked to the Pay of the Senior Executive Service)

Counselor (FE-OC)	Not less than 120 percent of GS-15 Step 1 and not more than 100 percent of Executive Level III
Minister Counselor (FE-MC)	Between 90 and 100 percent of Executive Level III
Career Minister	Between 94 and 100 percent of Executive Level III

Table 7.3. Executive Level Pay Scale, 2008

Executive level I	191,300
Executive level II	172,200
Executive level III	158,500
Executive level IV	149,000
Executive level V	139,600
GS-15 Step 1	95,390

Table 7.4. Career Trajectory: Years in Grade and Years in Service (Average)

			Generalists		Specialists	
	Grade	Midpoint Base Salary	Grade to Promotion	Service at Promotion	Grade to Promotion	Service at Promotion
Entry	06 to 05	50,000	NA	NA	5	8
level	05 to 04	61,000	NA	NA	5	15
Mid	04 to 03	75,000	3	4	3	5
level	03 to 02	93,000	4	8	4	9
	02 to 01	107,000	6	16	6	17
Senior	01 to OC	133,000	6	21	6	20
foreign	OC to MC	147,000	5	24	3	18
service	MC to CM	150,000	7	30	—	—

Note: Data based on 2006 promotions, 2007 salaries. Salaries rounded to nearest thousand, years to nearest integer.

and employment history, but most entrants begin at FS-06 or FS-05. Average time in grade and service at different ranks is presented in table 7.4.

Foreign service specialists are not routinely commissioned, and their appointment and promotions do not routinely require Senate action. They serve in job categories that include security, financial management, human resources, general services, information management, and medicine. Specialists apply for employment in their specialties and, like the generalists, enter the service after an oral examination and background and medical checks. Also like the generalists, they are evaluated for tenure, but their careers are influenced more by the job opportunities and needs of the service in their fields of specialization. Rank at entry depends on the job being taken as well as on background and attainments. The same pay table, set by act of Congress, applies to generalists and specialists—indeed, it applies to all members of the foreign service, regardless of the agency they work for.

Benefits are many and varied; the State Department's website provides a summary.[2] Of special note are certain benefits paid only to foreign service employees assigned abroad: a housing allowance, which provides either furnished quarters or a stipend; an education allowance, which sends children to certified overseas American schools where available, and which pays a fixed stipend where they are not; and home leave, which pays travel from the post of assignment to a home leave address in the United States as well as paid leave that may amount to six weeks for every two years abroad. An employee assigned to a post where family members are not allowed receives a separate maintenance allowance. These and certain other allowances are not subject to federal tax. Base pay and hardship and danger differentials are fully taxable.

Career Trajectory

A foreign service officer or commissioned specialist can expect a career of close to thirty years in three parts: entry level, midlevel, and senior service. The trajectory is predictable though the velocity for any individual is not. For those—the great majority—who begin their careers in classes six or five, the entry level usually lasts a bit more than four years, or two tours, and ends with tenure and promotion to class three. Passage through the middle grades, classes three, two, and one, may take a bit more than twenty years and end in voluntary retirement after age fifty, mandatory retirement for time in class or time in service (discussed below), mandatory retirement at age sixty-five, or promotion into the senior foreign service.

The career path crosses two thresholds: one from career candidate to tenured employee, the other to gain entry to the senior foreign service. "It's a flow-through system," said Rob Nolan, a career foreign service officer who headed both the career development and the performance evaluation offices in the bureau of human resources. "We hire bright people with the intention of keeping them for a finite period of time. If you're a generalist, we expect to keep you around for twenty-seven years, maybe a year or two more if you learn a hard language. Those who make it into the senior foreign service do so on average after maybe twenty-one years of service, and they stick around for another nine years on average, for a career of thirty or thirty-one years total, not that much longer. Either way, you should leave with a decent annuity." The figures bear him out.

The system is competitive but not cutthroat. Entry-level officers and specialists worry about gaining tenure, but 95 percent of them do. Midlevel personnel worry about being cut for failure to perform—what the service calls selection out, or involuntary separation. But over 90 percent of tenured officers make it to FS-01, the highest rank before the senior foreign service, and most of those who do not reach that rank resign or retire voluntarily. Of those who reach FS-01, about one-third go on to the senior ranks.

The passage from entry level through the middle grades and into the senior foreign service is not a random walk. There are six areas of competence—the core competencies—used to measure performance, achievement, and potential as a career progresses. What the service expects of its members in each area at the entry level, the middle grades, and in the senior service is laid out in precepts that are central to evaluation and professional development. The office of personnel evaluation reviews the precepts each year and makes adjustments as circumstances or the department's leadership dictate. The precepts for 2007 are reproduced in appendix B.

If few fail to get tenure, it is because the competitors are able, not because the standards are low. A career candidate begins with a five-year appointment. To gain tenure as a generalist, the candidate must satisfactorily complete two tours of duty, at least one overseas and at least one in consular affairs, and must achieve a reasonable level of proficiency in at least one foreign language.

The Foreign Service Institute teaches and tests language skills. FSI classifies languages by degree of difficulty:

- World languages: Western European languages closely related to English (e.g., French, German, Portuguese, and Swedish).
- Hard languages: languages more distant from English (e.g., Albanian, Finnish, Hindi, Russian, and Vietnamese).
- Superhard languages: Arabic, Chinese, Japanese, and Korean.

Critical languages are those with a severe shortage of qualified speakers. In 2007, these included Arabic, Chinese, Farsi, Urdu, and Hindi.

FSI measures proficiency on a six-point scale, with plus and minus signs to mark points between the integers. For the spoken language, the six points are defined as follows:

- S-0: Unable to communicate.
- S-1: Elementary proficiency; basic courtesy requirements; able to conduct very simple conversations on familiar topics.
- S-2: Limited working proficiency; able to satisfy routine social demands and limited work requirements.
- S-3: General professional proficiency; able to participate effectively in most conversations on practical, social, and professional topics.
- S-4: Advanced professional proficiency; able to use the language fluently and accurately on all levels normally pertinent to professional needs.
- S-5: Functional native proficiency.

A similar scale of R-0 to R-5 measures proficiency in reading.

FSI offers full-time training in about eighty languages at its Arlington campus. Distance training is available in many languages, and most posts offer training in the local language. In the superhard languages, FSI offers eighty-eight weeks of training: forty-four in Arlington, and forty-four more in Tunis, Taipei, Beijing, Yokohama, or Seoul. To gain tenure, a career candidate must test at S-3/R-3 in a world language, S-2/R-2 in a hard language, or S-2/R-0 in a superhard language or a hard language with a complex writing system (for example, Armenian). Proficiency at the S-3/R-3 level in more than one language is expected but not required for entry into the senior foreign service. Certain long-term language training does not count against time-in-class limits. Family members may usually receive language training, budgets permitting.

Management has the flexibility to bend the rules, or adapt them when individual needs are compelling. The standards are designed to ensure that tenured officers have the ability and potential to serve with full careers, through FS-01. An officer who needs a few extra weeks of language training, or who for some reason completed four years of service without exposure to consular work, will not necessarily be denied tenure for those reasons.

Tenure in the foreign service is not like tenure in the academic world. A tenured, midlevel generalist or specialist faces up-or-out rules that restrict the amount of time that can be spent in any one grade, or in the service, without promotion. Generalists who enter, as most do, in grade six, five, or four have a total time-in-service limit of twenty-seven years through grade one, with time-in-class (TIC) limits in each grade. Senior officers face a time-in-service limit of sixteen years, also with TIC limits in each grade (see table 7.5). In accordance with the needs of the service, and when justified by outstanding performance, time-in-class limits for senior officers may be waived. Retirement at sixty-five is mandatory.

Table 7.5. Time in Class, Time in Service (years)

| Class | Up or Out | |
	Time in Class	Time in Service
FS-04	10	27
FS-03	13	
FS-02	13	
FS-01	15	
FE-OC	7	16
FE-MC	5	
FE-CM	4	

Some foreign service officers let their careers just happen, but most try deliberately to acquire the mix of experiences, achievements, and skills that they need to be considered for the senior foreign service. Midlevel officers work on seven steps that lead up to and across the senior threshold:

- *Geographic experience:* Personnel regulations require that senior officers have three tours or six years dealing with one region (international organizations like the UN count as a region), plus two tours or three years in a second region, in the office of the secretary or one of the undersecretaries of state, or in certain other functions.
- *Languages:* Officers will not be considered for the Senior Foreign Service unless they speak and read a foreign language well enough to use it on the job, as determined by a test at the Foreign Service Institute (FSI). Strong candidates have brought their proficiency to a higher level, where they can give interviews and converse on any topic. Most senior officers have also learned a second foreign language. Skill in Arabic, Chinese, Hindi, or another critical language is a great help. "Languages," said a personnel officer, "are our rifles, our tanks."[3] For geographic purposes, long-term training at FSI's overseas facilities for languages like Arabic or Chinese counts as a regional tour.
- *Professional development:* By the time they reach the senior threshold, midlevel officers should have had a year altogether of career-related training.
- *Functional ability:* Officers should look for ways to broaden their experience without straying far from their areas of specialization. An economic officer, for example, might take an assignment where the most important work is management of resources, perhaps overseeing an aid program. A consular officer might do a political tour in refugee policy. A management officer might take on an economic assignment negotiating rules to regulate trade in militarily useful products and technologies.
- *Crisis management:* Midcareer officers can show their mettle in a crisis by serving in the department's operations center, where crisis is a permanent condition, or in a tour in country

undergoing violent change or recovering from war or natural disaster.

- *Leadership:* Officers rarely reach the senior grades without having run a large staff, for example as a deputy chief of mission or top management officer in an embassy. Three one-week leadership courses at the FSI are required. Officers should have at least one tour where they supervise a large staff.
- *Expeditionary energy:* No one will enter the senior foreign service without a tour—or two or three—in places that are difficult, dangerous, and lonely. Officers who best handle the hardest assignments will be best positioned to advance.

The Entrance Exam: Generalists

Members of the senior foreign service are at the top of their profession. Nearly all of them, however, began at the bottom with an experience powerful enough to create a bond among its survivors that lasts a lifetime—the foreign service exam.

Officers are members of an elite corps—just 6,400 in number—that is largely responsible for recruiting, hiring, assigning, promoting, and terminating its own members. This element of self-selection, even more than the pressure-filled and sometimes arcane nature of the work, gives the foreign service officer corps a cohesiveness that has critics as well as supporters.

Choosing a Track

Officers follow one of five career paths, which the service calls tracks, or cones. These are consular officer, economic officer, management officer, political officer, and public diplomacy officer. Candidates choose their preferred track early, when they register for the foreign service exam. The choice of track may have a modest effect on the chance of a passing grade; it has a major effect on the content of a foreign service career. Candidates with scant knowledge of the service need to educate themselves before they choose their track. They should take a look at the State Department's website, which offers a description of each track, and then read chapter 8 of this book.[4]

Taking the Test

The entrance exam in its several parts is a screening process so famously strenuous that successful candidates look back on it as a rite of passage. The exam has a clear objective: to identify and hire the candidates best suited to a foreign service career and representative of the American people. For those who give the test as for those who take it, the exam is a window into the service that reveals what the service prizes and rewards.

Registration

The State Department recruits new officers through its website, where candidates can register for the foreign service exam. (Other foreign service agencies have different hiring mechanisms, described in chapter 2.) Appointment to the foreign service is open to any American citizen between the ages of twenty-one and fifty-nine. There is no education requirement. Registration is in two parts: a straightforward application form, and a not-so-straightforward personal narrative. The narrative contains six questions and is meant to elicit a self-assessment of the skills, background, and experience that indicate suitability for a foreign service career. It is short but not easy to complete—most people will fret over it for a couple of hours—and the difficulty is intentional: it is meant to discourage those who would apply on a whim and prayer.[5]

The Written Exam

The next step is the foreign service written exam. The exam, which before 2007 was a once-a-year, blue-book-and-pencil affair, is now a computer-based test offered four or five times a year (and available each time for seven or eight days) at more than two hundred proctored sites around the country. Details are published on the State Department website.

The exam takes about three hours to complete and includes a biographical questionnaire, sections that test job knowledge and English expression, and an essay. All three sections are graded. Candidates with scores in the lower half do not pass; they are so informed and may not take the test again for a year. Candidates with scores in the upper half go on to further evaluation. Their files, including the registration, the personal narrative, and the essay, are sent to a panel of current and former foreign service officers, all of whom are members of a board of examiners trained by the department's Bureau of Human Resources.

The panel looks at the entire package of materials to decide which candidates will be invited to go on to an oral assessment, also conducted by members of the board of examiners. The panel gives favorable attention to candidates with knowledge of Arabic, Farsi/Dari, Mandarin Chinese, Hindi, or Urdu. Candidates who claim proficiency in one of those languages take a test by telephone, a conversation with a native speaker employed by the FSI. Speakers of Arabic are virtually guaranteed a ticket to the oral assessment.

The panel also looks at the career track indicated on the candidate's registration. If the service has a high demand for management officers but a low demand for political officers, and few candidates have selected the management track but many have chosen the political, the management candidates will be more likely than the political to advance to the next stage.

Some subjectivity enters the process, but the panels are bound by guidelines or precepts set by the Bureau of Human Resources. The precepts change from time to time, as experience brings in information about indicators of future success and as the needs of the service for different types of skills and backgrounds evolve.

The Oral Assessment
Step three is the oral assessment, a procedure that measures thirteen skills and qualities (or dimensions) essential to foreign service work (see table 7.6).[6] The oral assessment is a three-part exam that takes about half a day to complete. Each of the three parts has equal weight in the scoring, and here choice of career track has no effect on the outcome.

In the group exercise, three to six candidates take on roles as an embassy task force charged with allocating resources to various projects, with each candidate responsible for one of the projects and the group collectively responsible for reaching a final decision. In the structured interview, two examiners ask candidates about their background and interest in the foreign service; they also ask the candidates to address some hypothetical situations that they might face overseas—a natural disaster, perhaps, or civil unrest. Because the department has found that with people past behavior is a reliable guide to future performance, candidates are asked to connect their experiences to the skills and qualities they will need to succeed in the foreign service. Finally, in the case-management exercise, candidates have ninety minutes to read a narrative and quantitative brief on a complex management problem and write a memo proposing a way to deal with the issue.

When this ordeal is over, the examiners provide immediate feedback. Successful candidates get a conditional job offer—conditional, among other things, on a security background investigation and medical clearance. Unsuccessful candidates may ask questions about the process but will probably

Table 7.6. Thirteen Dimensions

Composure	To stay calm, poised, and effective in stressful or difficult situations; to think on one's feet, adjusting quickly to changing situations; to maintain self-control.
Cultural adaptability with	To work and communicate effectively and harmoniously persons of other cultures, value systems, political beliefs, economic circumstances; to recognize and respect differences in new and different cultural environments.
Experience and motivation	To demonstrate knowledge, skills or other attributes gained from previous experience of relevance to the foreign service; to articulate appropriate motivation for joining the foreign service.
Information integration and analysis	To absorb and retain complex information drawn from a variety of sources; to draw reasoned conclusions from analysis and synthesis of available information; to evaluate the importance, reliability, and usefulness of information; to remember details of a meeting or event without the benefit of notes.
Initiative and leadership	To recognize and assume responsibility for work that needs to be done; to persist in the completion of a task; to influence significantly a group's activity, direction, or opinion; to motivate others to participate in the activity one is leading.
Judgment	To discern what is appropriate, practical, and realistic in a given situation; to weigh relative merits of competing demands.
Objectivity and integrity	To be fair and honest; to avoid deceit, favoritism, and discrimination; to present issues frankly and fully, without injecting subjective bias; to work without letting personal bias prejudice actions.
Oral communication	To speak fluently in a concise, grammatically correct, organized, precise, and persuasive manner; to convey nuances of meaning accurately; to use appropriate styles of communication to fit the audience and purpose.
Planning and organizing	To prioritize and order tasks effectively, to employ a systematic approach to achieving objectives, to make appropriate use of limited resources.
Quantitative analysis	To identify, compile, analyze and draw correct conclusions from pertinent data; to recognize patterns or trends in numerical data; to perform simple mathematical operations.
Resourcefulness	To formulate creative alternatives or solutions to resolve problems, to show flexibility in response to unanticipated circumstances.
Working with others	To interact in a constructive, cooperative, and harmonious manner; to work effectively as a team player; to establish positive relationships and gain the confidence of others; to use humor as appropriate.
Written communication	To write concise, well organized, grammatically correct, effective and persuasive English in a limited amount of time.

be frustrated by the answers. Examiners will not tell candidates what they did well or badly, because they do not want to give repeaters an advantage over first-time candidates. In 2006 about one-fifth of those taking the oral assessment passed.

All candidates who go through the oral assessment must sign a confidentiality agreement that constrains sharing information. Still, everything a candidate needs to know about the test is on State's website, which gives a careful, detailed description of the entire examination process.[7]

How to Prepare

There is no one best way to prepare for the entrance exam. For the written test, old but still useful advice is to read the *New York Times*, the *Washington Post*, the *Economist*, or a similar publication every day for six months or a year—not just the international news, but political, business, and cultural news as well. The State Department's website offers an extensive reading list, weighted to books on diplomacy, diplomatic history, and foreign service, but no one needs to read it all. One successful candidate, applying after many years out of school, said his best move was to brush up with a high school advanced-placement American history textbook. The oral assessment will not reward cramming, but a candidate should review the thirteen dimensions and reflect on how they are revealed in his or her biography, performance, and behavior. An exercise in empathy might also help—what are the examiners looking for, and how will they know when they have found it?

Candidates can get plenty of unfiltered advice—some good, some bad, and some bizarrely obsessive—from two Yahoo! groups: FSWE for the written exam, and FSOA for the oral assessment. The most important single act of preparation is the simplest: Get some rest; it's a long day.

The Entrance Exam—Specialists

The five thousand foreign service specialists work in one of nineteen jobs in seven job categories (see table 7.7). Like the generalists, the specialists of the foreign service pass through a written screening and an oral assessment. Unlike the generalists, specialists are hired to fill specific vacancies.

Candidates for specialist positions also start at the State Department's website, which lists what positions are available.[8] The Jobs USA site of the federal Office of Personnel Management carries much of the same information.[9] To apply for a position, candidates fill out an online form, provide any

Table 7.7. Foreign Service Specialists—Jobs and Job Categories

Categories	Jobs
Administration	Facilities manager
	Financial management officer
	General services officer
	Human resources officer
Construction	Construction engineer
Information technology	Information management specialist
	Information management technical specialist
International information and	Regional English language officer
English-language programs	Information resource officer
	Printing specialist
Medical and health	Health practitioner
	Regional medical technologist
	Regional medical officer
	Regional medical officer–psychiatrist
Office management	Office management specialist
Security	Diplomatic courier
	Security engineering officer
	Security technical specialist
	Diplomatic Security Special Agent

other documentation requested in the vacancy announcement, and send in a two- or three-page biographical essay, including a section titled "Why I want this job."

Applications from candidates who meet the minimum standards for a position go to a panel of experts—not necessarily all foreign service specialists, but all experts in the particular field—for review. This qualifications evaluation panel sends the likeliest candidates on to what the department calls an oral assessment, although it includes a written exercise as well as an interview. Two examiners conduct the assessment. At least one is a foreign service specialist in the relevant field.

The assessment tests for the same skills and qualities that examiners look for in generalists, except for skills in quantitative analysis. Therefore, specialists can look to twelve of the thirteen dimensions in table 7.7.

The written exercise is a forty-five-minute essay on a topic the candidate chooses from a list. The interview, which lasts about an hour, covers motivation, experience, and technical skills. Feedback is immediate. Those who pass are asked to make three commitments: to be willing to perform duties outside their field of expertise; to be available to serve anywhere in the world;

and to support U.S. policies in public, regardless of their personal convictions. They then receive a conditional offer of employment on the spot.

Conversion Programs

Not all members of the foreign service enter through examination. "The State Department has many doors. Knock on them all, and one will open." Debi Fairman, who heard those words from a mentor, joined the State Department as a civil servant but then got the itch to work abroad. Civil servants have few opportunities for assignment overseas, but if no foreign service officer is available for a post, qualified and willing civil service officers have a chance. "They have to fill the hard-to-fill positions," she said. "If the foreign service pool is exhausted, and there's a civil service officer available, there can be a fit. For me it was a consular position in Georgetown, Guyana."[10] Her assignment to Guyana led to her eventual acceptance into the foreign service as a midlevel officer.

Debi Fairman's husband Jimmy went to Guyana as her dependent but found work in the embassy as an eligible family member. He started as the office management specialist (OMS) to the regional security officer and then filled in as OMS to the ambassador when the incumbent was away. He later took a course in general services at FSI and eventually received an offer to join the foreign service as a GSO specialist. He then considered whether to seek conversion from specialist to officer status.

The rules that governed the Fairmans' case are fairly stringent. A candidate for conversion to the foreign service officer corps must be a career civil service officer or a foreign service specialist with at least seven years of service, with four of the last six years in foreign service positions abroad. It is hard for a civil servant, though usually not for a specialist, to meet the overseas service requirement. Then the candidate must undergo an oral assessment and be approved by the commissioning and tenure board (see chapter 9).

The department is more aggressive in seeking officer recruits among foreign service specialists and civil servants at more junior levels. Under the department's Mustang program, a specialists in grades FS-08 through FS-04 and civil servants in grades GS-5 through GS-12 can enter the officer corps as career candidates eligible for tenure, provided they

- are at least twenty-one years old, with at least three years of service in the Department of State;

- have a college degree in a relevant field, or take the written exam and receive an acceptable score;
- designate a career track and complete an FSI, university, or correspondence course in that field equivalent to a semester of college training;
- submit an autobiography of a thousand words;
- are recommended by the qualifications evaluation panel to take an oral assessment; and
- pass the oral assessment.

The Agency for International Development also offers opportunities for conversion from civil service to foreign service. If AID has overseas positions with no foreign service employees available to fill them, the agency may turn to civil service volunteers at grade GS-13 and above. These civil servants join the foreign service initially as noncareer candidates, becoming career candidates after two years of satisfactory work overseas; they become eligible for tenure a year after that.

From Job Offer to Job

Between a job offer and a job lie a few important details. In particular, the State Department's Bureau of Diplomatic Security must conduct a background check that looks for drug use, alcohol abuse, employment misconduct, financial irresponsibility, application fraud, criminal conduct, poor judgment, and questionable loyalty to the United States. The presence of any of these factors will likely result in disqualification. The department's Office of Medical Services must decide whether to grant medical clearance, based on a medical exam that looks for conditions that create severe risks or otherwise limit worldwide availability. The background check and medical clearance are typically completed within ninety days.

Candidates with medical and security clearances are put on a registry, with those scoring highest on the entrance exam placed at the top (additional points for veterans and for tested language skills are added here). How quickly names move from the registry to the employment rolls depends on how many officers and specialists are being hired, and what tracks and specialties are most needed. Candidates not hired after eighteen months on the registry turn into pumpkins and have to start the entire process again. One goal of the 2007 reforms is to cut the time between passing the orals and taking the oath to about three months, from a pre-reform average of fourteen months or more. Whether this goal is achieved will not be known until 2008 or 2009.

How strait is the gate, and who passes through it? More than one hundred thousand people applied to become foreign service officers between September 2001 and February 2006. About 2,100 were sworn in. The new recruits had a median age of thirty-one. Four had earned an associate in arts degree; the rest had a bachelor's or graduate degree; 170 had master's degrees in business administration, and 86 had PhDs. More than 250 were lawyers, and three were medical doctors. Their work experiences were too broad to allow categorization, but well over half had worked overseas. Many had completed State Department internships in Washington or at an embassy overseas. Although there is no foreign-language requirement for entry, the 2,100 entrants had some degree of proficiency in ninety-six tongues.

Basic Training: A-100

The introduction to the service for new FSOs is a mandatory seven-week orientation course at the FSI in Arlington, Virginia, across the Potomac River from the State Department.[11] Foreign service specialists have separate orientation classes at FSI, as do State Department civil service employees, though the classes may meet together when schedules permit.

The officers' orientation course is called A-100, after the number of the basement room in the old State building where junior officers met for training in the late 1940s. The courses are individually and consecutively numbered; more than 130 classes have convened since the count began. In recent years there have been spring and fall classes, generally with forty to sixty officers, although sometimes with as few as twenty or as many as seventy-five.

New officers are sworn in twice. An official from State's Bureau of Human Resources administers the oath of office on the first day of the first week of A-100 training, because until the oath is taken, new officers cannot draw their pay.[12] On the last day of the seventh week, in a splendid room on the top floor of the State Department, the new officers are sworn in again. The secretary of state of usually attends and speaks at these occasions; it is one of the few ceremonies in a service notoriously shy about pageantry. The moment is memorable, not least because the new officers may not see a secretary of state again for many years.

The oath is the same on both occasions:

> *I do solemnly swear (or affirm) that I will support and defend the Constitution of the United States against all enemies, foreign and domestic; that I will bear true faith and allegiance to the same; that I take this obligation freely, without any mental reservation or purpose of evasion; and that I will well and faithfully discharge the duties of the office on which I am about to enter.*

Between the first and second oath, the new recruits spend every workday, some evenings, and an occasional Saturday learning about what they have gotten into and what lies ahead. There are no papers, no exams, no grades. The sole requirement is perfect attendance, with some allowance for illness or emergencies, but not much else.

There's little training in the art or skills of diplomacy. (An exception: two days of work on "composure under fire," or how to address a hostile audience on a tough subject like Iraq, or U.S. relations with Israel.) The A-100 is orientation, not training, which is done mostly on the job. Marcos Mandojana, an economic officer on his third tour of duty, recalled: "To be honest, seven weeks of A-100 does very little to build diplomatic skills. Mostly it tells what State is. We did enjoy hearing the experiences of the people who came to talk to us, but there was nothing about démarches or writing well. And you get to know your classmates. It built esprit de corps."[13] Another officer complained of FSI's fire hose approach: "My criticism then, and probably now, is that while each unit was useful, my mind was not big enough to handle all of them packed into eight or nine weeks. Two hours of this, two hours of that—it goes by too fast, it's a blur. It's like a European vacation when you're eighteen; you can't remember what happened in which country."[14] Once real work begins, the FSI lessons come back to mind. "What stuck with me," said Clayton Hays, "was dealing with foreign service nationals, the importance of cultural differences, gender roles, etc. At the time it seemed like a waste of time, but when I got to China I realized I wasn't in Kansas any more. I had to be sensitive. A-100 was helpful that way."[15]

At some point during the course—usually about the third week—the class goes to an off-site location for leadership and team-building exercises. And team-building works. Class members stay connected. They watch each other's progress throughout their careers and beyond, in a spirit that is at once cooperative, competitive, and simply curious. As their paths cross and recross—which they will—they turn to each other for inside information, support, gossip, and advice.

"I stay in touch with classmates and like most A-100 courses we have a group listserv," a first-tour officer explained. "There is almost daily information about people and where they are in life. It is a great support network, especially when it's time to bid on assignments."[16] Deborah Ann McCarthy, an FSO with about twenty-five years of service, said: "There is an active networking system that begins with the people you entered with, the A-100 course. It's the essential network. I've maintained those contacts."[17] When the first member of the class becomes an ambassador, the others will say, "I knew her when."

The emotional energy of every new member of the service is focused on the first assignment. New officers get advice on available jobs from a career development officer in State's bureau of human resources, and, with an active imagination and an atlas at hand, they picture life at each post: Chennai, Chengdu, Chisinau, Gabarone, Guangzhou, Guayaquil. From the list of openings, they put in bids on the jobs they want, in order of preference. All this happens in the first two weeks.

Assignment anxiety ends in week six, on flag day, when the class meets in the FSI gym with a class mentor—one of four foreign service officers who work with each A-100 course—who announces the postings and gives each officer the flag of the country of assignment. Most people get what they want, or close to it. In the 132nd A-100 class, which graduated in February 2007, sixty-nine officers bid on seventy-two posts. Such is the variety of human desire, and the persuasive power of the career development advisers, that every officer was assigned to one of his or her top ten choices.

With assignments made, training has a sharper focus. Officers who need language skills stay at FSI. Officers heading to consular assignments, which await nearly all new FSOs, train at a mock American consulate. Within a few weeks, members of the A-100 class are dispersed around the world.

8

•

Foreign Service Functions—
Five Tracks

Foreign service officers (FSOs) are career candidates until approved for tenure by a commissioning and tenure board. New FSOs, whether they start at the entry level or (as some do) in the middle grades, have five years to make the cut. The first two tours, normally two years each, are critical. In nearly every case, the first tour is overseas, as are the great majority of second tours as well. These first two tours give candidates a chance to size up the service, and vice versa.

Entry-level officers don't always have the chance to spend time working in the track they chose when they signed up for the foreign service exam. The service must fulfill the demands that law and regulation place upon it to screen foreigners who want to come to the United States. Entry-level officers carry a lot of that load. As a result, for most new officers the first tour, and sometimes the second, is largely or wholly in consular affairs. Work in the track of choice may not begin until tenure has been awarded.

Consular Affairs

Consular officers have two primary duties: to administer the visa provisions of U.S. immigration law, and to provide welfare and protective services to American citizens abroad. Consuls and vice consuls meet more people, and more kinds of people, than anyone else in an embassy, usually under unfavorable conditions and rarely with time to chat. They see a society's middle class and underclass, not just its elites. They get little credit when things go right but lots of blame when things go wrong. They have commissions that allow them to perform consular functions; since most ambassadors don't have comparable commissions, if consular officers hang tough on a decision they are hard to push around. They have tradition and history on their side, and also a flag:

a white *C* surrounded by thirteen stars on a blue field, displayed in consular waiting rooms and offices. They put up with a lot of routine and drudgery, but they have some spectacular adventures and, always, the best stories.

No one enters the foreign service with a background in consular work. Training is extensive and essential. New officers heading out to consular assignments pass through the Foreign Service Institute's courses at ConGen Rosslyn (ConGen for consulate general, Rosslyn for the Arlington, Virginia, neighborhood where the facility is located). The program gets high marks. Consular officer Marcos Mandojana explained: "I got consular training at FSI, and I thought that was good. They split it up into nonimmigrant visa [tourist, business, student], immigrant visa, and American citizen services, just like the posts. There were examinations for each phase. Lots of role play. We visited prisoners in jail with realistic settings, like rats in the cells. We did interviews. I think you know quite a bit about the rules when you finish. You know what the resources are, who to contact."[1]

Visas

Visa work absorbs the bulk of consular resources. A visa, usually in the form of a stamp—a fraud-proof, machine readable, printed photo ID—in a foreign traveler's passport, indicates a consul's approval of a request for permission to the enter the United States. Possession of a visa does not guarantee entry, which is controlled at the port of entry by officers of the Department of Homeland Security, but it is extremely rare for holders of valid visas to be turned away on arrival.

About 6.5 million people apply each year for nonimmigrant visas (for people who intend to leave the United States after their visit), and about 685,000 apply each year for immigrant visas (for people who plan to stay). Under regulations issued after September 11, 2001, every one of these applicants must be interviewed in person by an American consular officer.[2]

The busiest visa post in the world is Manila, which was Marcos Mandojana's first post:

> *You spend the first couple of days observing another junior officer on the line. Nonimmigrant visas were the heaviest workload. Immigrant visas were mostly paperwork, but we often did over a hundred cases a day per person. It was grueling. Manila was number one in output that year. You start slow, but with a little experience you can speed up. You begin to recognize patterns of fraud. FSI had given me six months of training in Tagalog, and when the applicants whispered to each other, "cry now," they didn't know I understood.*

> *Everything was done by appointment so we had to see everybody who came in. We stayed at work until we saw everybody with an appointment. It was like a machine. They were getting rid of backlogs; there were twenty-six officers doing consular work. We frequently worked Saturdays. We did get paid overtime—you can get overtime or compensatory time until you're tenured.*[3]

Nonimmigrant visa (NIV) work consists largely of trying to determine, in about a minute and a half, whether an applicant is likely to violate the terms of the visa he is applying for and to stay in the United States illegally. The work can be depressing and frustrating. One NIV officer, a lawyer, explained: "The law tells me to make a decision on whether they're coming back or not. But I don't know whether my country really cares who's coming back. There are people who stay two or three years illegally, and they get an automatic waiver from the Department of Homeland Security. I feel at times, what's the point? It's not my job to make policy, but this doesn't make a lot of sense."[4]

The workload can be daunting. At many posts, visa work provides employment opportunities for foreign service spouses or other family members, though only commissioned officers can conduct interviews and issue visas. A supervisory consular officer in Buenos Aires, a relatively low-pressure post for visa work, described the scene in 2005:

> *There are eight entry-level officers and one family member in the section. None of the officers is consular cone and all but one are on two-year assignments to the section. One is a rotational officer. I don't think any of them resent the work or the assignment, though a big part of my job, and the part I love, is to help them see the value and the challenges of the work they are doing. I try to get them to see that it's not just ticket punching. I know that some of it is grunt work and not intellectually stimulating, but I think that officers who resent the consular tour often suffer from poor senior management. I'm an evangelist for the consular cone and I try to help the officers understand that their performance here will show their potential for leadership and performance in other jobs. We're fortunate because nearly all who've cycled through have played nice with the other kids and taken their jobs seriously. I take satisfaction in the fact that one officer, on a rotational tour, even asked to come back to the section. I think 9/11 showed that our work really matters.*[5]

American Citizen Services

Consular officers will tell you that work on a visa line is "probably the same the world over."[6] But on the other side of the shop, the one serving American citizens, there is plenty of variety. Replacing lost or expired passports, notarizing legal documents, processing Social Security and veterans' benefits for persons living abroad, and other tasks may seem routine, but the legal puzzles of who is entitled to what can be fascinating. Every consular officer can tell stories of high drama about Americans, not all innocent and not all victims, who are caught up in political strife, swindles and scams, natural disasters, or who are dealing with illness, accident, or unwelcome justice.

Besides his visa work, Marcos Mandojana handled welfare and protection for Americans in the Philippines:

> *There were lots of Americans in jail. They were in for drug trafficking, murder. The prisons were very primitive, overcrowded. It was kind of scary to go there, really.*
>
> *What's it like to visit a murderer? At the maximum security prison there were five Americans, one in for murder. He had chopped up his wife's lover when he found them together. He was rich, he owned car dealerships in the Philippines. He had apparently bribed jail officials. He had donated computers to the jail. He didn't have to wear a prisoner's uniform, and he lived in one of the guard's quarters.*
>
> *There were shantytowns inside the jails, with huts, and that's where everyone else was, including the other Americans. A stark contrast. They had their own little economy in there, with little stores, kiosks, a little hospital. The prisoners protected each other. It was bizarre; there were thousands and thousands of people inside. These guys had been in jail for about eight years. Another guy was in jail for child molesting. One of the training exercises at ConGen Rosslyn was based on that individual.[7]*

Mandojana saw the intersection of consular and political work when the violent Muslim separatist group Abu Sayyaf kidnapped first one and then three more Americans and held them hostage on a remote southern island. "I went down there three times with U.S. Marines, accompanied a congressman down there. One day I got to my office and there was a towel with a femur and part of a skull—the remains of a hostage who had been beheaded."

Crisis Management

Responsibility for Americans in trouble often puts consular officers into crucial positions during times of crisis. Sean Murphy was chief of the consular section in Kuwait in 2002 and 2003 as the crisis with Iraq deepened and the war began. The American community in Kuwait numbered about twelve thousand, and, Murphy said, "everybody believed that Kuwait was going to be the main target" for Saddam Hussein's chemical and biological weapons.

Murphy recruited members of the community as wardens to act as liaisons between the community and the embassy, and to rehearse evacuation scenarios with the Marines. In early 2003 the embassy established what it called authorized departure, triggering clauses in many employment contracts that allowed paid travel out of Kuwait for those who wished to leave. Many did, and Washington ordered evacuation of the rest in March.

> We had a very small staff, four officers and nine foreign service nationals, but we kept track of departures and kept the community informed about how to get out, the state of the airport, the border with Saudi Arabia, what documentation the Saudis required, any guidance we had.
>
> My family left five or six days before the war started. The work was intense, sixteen-hour days. I worked forty-five days in a row. I went into Iraq, to a base at the port of Um Qasr, in June 2003. Freelance American business people were popping up, running afoul of the military, and a national guard unit had detained a couple of them. The department wanted us to see what was going on. There were also Iraqis with relationships with the U.S. military who for various reasons couldn't go home. Our military wanted State to take them to the United States, which wasn't going to happen. There were some very sad cases, but we couldn't do anything for them.
>
> There was tremendous augmentation in the staffs of other agencies, but no increase in State's staff that I recall. The one big thing they did for us was to give us a six-week grace period for sending in personnel evaluation reports.[8]

Status

For many, if not most, officers, mandatory consular assignments were hard to get through but were ultimately beneficial. Even so, some fault the service for a one-size-fits-all approach to an increasingly diverse group of entry-level officers. David Caudill, a lawyer, joined the service in the management cone at age forty-one, after ten years in elective office in Clermont County, Ohio. His first tour was in consular affairs, and it was "a good experience," but, he added, "the foreign service doesn't know what to do with entry-level officers who have had previous careers. When I was thirty-one, I was running an office [county clerk] with more people, and spending more money, than most embassy section chiefs. There are a lot of people like me coming into the service now, but the service hasn't adapted. If the foreign service could harness the talent, instead of treating everyone like a twenty-two-year-old graduate, we would be a better service."[9]

Some see consular work as a detour from their intended career path. "I have a lot of respect for consular work, I even enjoy it. But it's about retaining talented people. 'Wow, this is going to be four years of my career that I'm going to dedicate to work that isn't what I planned for. It isn't what I signed up to do.' I think that's the biggest gripe."[10]

Consular officers are sensitive about how they are regarded inside the service. Officers in substantive political, economic, and public-diplomacy positions often look on those in management and consular affairs as engaged in work of lesser importance. Marcos Mandojana saw the contrast when he transferred from the consular to the political section in Manila, while continuing to work on the Abu Sayyaf kidnapping. "In the consular section you're in your own little world. You might have an occasional brown-bag lunch with the DCM. In the political section, however, I worked with everyone: the ambassador and DCM, the regional security officer, the drug enforcement administration, everyone."

Murphy had a different view:

> Initially consular work appears to be less prestigious to some, but these perceptions change as you rise through the ranks. When you compare one-level jobs [section chief] in an embassy, who supervises the largest staff? Since 9/11, visa work is seen as national security activity. We're first in line to get new equipment, we have some status and some clout.[11]

Economic Affairs

The only career foreign service officer to serve as undersecretary for economic affairs is Alan Larson, who held that position from 1999 to 2005. (Larson was also the only undersecretary of state appointed by President Clinton to survive the transition to the administration of George W. Bush.) Larson holds a doctorate in economics from the University of Iowa, but he insisted that "you don't need training at the doctoral level. You do need a grounding in core economic concepts. You want to be able to think like an economist, to use the tools of economic analysis. You need to know enough to recognize junk arguments."[12]

Economic officers deal with businessmen, bankers, investors, producers, bureaucrats, academicians, and real and phony experts in every field of human endeavor that can be turned into cash. They handle a broad and growing range of issues that have significant economic content: finance and monetary policy, of course, but also trade, intellectual property, energy, environmental protection, science and technology, prevention of AIDS, bribery, and money laundering. For the most part, it is hands-on work. "You should have practical knowledge of how business works, and you should think pragmatically," Larson explained. "We don't need the academic approach, the one that says, 'We know it works in practice, but does it work in theory?' If we know it works in practice, that's all we need. In much of the world, in its far reaches, American business has no one but the embassy to turn to. We need to know our stuff."

Economic work involves reporting, analysis, advocacy, and negotiation. Reporting and analysis are more field work than desk work. Sitting in an office rarely answers questions about what drives markets, who owns what, or where the opportunities and risks are for exporters and investors. Nor does it answer questions about money laundering, bribery, environmental degradation, child labor, or any of the other issues that Americans care about. Senior officer Deborah Ann McCarthy remembers:

> *When I came into the foreign service, I expected to do economic analysis. I was a loan officer in a bank before I joined, and we had economists advising us on the economic situation, so that's what I thought I'd be doing. What I didn't expect, and really wasn't prepared for, was how to use my skills to promote a specific U.S. agenda: pushing for trade agreements, pressing for protection of intellectual property, urging compliance with an IMF agreement. In practice, you do the analysis, but you have to be an advocate. You've got to market the U.S. position and back it up with your analysis and knowledge of the situation.[13]*

In Washington or overseas, economic officers rarely put on solo performances. Sometimes they are in the lead, but often they are supporting actors, with top billing going to the Treasury, the U.S. Trade Representative's office, or some other agency with a claim to the issue. Teamwork is essential to success overseas or in Washington.

Bill McCahill, an economic officer, was the deputy chief of mission in Beijing during the 1997 to 1999 negotiations on Chinese accession to the World Trade Organization (WTO).

> *The focal point was the U.S. trade representative, Charlene Barshefsky. The State Department in Washington wasn't much involved, and until the end of the process the Secretary did not seem interested. But the embassy was vital.*

People all around the embassy were engaged, drawing energy from the sense that we were involved in something historic. Between negotiating sessions, we did reconnaissance. Everyone with contacts in the Chinese agencies involved would go out and gather information, so we could put together a picture of the whole Chinese side. Our economic section, about twenty officers, had some really good macro guys. They were plugged into what is now the State Planning Commission, the finance ministry, the central bank. We had about fifteen foreign commercial service officers, superb people, who worked the trade ministry and the ministry of information industries. And five or six agriculture guys. We used the consulates too, especially in Shanghai, Guangdong, and Guangzhou. Everyone who spoke Chinese contributed. I was the coordinator, the ringmaster. And I did reconnaissance of my own, with a back channel to Premier Zhu Rongji, through an aide whom I would meet on Saturday afternoons.

We had two young economic officers with really good Chinese. They would take a train out to the sticks, then hop on a bus and spend a couple of days in the countryside talking to farmers. Then they'd go back in six months or a year and do it again. They wrote some terrific stuff on rural China, where the migration of millions of peasants to the cities was already under way. Understanding the changes and the pressures on the government gave us insight into Chinese negotiating positions. It was great reporting.

We were deeply engaged with the American business community, through the local AmCham [American Chamber of Commerce] and meetings with a steady flow of visitors. We briefed the AmCham regularly, and sometimes there were three hundred people in the room. We were careful listeners and sturdy advocates. The administration was counting on the business community to lobby the deal through Congress, so government and business were hand in hand.[14]

Teamwork and coalition-building were also the keys to economic diplomacy after September 11. Within days of the attack, the State Department began to develop a plan to provide economic support to allies in the war on terrorism, tailoring support to the needs of each country.

The immediate center of attention was Pakistan, with which relations had long been strained.[15] The United States would need Pakistan's support for any challenge to the Taliban in neighboring Afghanistan, but providing that support would create costs and risks for Pakistan's President Pervez Musharraf, who faced constant pressure from Islamic extremists.

Musharraf sought, among other objectives, U.S. help in reducing Pakistan's foreign debt and in improving its access to foreign markets. State immediately put together an interagency financial team, led by Undersecretary Larson, that put together a plan to reschedule the payments Pakistan was due to make to official foreign creditors. "We wanted to provide real relief as quickly as possible, without using appropriated funds," said Larson, who led a mission to Islamabad before the end of October 2001. "We faced a tough situation on the trade side, where customers for Pakistan's textile products were nervous that supplies would be disrupted. We met with buyers and told them that Pakistan was an ally, that we wanted orders to continue. We were using military transports to carry supplies into Pakistan, and we said we could consider using those aircraft to carry textile products out on return flights. That calmed things down."[16]

These measures were in place before the end of 2001. Later, with congressional approval and appropriations, Washington expanded debt relief, increased foreign assistance, and increased access to the U.S. market for Pakistan's textiles.

It took a more multilateral approach to aid other key allies. Even before the Taliban were driven from Kabul in November 2001, State's economic team had begun to rally global support for the new regime taking shape in Afghanistan. The State Department hosted the European Union at a November meeting on aid that worked out elements of a common approach. A follow-up meeting in Brussels in December, and the larger International Conference on Reconstruction Assistance to Afghanistan in Tokyo the following month, garnered pledges of $4.1 billion in support from sixty-one countries (including Iran), with roles for the World Bank and for various nongovernmental organizations. "Those pledges weren't all fulfilled," Larson said, "but there was a really big buy-in.".

Support for Iraq after Saddam was harder to put together. As with Pakistan, debt relief was a major component.

> The Europeans were divided, but the United Nations Development Program hosted a meeting in June 2003 in the General Assembly room that got things moving. The United States set as a goal the cancellation—not the rescheduling, the cancellation—of 80 percent of Iraq's foreign debt by end of 2004. To get there, State led a collaborative interagency effort that, in my thirty-two years in the service, had no precedent. Every agency used its best contacts. [Treasury Secretary] John Snow and [Treasury Undersecretary] John Taylor went to the Germans. I went to the Japanese and brought them in, somewhat against their inclinations. The National Security Council dealt with the Russians, who were being asked to write down more than 80 percent of what they were owed, because of the changes in the value of the ruble. We brought in Saudi Arabia. We achieved our objective. In the end the cancellation of debt could not save Iraq's economy, but it was a great accomplishment for economic diplomacy.[17]

When the State Department polled foreign service officers to learn what skills they believed would be most in demand in the future, economics was the top choice.[18] "I would agree with that," Larson said. "The latest wave of globalization is such a powerful force. It has been of tremendous benefit to the United States, but there is the sense in the country that our economic dominance is eroding. That places greater pressure on economic diplomacy. Economic issues are at the center of our most important international relationships, with China, Japan, Europe, Mexico, Saudi Arabia, the Gulf states. Foreign service officers without economic skills won't be up to the job in the years ahead."

Management

Management officers are the inside guys of the foreign service, taking care of the money, the buildings, the data, and the people. They deal less with abstractions of foreign policy and more with the daily work of getting things done.

In Washington, management officers have natural homes in the department's Office of the Undersecretary for Management, the Bureau of Administration, the Bureau of Human Resources, and the Bureau of Resource Management. But every bureau in the department has an executive office, the management hub for the bureau's activities. Management officers posted abroad look to the executive office of their regional bureau, and specifically to a post management officer in that office, for support.

Management officers overseas attend to the safety, health, and well-being of all staff, and to the hiring, training, assigning, paying, and dismissing of locally hired employees and contractors. They buy, sell, rent, and maintain all the civilian facilities used by the U.S. government abroad, and do the same with the equipment—from fleet vehicles to chemical toilets—that keeps an embassy in operation. They do IT, including communications, network security, and record-keeping. They pay the bills, keeping embassy sections and agencies inside their budgets. They know—or should know—where each dollar, ruble, peso, yuan, euro, lev, or ringgit came from, and where it went, and why. With the regional security officer, they essentially control, directly or indirectly, all of the embassy's resources.

Management officers deal constantly with foreign officials on issues like employment law (for embassy employees and contract labor, and for American family members seeking jobs outside the embassy), taxes and exemptions, foreign exchange controls, customs clearances, building codes, and driving licenses and violations. Their work directly affects the quality of life for embassy employees and their families, and in many places for the broader American community as well. They have a supervisory or custodial role with regard to facilities run by or linked to the embassy; these facilities are a lifeline in many parts of the world—an American overseas school, an embassy clinic, a commissary. People look first to management officers when a physical crisis strikes—a natural disaster, a riot, a bomb, or an epidemic.

The four key people in an embassy are the chief of mission, the deputy chief of mission, the regional security officer, and the top management officer. If two of these four are first-rate performers, the embassy will be a well-run place; if three, it will be well run and happy; if all four, at least one is due for a transfer.

A Real Foreign Service Experience

Frank Coulter, acting assistant secretary for management as this is written, began his career as a management officer on his second tour, in Kaduna, Nigeria. Kaduna is closed now, but like many posts today it offered what FSOs call "a real foreign service experience." Electric power was off three to six hours a day, five days a week. Water was shut off twice a month. Cobras, black mambas, and malaria were daily hazards, along with street crime and break-ins. Riots punctuated the tension between Muslims and Christians in the majority-Muslim city. "We all rely on each other in a place like that. Everybody needs to pitch in. I learned a lot about generator maintenance, and I got a lot of calls at home. Good management—I mean taking care of the basics and responding quickly—is the key to success, because nothing happens if stuff doesn't work."[19]

A small, stressed post is a great place to learn how to manage a crisis. Coulter's lesson came when three of the consulate's locally hired maintenance engineers were severely injured while repairing a leaky fuel tank. Coulter took charge of the rescue effort. "I worked out through concentric circles of support, using phone patches through the State Department's operations center to the embassy in Lagos, the bureau of African affairs at State, the U.S. Air Force in Wiesbaden for medevac support, and even diplomats from other countries. Cooperation and teamwork are essential in a crisis. It was inspiring to see how it all worked."

Coulter was put in charge of renovating the building, said to be among the worst in the department's inventory. "For a second-tour junior officer, it was a thrilling ride. I had about three and a half months to get the plans, contract the work, and complete the renovations. I had support from Lagos, the Africa bureau's executive office, the foreign buildings office [now the bureau of overseas building operations], the bureau of administration, and security. I felt I had the authority to go with the responsibility, and I used it. It may have been the high point of my tour."

Specialists

Management is probably friendlier to specialists than other foreign service tracks. Eric Khant, a foreign service specialist in human resources now at grade FS-1, served six overseas tours and a tour in the department before assignment in 2006 as counselor for management affairs at a medium-sized embassy, one of the few specialists to head an embassy section. Russ King began his career in 1967 as a specialist, working as a communicator, before entering the officer corps through the Mustang program. He retired as a minister counselor in the senior foreign service and now fills management gaps around the world "when actually employed" (see chapter 3). There are scores of similar stories.

Responsibility in management can come early, as it did with Coulter. "Relatively junior people volunteering for places like Baghdad or Kandahar have opportunities for tremendous responsibilities, way beyond anything they can get on the outside," Russ King explained.[20]

The skills learned on the job in entry-level management tours overseas are resourcefulness, creativity, and leadership, meaning the ability to make a decision, act on it, and stand by its consequences. These skills get tested in the middle grades, when managers are often charged with meeting a rising workload and a more complex, challenging mission, with no increase in resources—the hated "do more with less." Managers are tugged in opposite directions by contradictory imperatives. The department's office of right-sizing, part of the office of the undersecretary for management, wants to keep our overseas presence down, but the assignments people want the family of an employee sent for a year to Iraq to be able to stay at their overseas post. The secretary wants more one- and two-person American presence posts, but security issues and the lack of a float for long-term language training make that decision hard to carry out. Managers have to strike the balance and get it right.

Serving Many Masters

Much of the diplomacy of management work is intramural, turning independent, suspicious, and sometimes rivalrous agencies into a team. The Department of State typically is one among many U.S. government agencies at an overseas post—when he served in Manila, Russ King counted fifty-two agencies with employees in the Philippines under the authority of the U.S. ambassador—and at many posts it is not even the largest. Agencies at a post share support services such as communications, budgeting, personnel management, transportation, housing, building operations, contracting, and so forth, under the government-wide International Cooperative Administrative Support Services (ICASS) system, which the Department of State administers.

ICASS is lunch with separate checks. Each agency, at least in theory, pays only for the costs of the services it uses. Washington provides a budget to the embassy's ICASS council, where every agency is represented and the chairmanship rotates among them. The council decides what services will be provided, who will provide them, and who will pay.

"The ICASS council is your master," said Russ King. Making it work takes constant attention. There are jealousies. Well-funded agencies can take better care of themselves and their people than can others. Because the ICASS council operates by consensus (or rarely by a two-thirds unweighted vote), small agencies can sometimes stop large agencies from doing what they want to do. A good management counselor has to know what needs to get done, how much things cost, and what rules and regulations apply. Then he or she has to apply this knowledge diplomatically, working with the council chairman and bringing the agencies together behind the chief of mission.

"We provide services to all agencies so they can do their job," said Eric Khant. "Ideally, good management is out of sight and out of mind, like the engine room in a ship. People shouldn't have to worry about what we do."[21]

Political Affairs

Political officers are still kings of the foreign service hill, despite repeated efforts to topple them. With their economic colleagues, political officers carry the burden of bringing foreign governments around to the U.S. point of view.

With their colleagues in public diplomacy, they present U.S. views and values as persuasively as possible to local audiences. Their reporting and analysis of the situation in their countries of assignment, along with reporting from clandestine sources, are often the starting points for policy. Calls for transformational diplomacy—for less reporting and more field work—are aimed mostly at them. Even so, their influence on policy formation is often strong, and when it is not their frustration level rises. They are supposed to guard reality against wishful thinking. They need thick skins.

The political portfolio covers internal politics, relations with third countries, multilateral affairs, nuclear nonproliferation, environmental affairs, narcotics and crime, human rights, labor, and refugees. It also covers political-military affairs, including alliance relationships; military-to-military relations; manufacture, sale, purchase, and trade of weaponry and goods and technology with military application; arms trafficking; disarmament and demining; and international peacekeeping. In larger posts political work is divided among several officers, but in smaller posts one or two officers cover a great deal of ground.

Given the importance of their work and the prestige attached to it, it is surprising that political officers receive so little preparation. The training that consular officers receive before their first assignment has no parallel in the political track, or in economic affairs or public diplomacy for that matter. In these areas, on-the-job training, or OJT, is the rule. OJT? Call it SOS, for sink or swim.

"I kept thinking," said Richard Miles, "my boss is going to come in and tell me, 'Richard, this is how it's done. This is how we pick a subject to report on, this is how we make contacts.' Never happened. You learn by doing, or you don't learn. I think I probably just asked a colleague, or tried to copy what people I respected were doing."[22] Miles, a midlevel officer, had his first exposure to political work during his first tour (in Barbados, which is not what FSOs call "a real foreign service experience") and went on to political assignments in Berlin, the department, Buenos Aires, and the National Security Council staff.

To make local contacts, Miles accepted every invitation that came his way. "I was pretty low on the totem pole, so I wasn't asked to glamorous events. The socializing wasn't easy. When I started out in the foreign service, the Myers-Briggs assessment marked me as a slight introvert. Now I'm a slight extrovert. It's part of the job. It doesn't come naturally to me, but I realized very quickly that it's one of the things—well, you've got to be that way or you're not going to succeed."[23]

Harry Kamian had better supervision but came to the same conclusion:

> *At my first post, [in El Salvador during that country's long civil war in the 1990s,] I had an outstanding adviser who took mentoring seriously. He explained why the job was important. He set it up as, here's our role, supporting the peace process here. He told me that Washington is interested in progress and setbacks in human rights, and how U.S. programs are working (or not) to help institutions in El Salvador function. And what's the military up to? That's always a concern.*
>
> *How do you get that information? Well, you have the press, political party contacts, UN officials, the NGOs. Mostly you go out and meet people. Rather than send me out on my own, he took me with him, so I got to see how he would ask questions and exchange information.*

Kamian learned his Spanish in school and gained fluency during a year as a visa officer. Miles had been an army intelligence officer in Germany before joining the foreign service and could work in German when he arrived in Berlin. Having the language and the courage to use it are important. In the Berlin embassy, said Miles, one supervisor stayed in his office, went nowhere, and did little; sketchy language skills may have been the reason. Kamian experienced the reverse: "Other officers [in El Salvador] were absolutely first rate. I tried to learn from them."[24]

Richard Miles didn't have the guidance that Kamian received in El Salvador. He found it hard to figure out what Washington wanted:

> *In Barbados and Berlin, I thought I was a reporter, looking for interesting stories to tell. Only later, when I served in the department, did I realize that Washington has an agenda, for the world, for your region, for your country and for your post. Washington doesn't always make its needs clear, sometimes you have to figure it out. But if your reporting isn't relevant when it arrives, no one will read it. I mean, I knew that on an intellectual level, but I didn't really understand it until I saw it from the Washington end. You're not writing term papers, and you're not a stenographer. You have to pull out the important elements of information and put them together in a way that is useful.*

There can be tension in the political track between those who hope to shape events and those who observe, report, and wait for instructions. Miles's ambassador in Germany often said, "we're not just about reporting, we're about doing stuff. We have to figure out what to do and tell Washington we're going to do it unless they stop us." Yet when the State Department describes what political officers do in the careers section of its website, it makes their work seem passive and detached, more observation than transformation: They develop contacts, assess developments, make recommendations, communicate with foreign governments, support high-level visits, advise policymakers, and implement and participate in developing policy.[25] It's a pretty gray description of what is really a vibrant and sometimes thrilling job.

Elsewhere in this book we've seen junior, midlevel, and senior political officers at the top of their game: Toby Bradley organizing local elections in a Shiite region of Iraq, Vincent Campos struggling to win the confidence of Iraq's Sunni minority, Steve Mann (a consular-track officer who spent his career doing political work) negotiating pipeline politics in Central Asia, Jimmy Kolker organizing U.S. government participation in the global struggle against AIDS. Every day in the news you can see career foreign service officers from the political track entrusted with and carrying out the nation's most delicate negotiations. Here is Chris Hill, dealing with North Korea (and China, Russia, South Korea, and Japan) on North Korea's nuclear weapons program; there are Ryan Crocker and Marcie Ries talking with Shiites, Sunnis, and Kurds about the future of Iraq; or Anne Patterson managing our can't-live-with-him, can't-live-without-him relationship with Pakistan's President Musharraf. These are the challenges that political officers aspire to take on, and that the best will master.

Public Diplomacy

Public diplomacy, which goes over, under, around, and through governments to communicate a U.S. message to a wider, less official audience, suffered more from the depredations of the 1990s than any other area of American representation abroad. When the cold war ended, the executive branch and the Congress both seemed to conclude that the enterprise had lost its purpose. They cut funds, let staff go, closed American libraries and cultural centers overseas, and reduced the languages, hours, and reach of official broadcasting. In 1999 they abolished the U.S. Information Agency and folded it into the Department of State, where it was received like a cornerback on a baseball team. The office of undersecretary of state for public diplomacy, created in 1999, sat empty for three of its first six years. Integration is still imperfect.[26]

"When you walk down the halls at Main State," said Marcia Bosshardt, "people don't say hello, they don't talk to anyone. That's the culture. A lot of FSOs are analytical, risk averse, introverted, maybe a little bit full of themselves. But for public diplomacy you need a different kind of person. In public diplomacy you talk to everyone." Bosshardt, a foreign service officer who began her career in the U.S. Information Agency, teaches media tradecraft at FSI. But, she says, "some things you can't teach. You have to recruit for the traits a public diplomacy officer needs: proud of our country, outgoing, a good listener, comfortable in any company, with the kind of fearlessness that is willing to make mistakes in a foreign language and keep going."[27]

Public diplomacy is a relatively new term. The website of the USIA alumni association traces it to 1965, but the expression was rarely used before the 1990s. [28] American officials define public diplomacy by its purposes: to understand, engage, inform, and influence foreign publics and policymakers, and to broaden the dialogue between American citizens and institutions and their counterparts abroad.[29] Public diplomacy officer Caryn Danz explained that these verbs are a progression:

> *First, you have to understand the people in the place where you are, their culture, their values, their history. Then you can engage them, establish a relationship, a dialogue. When you have a relationship of confidence, you can inform them, tell them things they may not know about the United States, our values, our foreign policy. You can explain things in a nuanced way, in a way that relates to their world view, not ours. And then, hopefully, you can influence their thinking and their behavior. It's a long process, it can take years, but when it works it can be very powerful.*[30]

American public diplomacy comes at this task from two sides: cultural affairs, and press relations and information. Cultural affairs include exchange programs that move in both directions, selecting and funding foreigners coming to the United States and, in smaller numbers, Americans going abroad. Information and media relations deal with the daily or hourly push and shove of the news. Many embassies will have a cultural affairs officer and an information officer, both reporting to a public affairs officer (PAO). At smaller posts, one American officer will cover both jobs. At every post, public diplomacy relies heavily on the skills, contacts, and bicultural understanding of foreign service nationals.

Public diplomacy is a tool in the service of policy. "In the last fifteen years there has been a tighter link between public diplomacy and policy," Betsy Whitaker, a senior foreign service officer, said. "We expect public diplomacy officers to be part of the ambassador's inner circle and to work hand in glove with other embassy sections." For example, to encourage adoption of legislation protecting intellectual property, public diplomacy officers identify performers, writers and publishers, film producers, and others who stand to benefit from stronger copyright laws. Economic officers identify the scientists, engineers, and business owners who gain from patent and trademark protections. Political officers identify the legislators with the greatest influence over the issues, and the jurists whose opinions weigh most heavily. Cultural affairs officers invite key players to the United States with U.S. government support for visits that may last five or six weeks, to meet with their U.S. counterparts and with whomever they wish to see. "When they help design their own program, hear all points of view, and reach their own judgments, that's when these visits are most effective," said Caryn Danz.

Or so we think. In public diplomacy it is often hard to measure success. "We need to understand," said Betsy Whitaker, "that changing attitudes won't happen by next Tuesday."[31] The department uses extensive polls, surveys, and follow-up surveys to determine whether educational and other exchange programs do what they are intended to do.[32] On the press and information side, minutes of air time or website visits or column inches of print are easy to count, but their effect is rarely obvious. Some successes are hard to document, much less quantify. "There's a lot we keep out of the press and off the air," said Bosshardt. "When the press trusts you enough to check their stories with you, you can stop misinformation before it starts. You can't easily get credit for this."

Public diplomacy officers should be well positioned to move into the senior ranks. They often have opportunities fairly early in their careers to manage programs with substantial budgets, to supervise large staffs of foreign service nationals, and to face the public and the press in more than one language. "There's not a lot that separates a public diplomacy officer from a political officer," Betsy Whitaker pointed out, "except perhaps the operational component, and understanding money and how to move it." Public diplomacy officers with fifteen or twenty years of experience should have the skills and background the service looks for in making assignments as deputy chief of mission and promotions to the senior foreign service.

9
·
Assignments and Promotions

Three great mysteries of the foreign service are who gets in, who goes where, and who gets ahead. Who gets in and who gets ahead are vital to insiders, but who goes where is the hinge of the system. Whether the service can pass the day-to-day test of performing its mission depends on getting the right people to the right place at the right time.

If past recruitment, training, and promotion had been consistently wise, prescient, and fully funded, the service would always have individuals with the right skills, experiences, and ambitions to fill all its positions. And if recruitment, training, and promotion are wise, prescient, and fully funded today, assignments will be easy to make tomorrow. But wisdom and prescience are not always abundant, and money is scarce, so assignments are and will ever be a struggle.

Who Goes Where

Foreign service officers and specialists are available for duty anywhere in the world—it is a condition of employment. The people and the positions, however, are not fungible. A consular officer who speaks Turkish may not work out as a security officer in Khartoum. A Russian-speaking political officer in Minsk may not be the right choice to deal with investment disputes in São Paulo or Guangzhou. A married Arabic-speaking political officer who has served in Iraq may have exactly the skills and personal relationships that are needed there, but for how long should the service require separation from family? In the course of a life in the service, events occur that may limit availability: a spouse's illness, a child's disability, an aging parent's demands for care.

Assignments in today's foreign service are made through a formal process that is largely transparent, and a parallel informal process that is largely opaque. In the formal process, the Bureau of Human Resources advertises positions that are coming open on the department's intranet, and members of the foreign service who are due for new assignments submit requests or bids for the positions in order of preference. Then a panel of officials of the Career Development and Assignments Office of the Bureau of Human Resources (HR/CDA) makes the assignments, based on the needs of the service, the views of the bureaus, and the preferences of the employees. Panels meet weekly and decide on hundreds of cases at each meeting, spending on average less than a minute on any one assignment. Any panel decision may be appealed to the director general.

The formal process is strongest where first- and second-tour officers and specialists are concerned. At midlevels and, especially, at senior levels, an informal process tends to preempt formal decisions.

Where entry-level officers and specialists go and what they do on their first and second tours depends heavily on the Bureau of Human Resources, acting through career development officers (CDOs). Newcomers to the service get a list of available openings and have a chance to bid on their preferred assignments, but their CDO guides them and urges them to submit bids that are realistic. The CDO aims first to fill service needs, for example, for visa officers, and only then to make use of the talents that the new recruits bring into the service. From the point of view of the employee, the bidding process is one in which the best is the enemy of the good: preferences will likely be accommodated if they are within the range of expectations that the CDO lays out. Those who buck the CDO's advice may find themselves headed for assignments they do not want, and with budding reputations as troublemakers they may not want either.

CDO influence, however, can ebb quickly. New employees who take a hardship tour on the first or second assignment improve their chances of getting their first choice on their second or third assignment. By the third tour, they will probably be awarded tenure and will enter the middle ranks.

Officers and specialists in the middle grades need to do more work to line up the next assignment. Employees whose tours are coming to an end should not wait for the department to announce vacancies; they should be checking informally with friends and colleagues to advertise their availability and find out what opportunities are likely to be available. Those who hear of a job that appeals to them should go out and do a little self-promotion. They might introduce themselves by e-mail to the ambassador, the deputy chief of mission, and the immediate supervisor, explaining why they want the job, why they would be good at it, and why all concerned should want them at the post. They should also be in touch with the Washington office in charge, usually the executive office in the appropriate regional bureau, because the objective is a handshake (informal) agreement with the bureau that can be reported to the CDO. When the CDO is confident that both parties have agreed—no deal if there's only one hand shaking—the CDO marks the position unavailable on the intranet. The deal is not closed until the formality of an assignments panel is complete, but it is rare for a handshake agreement to be broken without good cause.

Lobbying the posts and bureaus for a job is only half the game. The bureaus also go out and recruit, and they vet their prospects. For example, if the Beijing embassy needs an officer with a background in civil aviation, the Bureau of East Asia and Pacific Affairs (EAP) may scout around for active and former members of the Office of Aviation Negotiations who might be available. If it finds a suitable candidate, EAP would pitch the glories of Beijing, or at least the opportunities for achievement and advancement that service in China presents. At the same time, EAP might ask the candidate's colleagues, supervisors, and subordinates to comment on his professional skills, work habits, and past performance—an exercise called a 360° review. All this bureau activity is outside the formal assignment process, but it plays a large and often decisive role.

To prevent the comfortable positions from disappearing early from the list of open slots, the department acknowledges handshake agreements only in a certain order—the same order in which formal assignments are made. In the summer of 2008 (most transfers take place in the summer, during school holidays), there were 3,577 positions to be filled, of which the 252 positions in Iraq were assigned first, followed by those in Afghanistan and other unaccompanied posts (i.e., posts where the employee's family members are not permitted to go). More than 750 overseas jobs—including those in Iraq and Afghanistan—meet these criteria. Because assignments to these jobs are normally for one-year tours, all these slots—about 7 percent of all foreign service positions, more than 10 percent of all overseas posts—must be filled each year. Unaccompanied posts accounted for about 20 percent of the 2008 summer assignments.[1] Only when these unaccompanied jobs are filled will the assignments process move on to a second group of positions, where dependents can join the employee but where the department pays a bonus for hardship and danger that totals 15 percent of base pay or more. About three thousand positions meet these criteria, and about one thousand must be filled each year. Within this group, posts that are historically hard to staff or that have critical needs get priority.

Together, the unaccompanied and other hardship positions account for about half of all overseas positions. When they are filled, the other positions are processed. Handshake agreements on the second or third group of posts have no effect until the first group of assignments is settled.

Midlevel officers and specialists can expect to serve two tours in posts that have a hardship-danger differential of 15 percent or more. A tour of duty in at least one such post is a prerequisite for promotion into the senior ranks. One of those tours will likely be without family, or with adult family members only. An employee who has done his fair share—a term of art with a squishy definition—is not expected to be asked to serve in another hardship post.

The persistent notion that veterans of service in difficult and dangerous posts typically go on to Paris, London, and Rome is not correct. Sylvia Bazala, the deputy chief of mission at the embassy in Sarajevo from 1998 to 2000, said that "when Kosovo blew up, some of the people in the embassy wanted to curtail to go to Kosovo. Many of the same people later went to Afghanistan, and to Iraq. They want to be in the front lines. I'm glad we have these people."[2] Assignment officers said the same thing: There is a contingent of foreign service officers and specialists, uncounted but sizable, that willingly takes on more than its fair share of the toughest jobs.

Senior officers are pretty much on their own. "By the time you're an FSO-1, if you haven't figured out how to go about getting an assignment, you're probably not qualified anyway," a member of the career development office observed.[3]

Deputy Chief of Mission

Assignments as deputy chiefs of mission (DCM) are handled differently. A DCM committee of senior department officers, chaired by the director general of the foreign service, identifies a slate of candidates for every vacant DCM position. The committee sends the names to the chief of mission, who makes the selection. Similarly, the deputy secretary of state chairs a committee—the D committee—that identifies candidates to be deputy assistant secretaries of state and sends the names to the secretary for approval. The D committee also identifies career foreign service officers as candidates for ambassadorial appointments and forwards those names to the secretary with a recommendation, usually accepted, that she send the names on to the White House office of personnel. That is where State's input ends. White House decision making, at least when viewed from the Department of State, is a black box.

In the trajectory of a typical foreign service career, assignment as a DCM is a point of inflection, often the last overseas job for an officer at the top of the middle grades or the first for one newly promoted to the senior ranks. Foreign service officers believe that promotion boards want to see that DCM ticket punched. Good performance as a DCM is taken as evidence of broad substantive knowledge and leadership and management skills that are hard to demonstrate in narrower, smaller jobs. Poor performance often signals the end of the line.

Most foreign service officers who become chiefs of mission were a chief of mission's deputy for one or two tours. But not for three. "You shouldn't be a DCM more than twice," an ambassador said. "That's a bad sign." Of course, many DCMs are never named ambassador despite honorable service in the number two role.

It is a foreign service article of faith that DCM is the toughest job in an embassy. The assertion may not stand up to scrutiny, but its widespread acceptance suggests that DCM is, as one ambassador said, "the quintessential foreign service job. It's coordination. If the institution is aiming at anything, it's aiming at producing ambassadors and DCMs."

The mating dance between an ambassador looking for a deputy and a would-be DCM looking for a post is *Animal Planet* material. Every DCM has a "how I got my job" story to tell. Emi Yamauchi's story shows the perseverance, luck, and old-boy networking that enter into most DCM assignments.

Yamauchi's first bid on a DCM position failed when the ambassador chose a civil service employee. (The American Foreign Service Association protested on principle the award of a foreign-service position to a civil servant, to no avail.) Three years later, while serving as American consul general in Ho Chi Minh City (Saigon), she received a call from the ambassador who had turned her down, offering to help with her next assignment. So he did, putting in good words for her with the front office of the Bureau of Western Hemisphere Affairs, which passed her name on to Secretary Powell's executive assistant, Craig Kelly, who was then the likely future ambassador to Chile.

Kelly did not know Yamauchi, but he liked her background in public diplomacy and her mix of Asian and Latin American experience. That would be a good fit, he thought, with his own history as a political officer with service in Latin America and Europe. Chile was then preparing to host the summit-level Asian Pacific Economic Cooperation (APEC) forum, which lent importance to the Asian angle. Kelly checked Yamauchi out with people he knew who knew her: the assistant secretary for East Asian and Pacific affairs, the ambassador to Colombia, and her deputy in Ho Chi Minh City. Satisfied, he called her from Amman, Jordan, at four in the morning, their first conversation. Eventually they met in Washington, where Yamauchi was taking soundings on assignments, including another promising DCM possibility. Two additional phone calls, the last from Colorado to Chicago, closed the deal. Yamauchi finally took up her post nine months later, almost a year after the mating dance began.

Tandem Couples

Assignments are critical moments in every foreign service life. Only ten or twelve assignments will fill thirty years. When husband and wife are both members of the service, each assignment can pose a challenge to a marriage as well as to a career. The nearly six hundred tandem couples comprise about 10 percent of the foreign service, and they and the department have extra work to do at assignment time.[4]

First, each spouse in a tandem couple must tell the assignments office in writing of his or her desire to be assigned with the other spouse, if that is the case. The career development and assignments office is suspicious, or cautious, and will not let one spouse speak for the other. By its etymology, the word *tandem* means one in front of the other, like a tandem bicycle—not one alongside the other, like a yoke of oxen. Many tandem couples decide that one will lead and the other will follow, sometimes taking turns tour by tour; in that case, couples need to tell the assignments office which spouse's career takes precedence. If one spouse is an entry-level officer, there is no choice. The department gives priority to ELOs, to ensure that their assignments give them a fair shot at gaining tenure.

When a tandem couple wants to stay together, the department tries hard to accommodate by assigning them to posts that have two vacancies at the appropriate ranks and in the appropriate areas, but within the rules that prevent an employee from supervising a family member. That is easy enough to do for a Washington tour, but overseas it works only in the larger posts: there are no tandems at Recife or Bangui or Peshawar or Chiang Mai. At the same time, the department promises not to allow marital status to give any employee an advantage in assignments or in chances for promotion. Taking care of tandems without denying desired assignments to nontandems is difficult, and it grows harder as the number of unaccompanied posts is rising. Nevertheless, most tandems say they have managed well.

Philo Dibble and his wife Elizabeth rose to the senior levels of the service. In 2006, both were serving as deputy assistant secretaries of state, Philo in the international organizations bureau, which deals with the UN, and Elizabeth in the Bureau of Near Eastern Affairs, which deals with the Middle East. "We became a tandem couple in 1987," Philo said.

> We've been very lucky. We've played by the rules, we've made some compromises. We probably spent more time in Washington than either of us would have done if we were independent. We're both economic officers, and for most of our careers we've been at the same grade, so that limited our choices, given antinepotism requirements. We've been flexible. For example, in Pakistan, my wife did an economic job while I did narcotics work, because that's what was available. Had I insisted on an economics job, we couldn't have gone. Except for a year in Milan, where my wife took leave without pay to be with the kids, we've tried to do that all the way through. In senior positions it becomes more difficult. I don't think we'll be able to go out as a tandem again. Our choices are for one of us not to work, to separate, or to go to one of the three or four places where there is more than one mission.[5]

Like the Dibbles, the Byrds met overseas. Robin Byrd, whose father was a military attaché, joined the foreign service as an information management specialist in 1988 and was assigned first to Riyadh ("couldn't drive, but didn't have to wear a veil") and then to Moscow, where she met Lewis Byrd, a Bechtel employee working on construction of the new Moscow embassy.[6] They married, and in 1992 Lewis applied for a position as a foreign service facilities management specialist. Then Robin was posted to Santiago, Chile, and Lewis, still waiting to be called for an interview, went with her as an unemployed spouse. Lewis got his interview in January 1994; he passed and was assigned to Nairobi. About six months later, the department curtailed Robin's assignment in Chile and assigned her to Nairobi as well. They served as a tandem couple there and in Addis Ababa, returned to Washington in 1999, and soon thereafter left the service. It was a decision they came to regret. Lewis remarked, "every time I saw a plane go over I wondered where it was going."[7] The department granted their request for reinstatement in 2001 and restored their sick leave and seniority. They have served as a tandem couple since.

Jim and Joleen Derham, both foreign service officers, had a different experience. The Derhams worked at different levels and in different tracks. Joleen entered the foreign service as a management officer when her husband, an economic officer, was already in midcareer, several grades above her. "The department has made it very difficult every time we've changed jobs," Jim remembered, "overseas much more than in Washington. At times it's very stressful. The two of us may have different views on the importance of careers and jobs, on the alternatives. In our situation, where I'm the senior officer—consul general in Rio de Janeiro, deputy chief of mission in Brazil and Mexico—there are nepotism problems" that are handled erratically.[8] He added:

> In the case of Rio, I'm convinced the people who did the paperwork were not aware we were a tandem. I was consul general, she was the general services officer. Her boss was my subordinate, but no one said anything. In Brasilia, the ambassador agreed to review Joleen's performance evaluation, which would ordinarily be the DCM's job. Then the ambassador left post, and I was chargé for a year. But nobody checked, we handled things carefully to avoid favoritism, and everything worked out all right. When we went to Mexico, I was DCM, she was in the consular section, several layers below, and it should have been easy, but the department made it quite difficult.

Derham stressed two points about tandem couples. First, when the system is rigid, fight back. "If you're persistent enough, you're going to find a way. After Argentina we wound up coming back to the States, which is not what they wanted Joleen to do. 'Your career will be forever blighted,' they said, which was not the case.[9] The stakes are so much more important for the individual than for the system that the individual will fight harder and often prevail."

Second, "once you work it out, it's great. Getting up in the morning, you and your spouse going off to work, in interesting, reasonably remunerative jobs, it's great, it's definitely worth the effort."

"More Positions than People"

The assignments system, like much else in the foreign service, is under some strain. "Since the mid-1970s," said Chris Midura of the career development and assignments office, "assignments have been employee driven. Management has pretty much lost the ability to steer the process." He added that an employee-driven system doesn't work when the number of positions to be filled and the number of people available to fill them are out of balance. "Now we have more positions than we have people to put in them. We needed to re-establish our authority to meet high-priority goals. That's why we've introduced the practice of filling the most difficult positions first, to make sure they are taken care of. And that's why the director general wants to reduce the number of consecutive years a member of the service can spend in Washington from six to five" (which, after consultation with AFSA, he has since done).[10] The Foreign Service Act of 1980 provides a statutory cap of eight consecutive years of Washington duty for a member of the foreign service.

By 2007 the assignments process had become a game of musical chairs—but a backwards devil's version in which the object was to put the same number of people in more and more seats. At the end of 2007 more than 20 percent of positions worldwide were unfilled. Outside of Iraq, Afghanistan, and a handful of other very high priority posts, it is hard to find a place where some officer or specialist isn't covering two positions. "Two of us are doing three jobs, because they gave one person to Iraq," said a midgrade officer without rancor. "I was here in the embassy until ten o'clock last night, and I got here at seven o'clock this morning, and I have to work [Saturday]. There's no crisis here, but Congress still requires the same number of reports."[11] The same situation is repeated all over the world.

Stretch assignments, which place relatively junior officers in relatively senior positions, are increasingly common. Because the service took in so few new recruits in the 1990s, it has a serious shortage in the upper middle ranks today. Officers in grades FS-05 and FS-04 often take jobs normally filled by FS-03s and FS-02s. A stretch assignment is a great opportunity for an up-and-coming officer, but the opportunity comes with the risk that without experience and training, even abundant raw natural talent will not be enough to get the job done.[12]

Vacancies, stretch assignments, and shorter training cycles allow longer and more frequent tours in hardship posts, but at a heavy cost to the service's ability to carry out its duties and responsibilities around the world. In the longer term, the service needs to grow in numbers and attract entrants who expect to spend a substantial portion of their careers doing difficult work in dangerous places.

Who Gets Ahead—A How-To Guide

The foreign service puts a lot of time into its promotion system. Each member of the service, generalist or specialist, receives a full and formal written performance evaluation every year, in addition to oral and less formal reviews and counseling with his or her supervisor. It takes three people to prepare each written report: one to rate, one to be rated, and a third to review the other two. Each report becomes part of a personnel file, and five or six people on a promotion board review each personnel file each year. Members of the foreign service groan at the effort, especially in April, when most evaluation reports are due. They recognize, however, that time and effort are prices worth paying to keep a system in which the service picks its own winners by its own rules.

Counseling

Counseling, evaluation, and selection are the three parts of the promotion system. Counseling involves structured discussions between supervisor and subordinate to establish a clear understanding of what the job entails, what kind of performance is expected, and how well those expectations are being met. The supervisor (the rater), the subordinate (the rated employee), and a reviewer who is normally the rater's boss must certify in writing that they have discussed the work requirements. The rater and the employee must also document at least one of their counseling sessions.

Counseling often moves beyond the immediate job to discussions of career trajectory and professional development. A wise supervisor uses counseling to check out the view from the other side. Is the subordinate getting enough direction, or perhaps too much? Is he bored, or overwhelmed? Does he feel free to make decisions that involve some risk, or does he wake up in the morning thinking, "Will I be blamed today?" One way to find out is to ask, and then listen to the answer.

Evaluation

Evaluation is a formal process, with rules and regulations. The centerpiece of the process is the employee evaluation report, also called the EER or efficiency report, filled out each year for every American foreign service employee. The EER comes in two very similar formats: one for FS-1s and senior foreign service tenured officers only, the other for all other foreign service personnel, both generalists and specialists. All EERs are due in the Bureau of Human Resources on May 15 for an evaluation period that ends thirty days earlier, except for reports on untenured officers, which are due thirty days after the anniversary date of their assignment to the post or bureau.[13] Whenever possible, EERs are prepared on line, on the State Department's secure intranet.

The evaluation report begins with a statement of the work requirements, including *continuing responsibilities* and *specific objectives*. The rater, reviewer, and rated employee work these out during counseling and sign off on them no later than forty-five days into the rating period. The rest of the report is divided into three parts, completed in sequence when the rating period ends.

The Rater Writes

First, the rater checks off whether performance was satisfactory or unsatisfactory and then evaluates performance in about four hundred words. Length is important. Statements that spill outside the allotted space are not acceptable on paper and not even possible online. The narrative is keyed to the work requirements. How were the responsibilities of the job carried out? Were the specific objectives achieved?

Then, in another narrative of similar length, the rater discusses the employee's potential. The rater must check off whether an untenured employee should get tenure, but whether to recommend a tenured employee for promotion is optional. Just as the narrative discussion of performance ties into the work requirements, the narrative discussion of potential ties into six areas of competence—leadership, management, interpersonal skills, communication and foreign languages, intellectual skills, and substantive knowledge—that the State Department's Bureau of Human Resources has defined and negotiated with the American Foreign Service Association. A member of the service should demonstrate a rising level of skill in each area as he or she moves through the ranks. A rater needs to discuss with examples whether the rated employee has mastered the skills appropriate to his rank, and to show with reference to performance whether the rising level of expectations is likely to be met.

Because raters tend to overdo the positives (Brings order from chaos! Walks on water! Eats soft-boiled eggs with chopsticks!), the EER includes a block called *areas for improvement*. Here the rater indicates at least one of the six areas of competence in which the employee could do better. Examples are called for, but the block of space is mercifully small: fifty words or so will fill it. Despite this brevity it is a serious exercise. A discussion of areas for improvement should be part of regular counseling. In fact, nothing in the rater's section of the report should come as a surprise to the person who is being rated.

The Reviewer Comments

The rater has someone looking over his shoulder. Every EER includes a review statement, usually prepared by the rater's boss and always by someone in the chain of command. Ideally, the reviewer has independent knowledge of the employee's work and is close enough to the scene to be able to comment on the relationship between the rated employee and the rater. The ideal is not always met. For example, someone serving in a one- or two-person post may not be well known to the reviewer, and reviewing officers can be hard to find for ambassadors and assistant secretaries. (Assistant secretaries rate ambassadors in their region, including political appointees.) In most cases, though, the reviewing officer is close at hand.

The review statement also runs to about four hundred words, typically fewer. It should be less a new rating than a reaction to and commentary on the rater's judgments, from which it may or may not differ. Either way, the review should introduce new examples of performance and indications of potential, seen from a different perspective. The review also guards against a rating that is influenced by considerations that have no bearing on the employee's fitness or potential for service.

The Last Word

The last word belongs to the rated employee, who must be given five days to write it. "You must comment on your most significant achievements," the instructions say, but the rated employee may choose to not write anything or to elaborate on any aspect of the EER. Employees are also "encouraged to state your current career goals" with a five-year horizon, and for once, if the box is too confining, "continuation sheets may be used."

Anyone upset by what his rater or reviewer has to say does not have to argue it out in writing. Face-to-face discussions are a good idea, and changes can sometimes be negotiated. What the rated employee does write, however, is confidential, protected under privacy rules established in the Foreign Service Act of 1980. The rating and reviewing officers do not have access to it.

The last word belongs to a review panel that certifies that the rated, rating, and reviewing sections of the report comply with regulations, contain no inadmissible material, include examples to substantiate expressed judgments, and do not dispute matters of fact. When the panel signs off, the report is complete.

How to Write an EER

Efficiency reports can be a burden. They weigh most heavily perhaps on deputy chiefs of mission at large embassies. A DCM in most cases rates all the embassy's section chiefs (including agencies other than State) and reviews all the ratings that the section chiefs prepare. After writing a dozen ratings and two or three dozen reviews, it is hard to be fresh. Officers in this position need to attend to counseling throughout the year, so that they will have something useful to say when they sit down in April before a blank screen.

Files are fat. Selection boards read hundreds of reports. Short words, strong verbs, and plain language grab attention. Examples persuade, not adjectives. Almost every member of the service will at some point in a career face a time of testing and crisis. But in most years, most posts and most assignments lack drama. Don't fake it. Trust readers to discount hyperbole and value solid performance, fairly reported.

Career Development

All the agony and effort that go into an evaluation report are aimed at a tiny audience. Commissioning and tenure boards have six members, as do selection (promotion) boards. Award of tenure and promotion are separate actions, but the selection procedures in both cases are much the same.

Commissioning and Tenure Boards

Most career candidates are entry-level (junior) officers and specialists who have joined the service through a competitive process and have five years to be awarded tenure. A few career candidates start in the middle grades due to their specialized skills or employment history. A very few career candidates are senior officers, initially appointed as noncareer officers for limited periods, who decide to seek full career status. The commissioning of senior career candidates follows slightly different procedures than those described below, which apply to career candidates in entry-level and middle grades.

The director general of the foreign service appoints six members to each commissioning and tenure board. Five must be from the Department of State, including one from each career track, and the sixth must be from another foreign service agency. Regulations specify that at least one member of the board shall be a woman, and at least one a member of a minority group.[14] All must be ranked FS-01 or above. Members serve two-year terms and meet quarterly, or more often if needed. The American Foreign Service Association gets a chance to comment on the names proposed for appointment, but it has no veto power.

New foreign service officers who come in at the bottom, in grades FS-06 or FS-05, have five years and three chances to make tenure. They are promoted administratively, by action of the Bureau of Human Resources, up to FS-04, where the work of the commissioning and tenure board begins. The board reviews all FS-04 career candidates (untenured officers) for the first time after they have completed thirty-six months of service, for a second time after forty-eight months, and for a third time, if necessary, six months before the five-year period runs out.

The board also reviews new officers who are in the middle grades—FS-03, FS-02, and FS-01—after thirty-six months and again after forty-eight months of service. A third review, if necessary, takes place about sixty days before the candidate's time expires. Midgrade officers, including untenured career candidates, also face selection boards, which consider them for promotion. Any untenured midgrade officer who is promoted goes before the commissioning and tenure board immediately, regardless of length of service.

Selection Boards

Most selection (promotion) boards meet in the summer, from June to September, and they feel the heat. They consider all candidates for promotion, except entry-level generalists, who are administratively promoted from FS-06 to FS-05 and from FS-05 to FS-04.

Like commissioning and tenure boards, selection boards looking at generalists through FS-01 have six members, including five from the Department of State, one from each career track. Tracks are not relevant for promotion above the rank of counselor (FE-OC), the lowest rank in the senior foreign service. The sixth or public member comes from outside the department. Members of a selection board must be at least one grade higher than the grade under consideration, so most are FS-01s (senior officers). Specialists have separate boards, staffed by people knowledgeable in the specialty.

For generalists in the middle grades, two boards screen every file. The first ranks all members of a class, regardless of track, from top to bottom. The second goes track by track, looking for the best political, economic, consular, management, and public diplomacy officers. For generalists at FS-04, there is no second board, because assignments in grades FS-06, FS-05, and FS-04 are often not linked to an officer's track. Promotions from FS-04 to FS-03 are by classwide competition only.

Boards typically read the files several times. In a first screening, a file may get no more than ten or fifteen minutes of consideration. That is usually enough to allow a sorting into one of three piles: review for possible promotion, review for possible low ranking, and don't review. "You're moving fast," said Ambassador Rob Nolan, a former head of the office of career development and assignments, "but there are six of you. Usually it takes only two people on a board to get someone reviewed, sometimes only one."[15]

The second screening is quite detailed. "We use a forced-distribution point system," Nolan explained:

> You look at people typically in batches of forty. You rate them ten, nine, eight, and so forth. You only have a certain number of tens to give, a certain number of nines. You have to use all your rankings, including the twos and ones. It depends on the size of the pool and the number of slots, of course, but typically if you're not getting fives and sixes you're not getting promoted. It's important that rating, reviewing, and especially rated officers do a good job. If your file is sloppy, with typos, that sort of thing, the board can be affected. The rated officer can insist on fixing typos, grammar, spelling. We tell officers, it's your file, you own it. Act accordingly.

The Bureau of Human Resources decides for each promotion cycle where to draw the promotion lines based on current and projected staffing needs and budgetary constraints. In recent years, classwide competition has produced about a third of all generalist promotions, excluding promotions into FS-03. The two-thirds of promotions that result from competition within tracks (FS-02 public diplomacy officer against other FS-02 public diplomacy officers, for example) are allocated among the tracks in accordance with each track's share of total positions. This two-tier promotion system is intended to ensure that the service can identify and promote its best officers and still have the distribution of skills it needs throughout its ranks.

Officers who are close but fall short of the promotion cut-off line get a consolation prize: a meritorious step increase, which means a modest raise in pay. For senior officers, the same board that considers promotions also recommends awards of performance pay and presidential awards, which include cash payments.

In 2006, 26 percent of all foreign service employees were promoted, a share precisely in line with the 2002 to 2006 average. The total breaks down to 14 percent of the senior foreign service, 31 percent of foreign service generalists (excluding FS-06 and FS-05), and 21 percent of specialists.

Low Ranking

Selection boards look for the bottom as well as the top. For the middle grades, boards identify the bottom 5 percent classwide. (There is no low ranking of entry-level or senior officers. If entry level officers do not get tenure, their appointments expire. Similarly, senior officers who are not promoted face time-in-class restrictions that may force their retirement before the mandatory age of sixty-five.) A single low ranking has no consequences. An officer who is ranked low twice in five years in evaluations by different rating officers faces review by a performance standards board and possible separation from the service, which is called selection out.

"Low ranking is controversial," said Rob Nolan. "The evaluation form isn't designed for it. Evaluation reports may reveal the bottom two or three percent, but the rest is a statistical exercise. The selection board ranks all the names in each class, counts them, divides by twenty and draws a line." Across all the midlevel grades, fifty or sixty people face performance standards boards each year.

Precepts: How the Service Sees Itself

Evaluation and selection make no sense without a yardstick. For the individual, the work requirements discussed and signed off on at the beginning of the rating period are a pretty good guide to what is wanted. To compare employees with each other, or even to measure the same employee over time, something more is needed.

The servicewide yardstick of performance is the precepts, mentioned at the beginning of chapter 7. The precepts are words from on high about the skills and knowledge that should be mastered at different levels of the service. The State Department's leadership consults AFSA about the precepts, but the final product is a management document.

The precepts, which appear as appendix B, indicate perhaps better than any other document how the department sees the foreign service, and how the service sees itself. The precepts define, in clotted, almost unreadable language, what the service will reward with prestige, promotion, and rising levels of responsibility. Of course the service wants people who excel in every way, but the precepts suggest, as they should, which skills and traits are most valued. Does the balance tilt toward energy, decisiveness, leadership, and pursuit of advantage? Or toward sensitivity, discernment, teamwork, and pursuit of consensus? The service of tomorrow is in the precepts of today.

Part IV

·

The Future Foreign Service

10

·

Tomorrow's Diplomats

The wave of reforms that began in 2001 with Secretary Colin Powell's Diplomatic Readiness Initiative has not crested. Performance has not pleased the administration. "Who needs the State Department?" a senior administration official said in 2004, speaking of foreign service efforts at reconstruction in Afghanistan and echoing the speaker at the beginning of this book. "The military does a better job." This administration leaves office in 2009, but pressure for change has come from inside the service as well, and from inside the Department of State.

No wonder. At the end of 2007, close to 40 percent of foreign service officers and specialists had entered the service after January 1, 2000. These twenty-first century diplomats see a service under stress, inadequately staffed and inadequately skilled for the missions assigned to it. They want change, and they will make sure it happens.

What is not taking shape, however, is a classic battle of Young Turks versus Old Guard. The senior ranks are not filled with defenders of the status quo. On the contrary, the most carefully grounded proposals for reform come from some of the country's most experienced diplomats.

Project Horizon

The most elaborate of the several studies under way in late 2007 was Project Horizon, an exercise in strategic planning by fifteen foreign affairs agencies, among them the departments of State, Defense, Energy, Health and Human Services, and Homeland Security, as well as the Office of the Director of National Intelligence, USAID, and the staff of the National Security Council.[1] Project Horizon used both interviews with government officials and outside experts and a formal methodology to develop a set of five scenarios, or alternative futures.

"The scenarios are not forecasts," said Sid Kaplan, head of State's Office of Strategic and Performance Planning, "at least not in the usual sense of the word. They are detailed descriptions of the diverse environments in which agencies may have to operate."[2] Summarizing the scenarios in a sentence or two misrepresents the depth of the full product but still indicates the value of the approach:

1. Asian megacorporations increasingly dominate a global economy, at the expense of European and American military and economic powers.
2. In a world of freedom, opportunity, and technological progress, the U.S. government is overextended operationally, and activist democracies challenge the United States in unexpected ways.
3. Persistent terrorism, nuclear proliferation, and economic turmoil present constant and changing threats, the most dangerous situation the United States has faced in more than fifty years.
4. Political and economic power is increasingly organized on regional rather than national or global lines, creating a tense and highly competitive world with multiple points of friction.
5. Hypercapitalism has created new and powerful forms of organization that leave public institutions increasingly weak by comparison, setting up potential global conflicts between profits and principles.

All five scenarios—none of which, for planning purposes, should be considered more valid than the others—share certain features:

- new connections between formerly segregated issues, such as health and national security;
- shorter decision cycles, as global media extend their reach and reduce the time between event and reaction;
- a rising importance of transparent global rules and standards, and growing (if temporary) advantages for those who abandon the norm;
- the proliferation of strategically significant, networked global actors, including profit-seeking corporations and religious and issue-based organizations; and
- new opportunities to counter traditional forms of power with disruptive technologies, strategic communications, and control of critical resources.

"Diplomat of the Future"

Will the foreign service have the skills it will need for any of these new worlds? Marianne Myles, a career senior foreign service officer in the State Department's bureau of human resources, heads the Diplomat of the Future project. "We can't take a snapshot of the future," said Myles, "but we can identify trends."[3]

Myles brought in David Dlouhy, who before his retirement from the foreign service had worked on Secretary Powell's Diplomatic Readiness Initiative (see chapter 2, note 59). Dlouhy said, "We're going about our work in a systematic, documented way. To identify the conditions in which we will have to operate, the tasks we will have to perform, and the skills we will need to do those tasks, we did workshops with Project Horizon scenarios. We interviewed the Department's assistant secretaries, we did workshops on Iraq and Afghanistan. We're taking a survey of all 585 foreign service generalists who have served in Iraq or Afghanistan. And we're conducting a regular ten-year job analysis survey," which polls all 6,604 foreign service generalists to learn what work they are actually doing, what skills they use to do it, and what they think the service needs in the future.[4]

All this information feeds back into recruitment, hiring, training, assignment, and promotion. The data gathered, said Myles, "lets us design questions for the entrance exam, adjust the precepts, change assignments policy." New pre-employment precepts, she added, will eventually replace the thirteen dimensions that examiners use to evaluate candidates (see table 7.6).[5]

Dlouhy gave an example: "If you went from a position as an embassy economic-affairs officer to a provincial reconstruction team in Iraq, the work you're doing is something entirely different. But are the skills different, in nature or in intensity? That's what we have to figure out. Are the skills needed in hardship tours generally different than those in other tours? The answer seems to be yes. We need to make sure that's reflected in the precepts, which will govern recruitment, promotion, and assignments."

"What we've seen so far," said Dlouhy, "tells us empirically that the diplomat of the future will need the skills that the department's current management is looking for: more program management, more project analysis, more operational leadership. And languages, of course." Myles added:

> *Economic skills also. Our surveys say diplomatic battles of the future will be global and economic in nature. Some say that the United States in the future won't have the dominance it has enjoyed relative to the rest of the world, so that economic negotiations will be more difficult and more important. And if you're out there promoting democracy and the rule of law, you've got to be able*

to articulate the economic advantages, you've got to be able to answer the question, "What's in it for me?" You need to understand the linkages in a society—between regions, tribes, political parties—where the underlying economics are more important than the political overlay.[6]

Department of State 2012/2025

A diplomatic service that has all the skills will not be up to the job if the Department of State is unable to put those skills to use efficiently and effectively. A third project, Department of State 2012/2025, looks at this question.

The 2025 project, as it is often called, draws on the formidable expertise and authority of Tom Pickering, a retired career foreign service officer who served as undersecretary for political affairs and as ambassador to (in reverse chronological order) the United Nations, Russia, India, Israel, El Salvador, Nigeria, and Jordan. Pickering sits on the secretary's Advisory Committee on Transformational Diplomacy, appointed by Secretary Rice to examine how well the department is equipped for its mission in the world and to recommend areas for improvement.[7] The 2025 project is formally the work of that committee, which wants the department to take a long-term view of its structure and capabilities. What can be done now to anticipate the demands that will be placed on the department five and fifteen years out, and to prepare for them? Pickering and cochair Barry Blechman worked with the department's Bureau of Resource Management.

Their conclusions flow from the Project Horizon scenarios and are consistent with the Diplomat of the Future surveys. In the years to 2025, they contend, the use of military power will become politically more complex and operationally more difficult. The proliferation of weapons of mass destruction will raise the potential costs of conflict and make prevention increasingly vital. At the same time, continued U.S. military superiority will cause rivals to seek nonmilitary areas of competition. International law and multilateral institutions will grow in importance, as will legal and illegal transnational networks. The result? Diplomacy will be an increasingly decisive source of competitive advantage.

American diplomacy needs to be able to shape this difficult global operating environment in favorable ways. It also needs the capacity to respond quickly to emergencies and contingencies, and to support countries torn by conflict or wrenching social, political, or economic change. To meet the first of these tasks, the 2025 project calls on the department to apply more energy and resources to public diplomacy, the development of international law, the tools of economic and commercial diplomacy, and the global dispersion of science, engineering, and technology. To meet the second, the department should deepen the alignment of diplomacy and foreign assistance and learn better how to plan and carry out stabilization and reconstruction programs.

The 2025 project proposes a number of organizational changes to integrate strategic planning and policy execution across the U.S. government. It envisions a single interagency global-affairs plan and budget, to be examined by new national security subcommittees of the House and Senate budget committees. It also places public diplomacy in a new semi-autonomous agency in the Department of State, the better to bring coherence to the welter of government-to-government, private sector, and civil society relationships in which Americans are engaged. Its ideal is a more vertical Department of State, with far fewer people reporting directly to the secretary, and far greater emphasis on measuring performance and managing enterprise risk.

Overseas it calls for ambassadorial authority, weakened in recent years, to be restored, and ambassadors to be entrusted with greater responsibilities for planning. Foreign service nationals are an underused resource that can be more fully exploited. More planning and execution should take place at the regional level. Area combatant commanders need to be brought in, so that they are fully aware of civilian objectives and activities, and vice versa.

A Larger Service

The evidence is strong that since the end of the cold war, diplomatic tools have been allowed to weaken, absolutely and relative to the military. Today there is fairly broad consensus across the government and the foreign affairs community that America's diplomatic establishment must be upgraded. More secure buildings are probably helpful, and surely necessary. The technological changes that are bringing secure communications into the age of the Blackberry and the video conference will improve efficiency and lower costs. But the essential changes in American diplomacy are in the people, not the things.

All of the recent rash of studies of the foreign service see a need for greater numbers. *Embassy of the Future*, a privately funded study conducted by a Washington research institute, said that adding 1,050 officers and specialists to the State Department's foreign service would allow 15 percent of the service to be in training or transit without creating vacancies in other positions. The estimated cost was $273 million over three years.[8] The State 2025 project is more aggressive, arguing that the service should double in size by that year. Growth on that scale is about 5 percent per year above attrition.

The administration and Congress (through the Government Accountability Office) have been quick to point out where the foreign service and the State Department fall short, but up to fiscal year 2009 the administration has asked for little help, and Congress has denied even that. The National Security Strategy for 2006 ordered the State Department to improve "our capability to plan for and respond to post-conflict and failed-state situations," to "integrate all relevant United States Government resources and assets in conducting reconstruction and stabilization efforts," to develop "a civilian reserve corps, analogous to the military reserves," and to strengthen "our public diplomacy."[9] Tall orders, but the administration's budgets for fiscal years 2006, 2007, and 2008 asked for just 221, 100, and 254 foreign service positions over attrition—not enough to increase assignments to language and other long-term training, or even fill the vacancies in current staffing, much less allow a broader expansion of responsibilities and workload.

The budget requests were burka-modest, but Congress turned them down. The Foreign Affairs Council pointed out that, "of the 221 positions over attrition requested in FY 2006 . . . none was authorized and funded. In FY 2007, 100 over attrition were requested and none received.[10] The budget for FY 2008 received worse treatment. Congress rejected the request for additional hiring and also cut $200 million from State's overseas operating budget. The budget request for FY 2009, before the Congress at this writing, is bolder. It asks for money for an additional 1,076 foreign service positions in the Department of State and another 300 in AID. The increase, if granted, would put 300 more officers and specialists into hard-language training, and another 150 into professional training, mainly at the National Defense University, the Army, Air, and Naval War colleges, and other military facilities. It would add fifty new POLADs (foreign service advisers to U.S. military commanders), forty new officers in public diplomacy and cultural exchange, and two hundred new officers and specialists in diplomatic security and security construction.

The request also includes $249 million and 351 foreign service positions for a civilian stabilization initiative to create a civilian response corps as an antidote to the anarchy that spreads conflict and terrorism. The corps, with skills in areas like civil engineering, police work, agronomy, public health, education, and political organization, could deploy overseas on two weeks' notice. It would have an active-duty component drawn largely from State and USAID, a standby component drawn from many federal agencies, and a reserve component that could include civilians from state and local governments and from the private sector. The Senate, but not the House, authorized such a corps in the Reconstruction and Stabilization Civilian Management Act of 2006, and the president backed the idea in his 2007 State of the Union address, but the budget request did not go forward until 2008, when the funds were sought for FY 2009. Call it a leisurely approach to rapid response.[11]

The Institution, the Profession, the Career

The U.S. Foreign Service as an institution, the diplomatic profession, and foreign service careers have changed profoundly over the past sixty years. Change has not come easily. The foreign service and its guardian, the Department of State, have generally been slow to respond to new circumstances. They have rarely been adept at anticipating or preparing for shifting requirements, or at examining recent experience, identifying shortcomings, and making corrections. Across a broad range of issues—treatment of minorities, adoption of advanced information technology, coping with terrorism—both have needed repeated collisions with failure before finding a path to change.

Events and political decisions now demand that the foreign service use a wider range of diplomatic tools and deal with a wider range of actors than in the past. Preventing the emergence of failed or rogue states became a new imperative for American foreign policy on September 11, 2001. Members of the foreign service in this generation need to promote peace and stability in troubled regions, not only through negotiation of treaties in capitals, but also, where governments lack authority or scarcely exist, through political stabilization and economic reconstruction in cities, villages, and provinces.

The Institution

At the institutional level, the response to these demands includes the integration of foreign assistance and foreign policy, the rediscovery of public diplomacy, the redeployment of resources, and the conscious expansion of connections between official and unofficial American pursuits abroad, often under the name of public-private partnerships.

Functions like information and propaganda, cultural diplomacy, commercial diplomacy, and foreign aid have sometimes been consolidated in the State Department, and sometimes dispersed among several agencies (see chapter

2). Consolidation is the current tendency. The creation of the position of director of foreign assistance as a deputy secretary of state presages what the 2025 project called a deep alignment of foreign assistance and diplomacy. It hints at an eventual merger of the Agency for International Development into the Department of State and a possible convergence of the foreign service systems and personnel of USAID and State. There has been no comparable effort to consolidate the Commerce Department's foreign commercial service and the State Department's economic officers, although the Commerce Department's relative neglect of its commercial service and the growing role of ambassadors in commercial advocacy keep State's foreign service officers heavily—and successfully—engaged in commercial work.[12]

All foreign service agencies are adjusting the way they use their foreign service members to match changes in the global distribution of economic and political power and the shifting location of strategic threats. The number of foreign service posts is growing, and, if Baghdad is excepted, the average size of a post is shrinking. Positions are moving from western Europe to China, India, central Asia, and the Middle East. Redeployment by the Department of State includes greater use of one- and two-person "American presence" posts, which put diplomats close to audiences that are far from urban elites, and of no-person "virtual presence" posts, where interactive computer kiosks let foreigners stay in touch with the United States between visits from circuit-riding foreign service officers.

Connections between America's official and unofficial presence overseas have been growing in breadth, depth, and complexity. The unofficial presence—investors, exporters, importers, charities, groups that preach, teach, or advocate, and purveyors of the globally pervasive American popular culture—dwarfs the official presence in almost every way. The growing reliance of government agencies, and especially USAID, on private contractors to carry out their programs further blurs the line between official and unofficial activity and diminishes the visibility, authority, and influence of the U.S. government abroad.[13]

Foreign affairs agencies, American embassies, and the foreign service are still working out what kinds of relationships with these private entities best serve the public interest. For the resource-starved foreign service, the temptation is strong to see cooperation with the private sector as a way to spend private, unappropriated money for public purposes, but alignment of private and public interests can never be taken for granted. Relationships between embassies and the private groups operating in their countries are like diplomatic relationships between allies: they aim at maintaining the alignment of interests and working in tandem where possible, and, when interests diverge, at staying in close touch, avoiding open conflict, and finding areas of cooperation that can be expanded over time. The techniques of building and exploiting public-private partnerships are the subject of much study. The most successful examples are likely to be widely copied.[14]

The Profession

Changes at the professional level may be more fundamental. The foreign service did not have the skills required to perform the mission assigned to it in Iraq. Economic reconstruction required specialists in agronomy, sanitation, administration of justice, public finance, public health, and others not on the foreign service payrolls. The service turned to civilian contractors and military personnel, many drawn from the reserves, to do this work. The debate over the lessons to be learned has just begun.

The threshold question is whether the foreign service will again face a situation at all like the one it faced in Iraq. Is economic and political reconstruction in places like Somalia, Darfur, Palestine, or Mindanao part of the future of American foreign policy? If so, is the foreign service the right organization to take on the task? If it is, to what extent should the service rely on contractors to supply specialized personnel, and to what extent should it develop its own expertise?

Dennis Ross, the former Middle East negotiator, has speculated that aggressive and timely U.S. efforts to promote economic reconstruction and development could have strengthened Mahmoud Abbas against Hamas in the Palestinian territories and Hamid Karzai against provincial warlords and Taliban fighters in Afghanistan. Ambassador Henry Crumpton, the former CIA operations officer who served as the State Department's coordinator for counterterrorism from 2005 to 2007, said the United States should have "an expeditionary foreign service" skilled in nation-building, an idea that Secretary Rice also apparently favors.[15]

The service could be moving in that direction. The service has compiled an inventory of the skills and experience of its active and retired members, and of family members who choose to participate and will do something similar for its foreign service nationals.[16] These databases should identify what and who are available to meet a sudden need. But the civilian reserve corps for now is just a phrase, and an expeditionary foreign service is a long way off. They may never arrive.

The Career

The foreign service career is changing in important ways. The law of supply and demand suggests that for the next ten years or so, officers and specialists who are prepared for service in dangerous, difficult, or isolated posts, or who are eager and able to learn a critical language, will find a seller's market. They are likely to be rewarded with the assignments they want, the training they need, and the responsibility that creates opportunities for rapid advancement. But the pressure to take on hardship tours should not be exaggerated. Many, probably most, officers will spend no more than two or three years of a twenty-seven-year career in posts that take them away from their families.

In the past few years, the Department of State has come under pressure from within as well as from the outside to lift its level of skill and bring more rigor and consistency to the professional development of foreign service officers. The model most often cited is the officer corps of the armed services.

Secretary Powell reportedly said that foreign service officers are better educated than military officers when they begin their careers, but military officers are better educated than foreign service officers at retirement. The military has the capacity for methodically upgrading and updating officers' skills as they rise through the ranks. The foreign service does not, and it will not unless the number of officers is substantially increased. Until that happens, a foreign service career will be marked by conflicts between posts that need staff and staff that need training, and professional development will remain haphazard.

Foreign Service Pride

What will not change is the pride that members of the service can take in their careers. Foreign service officers and specialists feel that pride quietly. Inexplicably, neither the Department of State nor the U.S. Foreign Service as an institution does much to foster what should be a formidable esprit de corps. There are no insignia of rank except for an ambassador's flag. There are few traditions or ceremonies. Promotions and retirements generally go unmarked. Awards may be conferred by mail or in perfunctory group presentations. New diplomats and new ambassadors get a gaudy swearing-in, but otherwise a member of the service may pass a thirty-year career and see no pomp under any circumstance.

This public diffidence, and its obvious contrast with military display, emphasizes the difference between diplomats and soldiers. The foreign service may be what it is often called, America's first line of defense, but it relies on persuasion, negotiation, inducement, and threat, not on force. "Diplomats," wrote David Newsom, "live in realms that are conspiratorial, cynical and devious."[17] They can be, but often are not, plain talkers and straight shooters. They seek clarity but are comfortable with ambiguity. Their most prized skills are verbal, psychological, and manipulative. As David Brooks observed, these are not talents most Americans regard with moral admiration.[18]

The foreign service merits, but should not expect, the high esteem of the American public. Most diplomatic success is incremental, measured in small doses when it can be measured at all. Breakthroughs occur, but they are rare. Americans are impatient. They want results, and they easily blame diplomats for failing to deliver. Neither the State Department nor the foreign service has anything like a grassroots constituency.

The greatest part of the work of the foreign service is done quietly. Its achievements often pass unnoticed, as do its sacrifices. It bears repeating that since World War II, more American ambassadors than general and flag officers have been killed in the line of duty.

Foreign service officers salute the flag but rarely wave it. Within the service, as its members will tell you, patriotism and passion for the job run deep. A life in the foreign service is its own emblem.

Appendix A.
U.S. Department of
State Organization Chart

United States Agency for International
Development (USAID) Administrator

Director of Foreign Assistance (F)

Chief of Staff
(S/COS)

Under Secretary for Political Affairs (P)	Under Secretary for Economic, Business and Agricultural Affairs (E)	Under Secretary for Arms Control and International Security Affairs (T)	Under Secretary for Public Diplomacy and Public Affairs (R)

African Affairs (AF) Assistant Secretary	East Asian and Pacific Affairs (EAP) Assistant Secretary	Economic, Energy & Business Affairs (EEB) Assistant Secretary	International Security and Nonproliferation (ISN) Assistant Secretary
			Education and Cultural Affairs (ECA) Assistant Secretary
European and Eurasian Affairs (EUR) Assistant Secretary	International Organizations (O) Assistant Secretary		Political-Military Affairs (PM) Assistant Secretary
			Public Affairs (PA) Assistant Secretary
Near Eastern Affairs (NEA) Assistant Secretary	South and Central Asian Affairs (SCA) Assistant Secretary		Verification, Compliance and Implementation (VCI) Assistant Secretary
			International Information Program (IIP) Coordinator
Western Hemisphere Affairs (WHA) Assistant Secretary	International Narcotics and Law Enforcement (INL) Assistant Secretary		

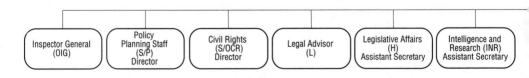

Inspector General (OIG)	Policy Planning Staff (S/P) Director	Civil Rights (S/OCR) Director	Legal Advisor (L)	Legislative Affairs (H) Assistant Secretary	Intelligence and Research (INR) Assistant Secretary

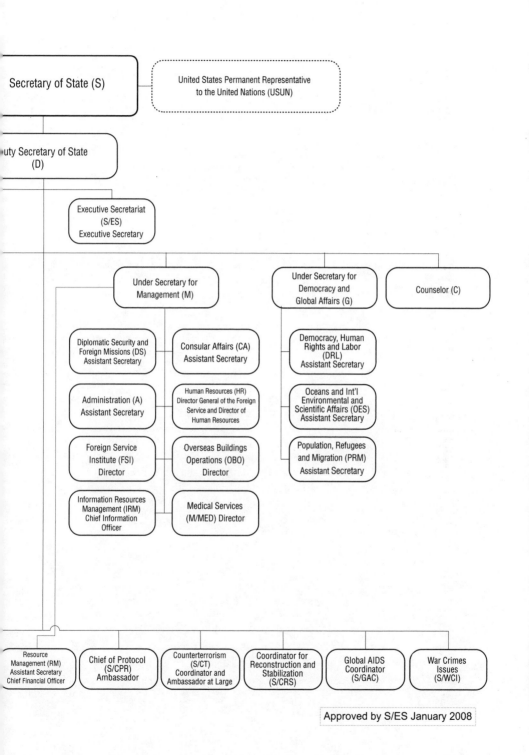

Secretary of State (S)

United States Permanent Representative
to the United Nations (USUN)

Deputy Secretary of State
(D)

Executive Secretariat
(S/ES)
Executive Secretary

Under Secretary for
Management (M)

Under Secretary for
Democracy and
Global Affairs (G)

Counselor (C)

Diplomatic Security and
Foreign Missions (DS)
Assistant Secretary

Consular Affairs (CA)
Assistant Secretary

Democracy, Human
Rights and Labor
(DRL)
Assistant Secretary

Administration (A)
Assistant Secretary

Human Resources (HR)
Director General of the Foreign
Service and Director of
Human Resources

Oceans and Int'l
Environmental and
Scientific Affairs (OES)
Assistant Secretary

Foreign Service
Institute (FSI)
Director

Overseas Buildings
Operations (OBO)
Director

Population, Refugees
and Migration (PRM)
Assistant Secretary

Information Resources
Management (IRM)
Chief Information
Officer

Medical Services
(M/MED) Director

Resource
Management (RM)
Assistant Secretary
Chief Financial Officer

Chief of Protocol
(S/CPR)
Ambassador

Counterterrorism
(S/CT)
Coordinator and
Ambassador at Large

Coordinator for
Reconstruction and
Stabilization
(S/CRS)

Global AIDS
Coordinator
(S/GAC)

War Crimes
Issues
(S/WCI)

Approved by S/ES January 2008

Appendix B. Foreign Service Core Precepts (July 2007)

Leadership Skills

Entry Level	Mid Level	Senior Level
Innovation		
Takes initiative to go beyond assigned tasks; identifies problems and proposes creative solutions; seeks to improve job and organization performance.	Develops insights into situations and applies them in the workplace; devises innovative solutions to make organizational improvements and policy adjustments.	Creates an organization-wide environment which encourages innovation; takes a long-term view and acts as a catalyst for constructive change' conceives and institutes organization-wide policy and program initiatives; anticipates and prepares for the future.
Decision Making		
Identifies issues within context of own job which require decisions of other action; arrives at recommendations in a logical, orderly manner, act confidently and decisively within own purview, consulting others as appropriate; is sensitive to needs and opinions of others.	Makes reasoned, effective, and timely decisions after considering all relevant factors and options, even when data are limited or conflicting or will produce unpleasant consequences; implements decisions and evaluates their impact and implications, making adjustments as needed.	Integrates policy and administrative factors into problem solving and decision making in a manner enhancing the entire organization; encourages staff to accept responsibility.

Leadership Skills

Entry Level	Mid Level	Senior Level

Teamwork

Entry Level	Mid Level	Senior Level
Applies what he/ she learns about team building to be an effective team member. Is open to views of others; works in collaborative, inclusive, outcome-oriented manner with U.S. and foreign colleagues; accepts team consensus.	Is an effective team leader, who creates an environment that facilitates full participation and an open exchange of ideas; fosters cooperation and collaboration among U.S. and foreign colleagues; motivates and guides team members toward a common goal. Actively develops the skills of subordinates, counsels them, and makes optimum use of their talents.	Is an effective team motivator, who inspires all staff to participate and contribute; encourages and develops a sense of pride and cohesiveness among staff; resolves work-related problems by mobilizing team skills and resources; develops and implements strategies to improve the workplace, morale, skills and achievements of team members.

Openness to Dissent

Entry Level	Mid Level	Senior Level
Demonstrates the intellectual integrity to speak openly within channels and a willingness to risk criticism in order to voice sensible dissent. Publicly supports official decisions, even when disagreeing with them.	Discerns when well-founded dissent is justifies; engages in constructive advocacy of policy alternatives; guides staff to do the same.	Accords importance to well-founded dissent and defends its appropriate expression.

Community Service and Institution Building

Entry Level	Mid Level	Senior Level
Participates actively in outreach or "community service" activities that contribute to employee welfare. For example, volunteers for Post or Department programs, initiatives, ceremonies, special events, blood and fund drives and other activities.	Participates actively in performance evaluation decision making and resource allocation activities (e.g., serves on Selection Boards or on post EER Review Panel); works on resource allocation committees (e.g., Housing Board); counsels personnel more junior in grade.	Participates actively in "institution building" activities that strengthen the Department as an organization. For example, recruits for the Department (e.g., serves as Diplomat-in-Residence or on the Board of Examiners); works on the Selection Boards' participates in Department mentoring program.

Source: U.S. Department of State, Bureau of Human Resources, unpublished material provided to the author.

Managerial Skills

Entry Level	Mid Level	Senior Level

Operational Effectiveness

Entry Level	Mid Level	Senior Level
Plans, organizes, and directs activities effectively; ensures that projects within area of responsibility are completed in a timely manner; accepts supervision and guidance; provides feedback to supervisors. Demonstrates commitment and moral courage by making difficult choices, by working with a sense of purpose, and by caring about the results.	Produces results in most effective manner; objectively analyzes the organization's strengths and weaknesses, and takes appropriate action.	Establishes effective management procedures and controls; encourages and rewards efforts or staff to enhance their effectiveness; foresees challenges to, and opportunities for, the organization and takes steps in advance to deal with them.

Performance Management and Evaluation

Entry Level	Mid Level	Senior Level
Participates in preparation of work requirements for self and works with staff in preparing their work requirements; develops plans to accomplish work requirements; ensures that staff are appropriately utilized, appraised, and rewarded; gives staff both formal and informal feedback on performance and potential; completes employee evaluations in accordance with standards and deadlines.	Establishes and clearly communicates broad performance expectations for unit; manages staff effectively, focusing on results; monitors plans to accomplish work requirements; delegates appropriately; creates a productive work environment in which employee's contributions are valued and encouraged; works to prevent and resolve personnel problems in a timely manner; ensures that the evaluation process is properly conducted and that counseling occurs throughout the rating year.	Establishes and clearly communicates organization-wide performance expectations in accordance with the Department's goals and objectives; inspires a high level of performance in staff; ensures the professional development and mentoring of staff; oversees possible improvements in human resource processes; works to prevent and resolve personnel problems in a timely manner; ensures that the evaluation and counseling process is conducted effectively and in accordance with standards and deadlines.

Managerial Skills

Entry Level	Mid Level	Senior Level

Management of Resources

Entry Level	Mid Level	Senior Level
Utilizes internal controls to protect the integrity of the organization and prevent waste, fraud, and mismanagement, reporting any instances where such problems occur; uses material and financial resources prudently; strives to produce highest return with lowest cost.	Ensures that effective internal controls are in place and work correctly; allocates resources efficiently, equitably, and in conformity with policy and regulatory guidelines; makes every effort to ensure that employees have the tools needed to work effectively.	Evaluates adequacy of internal controls and ensures implementation of improvements as warranted; holds managers accountable for the consequences of their resource policy decisions; seeks resource adjustments as needed.

Customer Service

Entry Level	Mid Level	Senior Level
Responds professionally, courteously and competently to both internal and external customers.	Balances competing and sometimes conflicting interests of a variety of customers; anticipates and responds appropriately to customer needs.	At the organization level, encourages customer-oriented focus, maintains or improves services organization-wide.

Support for Equal Employment Opportunity and Merit Principles

Entry Level	Mid Level	Senior Level
Takes diversity training and applies its principles to the workplace; treats all individuals with respect and without regard due to race, color, gender, religion, national origin, age, disability, sexual orientation; acts in compliance with USG and Department EEO policies.	Manages diversity by recruiting diverse staff at all levels and ensuring staff diversity training and awareness. Promotes diversity awareness through training; ensures by example and instruction, and verifies through monitoring and follow-up, that all employees are treated with fairness and respect; applies EEO and merit principles consistently; identifies and addresses situations giving rise to complaints and grievances based on issues of fairness in the workplace.	Fosters an organization-wide environment in which diversity is valued and respected; encourages the organization to realize the full potential of a diverse staff; provides personal leadership and vigorous support for EEO, merit principles, and fair employment practices.

Managerial Skills

Entry Level	Mid Level	Senior Level

Management of Sensitive and Classified Material, Information and Infrastructure

Entry Level	Mid Level	Senior Level
Practices good personal security. Takes full responsibility for handling and safeguarding sensitive and classified material, information, and infrastructure properly.	Encourages the practice of good personal security measures and serves as a model for others. Takes full responsibility for handling and safeguarding sensitive and classified material, information and infrastructure properly; ensures that effective procedures are in place to protect classified material, information and infrastructure and that established security regulations are being followed.	Promotes the practice of good personal security measures by employees. Takes full responsibility for handling and safeguarding sensitive and classified material, information and infrastructure properly; promotes security consciousness on an organization-wide basis; evaluates and monitors procedures to safeguard sensitive and classified material, information and infrastructure and ensures that necessary changes are made if current procedures are inadequate; holds managers accountable for the consequences of their security policy decisions.

Source: U.S. Department of State, Bureau of Human Resources, unpublished material provided to the author.

Interpersonal Skills

Entry Level	Mid Level	Senior Level

Professional Standards

Entry Level	Mid Level	Senior Level
Holds self accountable for rules and responsibilities; is dependable and conscientious; is composed, professional, and productive, even in difficult conditions. Treats all with respect.	Holds others accountable for rules and responsibilities; consistently maintains equanimity and a professional demeanor; maintains own motivation and encourages others to persevere in difficult circumstances.	Sets the standard for integrity and workplace behavior by example and instruction; does not lose composure under stress or in crisis; fosters a climate based on mutual respect and trust.

Persuasion and Negotiation

Entry Level	Mid Level	Senior Level
Learns to influence others; gains cooperation, while showing, in the spirit of mutual respect, understanding of others' positions.	Influences others deftly; fosters understanding of USG/Department views and positions and/or procedures and requirements; develops alliances with others; finds common ground among disparate forces and builds consensus; facilitates win-win situations.	Negotiates effectively on a wide range of issues in internal, bilateral, and multilateral environments; manages and resolves major conflicts and disagreements in an interest-based manner; manifests a faculty for astute compromise without sacrificing ultimate goals.

Workplace Perceptiveness

Entry Level	Mid Level	Senior Level
Demonstrates sensitivity in both domestic and foreign environments to status, protocol, and chain of command; responds considerately to the needs, feelings, and capabilities of others; shows respect for cultural differences.	Understands and deals effectively with relationships and aspirations; anticipates how others will react; frames own responses to achieve results.	Navigates easily in an environment of shifting relationships; anticipates socially sensitive issues and takes appropriate action.

Interpersonal Skills

Entry Level	Mid Level	Senior Level
Adaptability		
Adapts behavior and work methods as needed in response to new information, changing conditions, or unexpected obstacles; displays sensitivity.	Guides staff in adjusting to new environments and different value systems and cultures, while maintaining own standards and identity.	Anticipates and plans for change; exercises sophisticated cultural sensitivity in all circumstances.
Representational Skills		
Establishes and maintains purposeful and productive relationships with domestic and foreign contacts; interacts effectively in official and social encounters.	Identifies and cultivates key individuals and institutions; advocates U.S. interests through hosting and attending representational events.	Moves with ease at all social settings and levels; ensures identification, cultivation and periodic assessment of audiences important to U.S. interests

Source: U.S. Department of State, Bureau of Human Resources, unpublished material provided to the author.

Communication and Foreign Language Skills

Entry Level	Mid Level	Senior Level
	Written Communication	
Writes succinctly; produces written materials that are thorough; conveys analysis that highlights essential points and clearly explains the essence of the subject to the intended audience – whether mission management or senior Department official.	Writes clearly and persuasively; ensures that policy and operational issues are articulated in ways most helpful to the intended audience; assists staff to develop effective writing skills.	Exhibits full mastery of written communication; shows sophisticated ability to analyze, synthesize, and advocate in a timely manner; edits others' texts judiciously.
	Oral Communication	
Speaks in a concise, effective, and organized manner, tailored to the audience and the situation; speaks convincingly in groups and in individual discussion.	Speaks authoritatively to all audiences, demonstrating comprehensive understanding of issues and options; articulates policy goals persuasively; fosters an atmosphere of open communication and exchange of ideas.	Effectively argues complex policy issues; deals comfortably with the media and with the most senior levels of government and society.
	Active Listening	
Listens attentively; understands and absorbs others' messages correctly; reads nonverbal signals; summarizes others' views accurately and confirms accuracy of understanding; considers and responds respectfully and appropriately.	Instills trust in others which motivates them to speak openly and candidly; understands and respects cultural sensitivities and constraints in discussing issues and opinions; asks open-ended, incisive questions to ensure accuracy of understanding.	Adeptly discerns the innermost meaning and nuances of messages that others convey.

Communication and Foreign Language Skills

Entry Level	Mid Level	Senior Level
Public Outreach		
Develops public speaking and writing skills by seeking appropriate opportunities to present U.S. views and perspectives.	Seizes and creates opportunities to advocate U.S. perspective to a variety of audiences. Actively develops the skills of subordinates.	Deals comfortably with the media; is active and effective in public diplomacy, both in the U.S. and overseas. Contributes to and implements strategies to encourage a fair hearing for U.S. views and perspectives.
Foreign Language Skill (Generalists; Specialists as applicable)		
Meets language probation requirements; uses foreign language skills to enhance job performance; seeks to improve foreign language skills.	Attains general professional proficiency* in at least one foreign language, strives to acquire advanced level proficiency and/or general professional proficiency in additional languages; uses that skill effectively to communicate USG themes and to exercise influence; works to increase foreign language ability. *Generalists, to cross senior threshold, must obtain S/3-R/3 (i.e., general professional proficiency) in one language.	Maintains and/or develops proficiency in foreign language(s); uses skill to promote U.S. interests with a wide range of audiences, including the media.

Source: U.S. Department of State, Bureau of Human Resources, unpublished material provided to the author.

Intellectual Skills

Entry Level	Mid Level	Senior Level

Information Gathering and Analysis

Entry Level	Mid Level	Senior Level
Locates, evaluates, and quickly assimilates information; considers a variety of sources, cross-checking when appropriate; reorganizes information logically to maximize its practical utility and identify key underlying factors; recognizes when additional information is required and responds accordingly.	Has a sophisticated understanding of sources and their reliability; knows what to report and when; accepts that it may not be possible to base recommendations, decisions, or actions on comprehensive information; considers downstream consequences; guides and motivates staff to refine their own analytical skills.	Integrates fully a wide range of information and prior experiences in policy making; ensures that staff search out and evaluate information before making recommendations and decisions; recognizes situations in which information and analysis are incomplete and responds wisely; accepts accountability for self and insists on it for staff.

Critical Thinking

Entry Level	Mid Level	Senior Level
Identifies key information, central issues, and common themes; distinguishes fact from opinion and relevant from irrelevant information; identifies the strengths and weaknesses of various approaches; outlines realistic options.	Isolates key points, central issues, and common themes in a mass of complex information; can determine the best solution or action from a range of options; is objective in analyzing problems and judging people.	Analyzes and defines complex policy issues clearly, in terms which permit them to be dealt with in a practical way; encourages staff to analyze situations and propose options, giving constructive and instructive feedback; correctly senses when it is appropriate to take risks, and does so.

Intellectual Skills

Entry Level	Mid Level	Senior Level
Active Learning		
Seeks out new job-related knowledge and readily grasps its implications for the workplace; seeks informal feedback and learns from mistakes; recognizes own strengths and weaknesses and pursues self-development.	Develops own knowledge through broadening experiences, whether work-related, academic studies, or other type of professional development; develops plans to teach others in the workplace; provides informal feedback to colleagues and seeks feedback on own performance.	Anticipates the need for new information or knowledge for self and others; identifies sources of new information and communicates these sources to staff and facilitates access.
Leadership and Management Training		
Learns basic principles of effective leadership and management. Pursues formal and informal training opportunities.	Uses training opportunities to improve personal leadership and management skills to keep abreast of current theory and techniques. Applies the principles learned at FSI and other relevant courses on the job, e.g., by developing subordinates.	Actively promotes leadership and management training at the organizational level; as appropriate opportunities arise, works to enhance that training; applies principles of leadership and management training to foster organizational improvements.

Source: U.S. Department of State, Bureau of Human Resources, unpublished material provided to the author.

Substantive Knowledge

Entry Level	Mid Level	Senior Level
	Job Information	
Develops and applies knowledge needed in current assignment; learns factors which impact work; understands how job relates to organizational goals and U.S. policy objectives; uses FSI and other training to improve individual performance.	Has broad knowledge of job-related processes and practices; remains current on policies programs and trends that affect the organization; analyzes the interplay of forces influencing the achievement of policy and program objectives and makes reasonable recommendations. Uses training and other means to improve programs. Supports continuous learning of employees through both training and work opportunities.	Integrates thorough knowledge of issues arising in job to formulate and implement policies and programs; monitors internal and external sources for information and ideas; uses job knowledge to shape outcomes. Utilizes FSI training to raise level of organizational unit performance. Creates an environment and strategies to support professional development both through training and work opportunities.
	Institutional Knowledge	
Understands institutional realities which may affect work; understands the role and power of various offices and people, both domestically and abroad; cultivates and utilizes contacts in other organizational entities; uses institutional understanding to get things done.	Applies knowledge of institutional realities to policy and operational issues; crosses institutional boundaries in obtaining information and building support; operates on an equal footing with officials in other bureaus, agencies, foreign governments, business communities, academia and media; assists staff to comprehend the institutional influences within which they work.	Uses sophisticated institutional understanding to avoid problems and advance USG goals; ensures that staff are mindful of the importance of proper and prudent procedures in securing desired outcomes.

Substantive Knowledge

Entry Level	Mid Level	Senior Level

Technical Skills

| Learns and uses technical skills and technology as appropriate in job setting; understands the impact of technology on the workplace; seeks ways to use technology to enhance performance. | Continuously enhances own and staff's understanding of work-related technical skills and technology and their applications; advances policy and program goals through the use of available technology. | Promotes own and staff's full utilization of technical skills and technology to achieve bureau/mission goals; devises efficient and cost-effective strategies to integrate technology into the workplace. |

Professional Expertise

| Understands and applies Foreign Service procedures, requirements, regulations, and policies; assimilates Department of State and Foreign Service milieu; builds knowledge of U.S. and foreign environments; uses developing expertise in work situations. | Strives to deepen understanding of the Department of State and of the Foreign Service as a profession; uses expertise to evaluate policies and programs and to advise and develop others; is able to operate independently to further bureau/mission objectives. | Combines mastery of U.S. policy objectives and knowledge of foreign environments to advance USG goals; assists staff to develop Foreign Service skills and expertise, promoting a work environment that enhances their professional development. |

Knowledge of Foreign Cultures

| Develops and demonstrates knowledge of foreign cultures, values, and norms; appropriately applies foreign perspective to domestic assignments and host country perspectives to assignments abroad. | Has sophisticated grasp of foreign political, economic, cultural, and information environments; relates knowledge to fulfillment of bureau/mission goals. | Uses thorough knowledge of foreign environments to identify and seize opportunities to advance USG goals. Develops subordinates' understanding of how best to advance U.S. interests in a foreign environment. |

Source: U.S. Department of State, Bureau of Human Resources, unpublished material provided to the author.

Appendix C. Interviews

The authors are grateful to all those who gave their time to this project, including those whose names have been withheld. Those interviewed spoke for themselves, not for their agencies or employers.

Charles Alexander	February 14, 2006
Juan Alsace	August 28, 2006
Robert Batchelder	August 12, 2005
Davida Baxter	February 23, 2007
Sylvia Bazala	August 29, 2006
Barry Blechman	June 12, 2006
Marcia Bosshardt	August 6, 2007
Tobin Bradley	November 3, 2005
Rea Brazeal	January 26, 2006
Douglas Broome	January 31, 2006
John H. Brown	September 1, 2006
Jennifer Butte-Dahl	April 2, 2007
Lewis K. Byrd	August 10, 2006
Robin Byrd	August 10, 2006
Vincent Campos	February 15, 2007
Katherine Canavan	September 14, 2005
Joseph Castro	August 11, 2006
David Caudill	February 23, 2007
William N. Center	February 8, 2006
Andrew Chritton	June 23, 2005
Marguerite Coffey	July 27, 2006
Frank Coulter	November 15, 2005
Caryn Danz	July 25, 2007
Bill DePree	August 20, 2005
James Derham	July 10, 2005
Philo Dibble	October 26, 2005
Steve Dietz	April 27, 2007
David Dlouhy	January 27, 2006, July 20, 2007
Debi Fairman	February 23, 2007
Jimmie Fairman	February 23, 2007
Steve Gallogly	August 8, 2005
Robert Gallucci	June 9, 2007
David Greenlee	August 24, 2005
Marc Grossman	November 16, 2005
Linda Hartsock	June 23, 2005
Clayton Hays	August 12, 2005

L. Craig Johnstone	February 1, 2006
Harry Kamian	August 26, 2006
Sidney Kaplan	May 18, 2007
Steve Kashkett	August 29, 2006
Craig Kelly	October 2006
Christian Kennedy	July 20, 2005
Kristie Anne Kenney	August 26, 2005
Eric Khant	February 23, 2007
Russ King	August 10, 2006
Barbro Owens Kirkpatrick	September 28, 2005
Jeremiah Knight	February 22, 2007
Jimmy Kolker	May 25, 2007
Alan Larson	July 13, 2007
Rose Likins	December 13, 2006
Dana Linnet	April 2, 2007
Hugo Llorens	August 12, 2005
Robert Loftis	September 19, 2006
Rudolph Lohmeyer	May 18, 2007
Marcos Mandojana	February 8, 2006
Steven Mann	September 7, 2005
Kristine Marsh	March 3, 2007
John Marten	August 6, 2006
William McCahill	August 23, 2007
Deborah McCarthy	August 26, 2005
Sean McCormack	December 12, 2006
Christopher Midura	May 29, 2007
Richard Miles	March 10, 2006
Charnae Morris	March 8, 2006
Langhorne A. Motley	August 30, 2006
Sean Murphy	August 28, 2006
Marianne Myles	July 20, 2007
John Naland	May 17, 2007
Michelle Nichols	February 22, 2007
Robert Nolan	May 18, 2007
Cecilia Olea	August 10, 2006
James Pavitt	January 25, 2007
W. Robert Pearson	June 27, 2006
Brian Polley	July 6, 2006
John A. Ritchie	October 28, 2005
Adele Ruppe	December 14, 2005
Gregory Schiffer	February 8, 2006
William Schofield	November 15, 2005
Susan Shea	June 27, 2005
Thomas Skipper	December 14, 2005
Timothy Slater	August 10, 2006
David Stephenson	February 23, 2007

Diana Tasnadi	October 23, 2006
Robert B. Waldrop	October 28, 2005, December 1, 2005
Betsy Whitaker	December 13, 2005
Loren Willet	July 6, 2006
Ann Witkowski	July 19, 2007
Bryan Wockley	March 6, 2007
Emi Yamauchi	May 16, 2007
Ben Ziff	December 14, 2005

Appendix D. Websites

The following websites are especially useful, interesting, or both.

www.careerdiplomacy.com
The website associated with this book.

www.state.gov and http://careers.state.gov
Department of State. The department's careers site has information on foreign service and civil service jobs, and on student programs and internships. Sign up here to take the foreign service exam.

www.usaid.gov and usaid.gov/careers
U.S. Agency for International Development jobs page.

www.commerce.gov and commerce.gov/jobs.html
The Department of Commerce jobs page.

www.america.gov
A State Department website aimed at providing international audiences with "in-depth material on U.S. policies, culture and values."

www.usda.gov and www.fas.usda.gov/admin/jobs/jobs.asp
The Department of Agriculture jobs page.

http://adst.org and www.usdiplomacy.org
The Association for Diplomatic Studies and Training (ADST) website. The ADST advances understanding of American diplomacy and supports training of foreign service personnel. ADST maintains www.usdiplomacy.org, an online exploration of diplomatic history and foreign affairs.

www.afsa.org
The American Foreign Service Association. Back issues of the *Foreign Service Journal* are available at this site.

www.americanambassadors.org
The Council of American Ambassadors, an association of noncareer ambassadors.

www.americandiplomacy.org
An electronic journal published by retired foreign service officers and hosted by the University of North Carolina, Chapel Hill.

http://blogs.state.gov/
Dipnote, the official blog of the Department of State.

http://businessfordiplomaticaction.org
Public relations professionals in support of public diplomacy.

www.foggybottomsociety.org
The association of the State Department's civil service professionals.

www.nicholaskralev.com/WT-FS.html
Nicholas Kralev, a journalist with the *Washington Times*, wrote a series of articles on the foreign service in 2004. They are collected at this address.

www.osac.gov
Overseas Security Advisory Council, the link between the private sector and the Department of State on security overseas.

www.publicdiplomacy.org
The public diplomacy alumni association, formerly the USIA alumni association.

http://uscpublicdiplomacy.com
The Center for Public Diplomacy at the University of Southern California.

www.usdiplomacy.org and http://adst.org
An online exploration of diplomatic history and foreign affairs, published by the Association for Diplomatic Studies and Training.

Notes

Chapter 1

1. Rice, Remarks at town hall meeting.
2. Rice, Confirmation hearings opening statement.

Chapter 2

1. Acheson, *Present at the Creation*, 303.
2. Grove, *Behind Embassy Walls*, 95.
3. Kissinger, *White House Years*, 11.
4. Conversation between Nixon and Kissinger, November 13, 1972, quoted in Humphrey, *Foreign Relations of the United States*, Vol. II, 768.
5. Foreign service officers in the Nixon White House included Frank Carlucci (later secretary of defense), Lawrence Eagleburger (secretary of state), Anthony Lake (national security advisor), Winston Lord (ambassador to China), John Negroponte (deputy secretary of state), Peter Rodman (assistant secretary of defense), and Harold Saunders (assistant secretary of state).
6. In 1792, the United States had five diplomatic and sixteen consular posts abroad. By 1860, the numbers had grown to 33 and 279. When no American was available, consular commissions were sometimes given to third-country nationals.
7. Some writers ridiculed consuls, but others benefited from consular appointments, which were a form of federal support for artistic achievement. A list of nineteenth-century writers who served as consuls includes Washington Irving, Nathaniel Hawthorne, James Fenimore Cooper, William Dean Howells, James Weldon Johnson, and Bret Harte. Henry Adams served as private secretary to the minister of the American legation in London, his father, Charles Francis Adams. President Abraham Lincoln, who sent Charles Francis Adams to London, asked his secretary of state to use consular positions to "facilitate artists a little [in] their profession" (Goodwin, *Team of Rivals*, 703).
8. Trask, *A Short History*, 22.
9. Bierce, *The Devil's Dictionary*, 18.
10. Adams, *The Education of Henry Adams*, 1080.
11. Trask, *A Short History*, 26.
12. Quoted in Barnes and Morgan, *The Foreign Service of the United States*, 207.
13. Congressional efforts in 1995 to return the commercial service to the Department of State received wide support, but not wide enough: the measure died in committee.
14. The Trade Expansion Act of 1962 created the Office of the Special Trade Representative in the Executive Office of the President. Subsequent legislation

made the office responsible to both the president and the Congress, the only such office in the U.S. government. An executive order changed the name to U.S. trade representative in 1979.

15. The Office of War Information, established in 1942, was dissolved in 1945 and its foreign operations, called the U.S. Information Service (USIS) in most countries, were transferred to the State Department. In 1953 President Eisenhower transferred USIS and other overseas information activities from the Department of State to a new United States Information Agency (USIA), whose director reported to the secretary of state. USIA personnel were brought into the foreign service as foreign service information officers by act of Congress in 1968. Cultural activities including the Fulbright program were transferred in 1978, when President Carter renamed USIA the United States Information and Communications Agency (USICA). President Reagan restored the USIA name in 1982. In 1996 President Clinton vetoed legislation to abolish USIA and return its functions to State, but he signed the Foreign Affairs Reform and Restructuring Act of 1998 that abolished USIA (except for the Broadcasting Board of Governors and the International Broadcasting Bureau) and moved its functions to the State Department, effective October 1, 1999.

16. The Economic Cooperation Administration, set up in 1948 to administer the Marshall Plan, begat the Mutual Security Agency (1951) and the Foreign Operations Administration (1953). The Foreign Operations Administration begat the International Cooperation Agency (1955). The Foreign Operations Administration had been outside the Department of State, but the International Cooperation Agency was part of the Department. The International Cooperation Agency begat the U.S. Agency for International Development in 1961. USAID was set up as an independent agency. Its staff was not part of the career foreign service until passage of the Foreign Service Act of 1980, but its administrator reported to the secretary of state. In 1979, an executive order placed USAID under a new International Development and Cooperation Agency (IDCA), established outside the Department of State, though State retained control of security-related assistance programs. The Reagan administration allotted no staff or funds to IDCA, which effectively ceased to exist and was formally abolished by the Foreign Affairs Reform and Restructuring Act of 1998. In 1996, President Clinton vetoed legislation that would have abolished USAID and transferred its functions to the Department of State. The Millennium Challenge Corporation (MCC) was established by law in 2004 outside USAID to administer up to $5 billion annually in appropriated foreign assistance funds to promote good governance and economic freedom. The USAID administrator sits on the MCC board of directors, which the secretary of state chairs. In January 2006, administratively imposed reforms linked USAID more tightly to State and made the head of AID a deputy secretary of state, although the agency retained its autonomy.

17. Trask, *A Short History*, 29.

18. LaRue Lutkins, interview by Charles Stuart Kennedy, cited in Morgan and Kennedy, *American Diplomats*, 46.

19. Mee, *The Marshall Plan*, 215–16.

20. Kennan, *Memoirs*, 191–92.

21. Lauren, *The China Hands' Legacy*, 13. Hiss was tried and convicted of perjury in 1950 but was never charged with espionage. Readers who wonder about the disparity between the large number of employees dismissed for security concerns and the relatively small number believed to be involved with foreign powers may safely conclude that many were dismissed as security risks because they were believed to be homosexual.

22. There is no known recording or printed text of McCarthy's speech as delivered. This quote comes from an account by a reporter who was present. Frank Desmond, "McCarthy Charges Reds Hold U.S. Jobs," *The Wheeling Intelligencer*, February 10, 1950. Available at www.wvculture.org/history/government/ mccarthy.html. Other accounts vary only in detail.

23. Cited in Acheson, *Present at the Creation*, 365.

24. See Davies, "The Personal Experience."

25. See Kahn, *The China Hands*, 174–75. The accuser quoted here is Patrick Hurley, named ambassador to China in 1944. Hurley tried to promote a Communist-Nationalist coalition to fight the Japanese. His professional staff, the China hands, did not believe such an approach had any chance of success. The quotation is from Hurley's letter of resignation to President Truman in November 1945.

26. Kennan, *Memoirs*, 216.

27. John S. Service, fired in 1951, was reinstated in 1957 after the U.S. Supreme Court ruled that the department in dismissing him had violated its own regulations.

28. Grove, *Behind Embassy Walls*, 41. The aide is identified as Bob Fearey.

29. Nathan and Oliver, *Foreign Policy Making*, 17.

30. Quoted in Trask, *A Short History*, 35. The ambassador is Stanton Griffis, a businessman who served as ambassador to Poland, Egypt, Argentina, and Spain from 1947 to 1951.

31. For example, reserve officers had a separate pay scale, a source of continuing friction with the regular foreign service officers.

32. Bacchus, *Staffing for Foreign Affairs*, 201.

33. Ibid., 198–201. The 1980 act revived selection out for senior officers and extended it to secretaries, communications specialists, and other foreign service staff. Foreign service nationals (FSNs), local and third-country nationals employed by U.S. missions abroad, are by law members of the foreign service, but they are not subject to selection out. In this book, however, as in most usage, the term *members of the foreign service* means foreign service officers and specialists, not foreign service nationals.

34. The *New York Times* reported on August 13, 1974, that all five black ambassadors, all seven black USAID mission chiefs, and seven of the ten blacks who were USIA chiefs of section, were assigned in Africa (Thomas Johnson, "Black Envoys Seek More Non-African Posts," 4).

35. Quoted in the *New York Times*, "Report on Minority Progress Still 'Distressing,'" June 28, 1983.

36. The position of director of personnel was at the time separate from that of

director general. The officer who failed to win confirmation was Howard P. Mace (Benjamin Welles, "Women Winning State Department Cases," *New York Times*, February 28, 1972).

37.   U.S. General Accounting Office, *State Department*.

38.   Name withheld, interview, January 2006.

39.   Marc Grossman, interview, March 2005.

40.   L. Bruce Laingen, correspondence with authors, July 2005.

41.   Vance, *Hard Choices*, 329.

42.   Ibid., 340.

43.   U.S. Department of State, *Final Report and Recommendations*, appendix C. The seventy-two persons in the compound included thirty-seven Department of State employees, twenty-eight from the U.S. military (thirteen Marines, six army, six air force, and three navy), four from the U.S. International Cooperation Agency, one from the Foreign Agricultural Service, one from the Department of Education, and one private businessman. Three embassy officers, including the chargé d'affaires, were on their way to the foreign ministry building at the time the embassy was seized. They were effectively placed under arrest in the foreign ministry, where they stayed until their transfer to a prison in January 1981. Six people escaped the compound and took refuge in the Canadian embassy. Three months later they were smuggled out of the country under false identities provided by the Canadians, who then closed their embassy and withdrew all personnel. Thirteen were allowed to leave between November 18 and 20, after Khomeini ordered the release of "women and blacks." One hostage, Foreign Service Officer Richard Queen, was afflicted with multiple sclerosis and released in July 1980. Fifty-two hostages, including the three held in the foreign ministry, were released at noon on January 20, 1981, the last day of President Carter's term in office.

44.   Department of State, *Final Report and Recommendations*, appendix D. The murdered personnel include Ambassador John Gordon Mein, Guatemala, 1968; Public Safety Advisor Dan Mitrione, Uruguay, 1970; Ambassador Cleo A. Noel and Deputy Chief of Mission George Moore, Sudan, 1973; State Department employee John S. Patterson, Mexico, 1974; Ambassador Rodger P. Davies and administrative assistant Antoinette Varnava, Cyprus, 1974; consular agent John Egan, Argentina, 1975; Ambassador Francis E. Meloy, Jr., Economic Counselor Robert O. Waring and driver Zuhayr Mughrabi, Lebanon, 1976; Ambassador Adolph "Spike" Dubs, Afghanistan, 1979.

45.   A group representing most of the hostages later tried to sue the government of Iran, but federal courts upheld the validity of the renunciation clause of the agreement with Iran and rejected their case. Glenn Kessler, "Administration Blocks Ex-Hostages' Bid for Damages from Iran," *Washington Post*, March 19, 2006. The most recent federal court ruling came in 2002. The Supreme Court refused to hear an appeal in 2004. The Department of State repeated its opposition to claims by the hostages against Iran at a meeting with a group of former hostages in 2006.

46.   Steigman, *The Foreign Service*, 2.

47.   United States and Inman, *Report of the Secretary of State's Advisory Panel*.

48. For OSAC's membership, see www.osac.gov.

49. The predecessor of the Bureau of Diplomatic Security was the smaller Office of Security, which reported to the assistant secretary for administration.

50. The Bureau of Human Resources counted 4,733 foreign service specialists on December 31, 2005. Of these, 1,384 were diplomatic security special agents. Office-management specialists were the next largest category, numbering 845.

51. U.S. Department of State, *Partnerships for a Safer World*, 9.

52. For the distinction between ambassador and chief of mission, see chapter 5.

53. Tony Motley, interview, August 2007.

54. Gib Lanpher, telephone conversation with author, August 2007. Ambassador Lanpher noted that "a six-week ARB on Iraq, including salaries, travel, and per diem, costs less than one armored Suburban. Pretty good value provided the recommendations are given serous consideration."

55. Gates, Landon lecture.

56. Marquardt, "The DRI Rides to the Rescue," 21.

57. U.S. Department of State, *America's Overseas Presence*, 5.

58. Marc Grossman, interview, March 2005.

59. Grossman's inner circle included Bill Eaton, David Dlouhy, and Mike Polt. The original skunk works was a secret engineering department set up at Lockheed Aircraft Company in 1943 to develop jet aircraft. The name came from the "Skonk Works," a hidden still where denizens of Dogpatch, the fictional mountain community in Al Capp's Li'l Abner comic strip of the era, produced the stupefying Kickapoo Joy Juice.

60. U.S. GAO, *Staffing and Foreign Language Shortfalls*, 5. Looking back, the GAO calculated the cost of the DRI at $197 million.

61. In fact, they very nearly reached their goal. Of the 1,158 foreign service positions requested, the department obtained 1,069.

62. Foreign Affairs Council, *Secretary Colin Powell's State Department*, 3–4. See also Marquardt, "The DRI Rides to the Rescue." The Foreign Affairs Council is an umbrella group of eleven organizations, including the American Academy of Diplomacy, the American Foreign Service Association (AFSA), the Associates of the American Foreign Service Worldwide, the Association for Diplomatic Studies and Training, the Association of Black American Ambassadors, the Business Council for International Understanding, the Council of American Ambassadors, the Una Chapman Cox Foundation, the Nelson B. Delavan Foundation, and the Public Members Association of the Foreign Service, USA.

63. Foreign Affairs Council, *Secretary Colin Powell's State Department*, 4.

Chapter 3

1. Foreign Service Act of 1980, section 3904.

2. See chapter 6 for a detailed discussion of foreign service ranks.

3. The original building, which faces 21st Street, was constructed before World War II to house the War Department, which until then had shared space with

the State Department in what is now the Eisenhower Executive Office Building on 17th Street next to the White House. The War Department, however, moved to the much larger Pentagon, built in haste in 1943 and 1944, leaving the building at 21st and C vacant. State moved there instead in 1947 under pressure from the White House, which wanted to expand into the space that State occupied. State's new home was cramped, however, and was soon incorporated in a new and much larger building completed in 1960, with its main entrance on C Street at 22nd (see Acheson, *Present at the Creation*, 213). The new building was named for President Truman in 2000, and the original building, renovated between 1999 and 2007, was named the George C. Marshall wing.

4. See www.afsa.org/plaques.cfm. The American Foreign Service Association (AFSA) erected the first plaque in 1933 and the second in 1972. Names on the plaques are chosen by the AFSA governing board. The six who died in Iraq are Barbara L. Schell (helicopter crash, 1994); James Mollen (terrorist attack, 2004); Edward J. Seitz (rocket attack, 2004); Barbara C. Heald and Keith E. Taylor (rocket attack on U.S. embassy, 2005); and Stephen E. Sullivan (terrorist attack, 2005).

5. For a full list of State Department office designations and abbreviations, see www.state.gov/documents/organization/86890.pdf.

6. For a list of officials based in Washington with a rank equivalent to assistant secretary or higher, see www.state.gov/r/pa/ei/biog/c7647.htm. Including overseas personnel would sharply increase the ratio. Ambassadors count among officials with the rank of assistant secretary or above, and there are about 180 of them. State has about 18,000 direct-hire employees overseas, including 11,000 foreign service nationals, for a ratio of 1:100. Another 27,000 FSNs work under personal-service agreements. If these are included, the ratio improves to 1:250.

7. Foreign service nationals are subject to the employment laws of the jurisdiction in which they work.

8. The word *attaché* defines an official assigned to an embassy to perform a specific task. Although U.S. military personnel assigned to U.S. embassies still use the title *attaché*, the term is slowly passing out of use, along with other terms from French diplomatic usage, like *démarche, aide-mémoire,* and *note verbale.* In diplomatic rank, an attaché is ordinarily below a counselor.

9. The AFSA's official website can be found at www.afsa.org.

10. AID hires contractors to carry out many of its programs. The costs, including the contractors' salaries and other operating costs, are charged to AID's program budget. Not all foreign assistance flows through the AID budget, and what is budgeted in one year is generally spent in other years. That is why U.S. spending on foreign assistance as measured by the Organization for Economic Cooperation and Development (OECD) is close to $20 billion, more than double the AID budget.

11. Douglas Broome, interview, January 2006.

12. The same three d's—development, defense, and democracy—formed the basis for the policy recommendations of the report of the National Bipartisan

Commission on Central America, which Henry Kissinger, then former secretary of state, chaired in 1984.

13. Department of State, "New Direction for Foreign Assistance."
14. Craig Johnstone, interview, February 2006.
15. Ford, "Final Thoughts," 4. Ford, who joined the foreign service in the Department of State and transferred to the Foreign Commercial Service in 1980, later served as U.S. ambassador to Honduras.
16. Another sixty-seven foreign service officers and two-hundred foreign service nationals work in USDA's animal and plant health inspection service, which has employees in twenty-seven countries (data as of February 2006).
17. Charles Alexander, interview, February 2006.

Chapter 4

1. See Seitzinger, *Conducting Foreign Relations without Authority.* The Logan Act of 1799 does provide sanctions—fines and possible imprisonment—for unauthorized efforts by private U.S. citizens or residents to influence the behavior of foreign governments engaged in disputes with the U.S. government. A recent study by the Congressional Research Service found only one indictment (in 1803) and not a single prosecution under the Logan Act in its history.
2. See, for example, Steven Greenhouse, "Clinton Is Faulted on Political Choices for Envoy Posts," *New York Times*, April 13, 1994; Barbara Crossette, "Foreign Service Groups Urge Senate to Approve Ambassadors," *New York Times*, April 28, 2000. See also www.afsa.org/ambassadorsgraph2.cfm.
3. See www.state.gov/r/pa/ho/po/. The historian's page on the Department of State website lists all former chiefs of mission and principal officers of the department, distinguishing between career and noncareer appointees.
4. Robert Kimmitt (1989–91), Arnold Kanter (1991–93), Peter Tarnoff (1993–97).
5. Mike Lewis, "Gates is a big draw for visiting world leaders," *Seattle Post-Intelligencer*, April 17, 2006.
6. Nicolson, *The Evolution of Diplomatic Method*, 2 and 51–68. See also Berridge, *Diplomacy*, 111–12. This discussion deals only with European diplomacy because U.S. diplomatic practice is entirely derived from European traditions.
7. Quoted in Nicolson, *The Evolution of Diplomatic Method*, 68.
8. See http://untreaty.un.org/ilc/texts/instruments/english/conventions/9_1_1961 .pdf and http://untreaty.un.org/ilc/texts/instruments/english/conventions/9_2 _1963.pdf.
9. United Nations, *Vienna Convention*, 1961, Article 41, para. 1.
10. For a description of immunities and privileges enjoyed by U.S. diplomats posted abroad, see www.state.gov/documents/organization/22243.pdf.
11. *Agrément* is for chiefs of mission only. Others assigned to an embassy are simply reported to the host government as either diplomatic or administrative and technical staff. Some governments, however, reserve the right to approve military attachés in advance.
12. Berridge notes that before the Congress of Vienna, the reference point for

precedence was a list of primacy among sovereigns promulgated by the papacy in 1504 (the pope came first). In practice, diplomats had to negotiate precedence before each meeting (110–11).

13. See Transition Center, *Protocol for the Modern Diplomat.*

14. See www.royal.gov.uk/output/Page4943.asp.

15. See www.state.gov/s/cpr/rls/dpl.

16. Many ambassadors, including the coauthor, can attest to this story. One written account is in Grove, *Behind Embassy Walls*, 262.

17. Attributed to Sir Henry Wotton, British ambassador to Venice (1651); Freeman, *The Arts of Power*, 4; *Random House Dictionary*, 558. The dictionary's definition wrongly excludes persons who work for no national government (e.g., the UN secretary general) or who deal not with countries but with international organizations (e.g., the U.S. ambassador to the World Trade Organization).

18. Kissinger, *Diplomacy*, 683.

19. Kennan wrote his long telegram, as it was called, while bedridden with fever. In his memoirs, he says that "the effect produced in Washington by this elaborate pedagogical effort was nothing less than sensational. . . . It was one of those moments when official Washington, whose states of receptivity or the opposite are determined by subjective emotional currents as intricately imbedded in the subconscious as those of the most complicated of Sigmund Freud's erstwhile patients, was ready to receive a given message." *Memoirs*, 294. The telegram, Kennan explains, was the basis for his article, "The Sources of Soviet Conduct," which he signed *X*, in the July 1947 issue of *Foreign Affairs. Memoirs*, 354–67 and 547–59.

20. Barbro Owens-Kirkpatrick, interview, September 28, 2006.

21. Brent Scowcroft, remark to author, November 1992.

22. Comparisons to advertising are common. For example, see Roger Cohen, "Democracy as a Brand: Wooing Hearts, European or Muslim," *New York Times*, October 16, 2004. The comparison gained currency when Charlotte Beers, an advertising executive known for successful brand development, was named undersecretary for public diplomacy at the Department of State in October 2001. She served until March 2003.

23. Shultz, *Turmoil and Triumph*, 28–31. Shultz held a doctorate in industrial economics from MIT and worked as an arbitrator and mediator of labor disputes before joining the Nixon cabinet as secretary of labor in 1969.

24. Robert Gallucci, interview, June 2007. Gallucci described the negotiations with North Korea in a book he wrote with the two other members of the negotiating team. See Gallucci, Poneman, and Wit, *Going Critical.*

25. Destler, Fukui, and Sata's *The Textile Wrangle* is a cautionary tale of what can happen when negotiators outrun their domestic constituents. What began as a dispute over square yards of cloth built to a clash over control of Okinawa and led to the fall of the Japanese government.

26. Perkins, *The Department of State and American Public Opinion*, 282–83.

27. Kissinger, *Years of Renewal*, 628.

28. Carlucci, Foreign Affairs Oral History Collection.

29. Ibid.
30. Ibid. Kissinger's account of these discussions, written after Carlucci's interview, does not mention Carlucci's appointment with the president but otherwise supports Carlucci's account. Kissinger calls Carlucci "extremely astute" and notes "I had urged Carlucci's appointment and took his views very seriously." *Years of Renewal*, 629–34.
31. Carlucci, Foreign Affairs Oral History Collection.
32. Steve Gallogly, interview, August 2005.
33. For perhaps the first time in a negotiation of this type, many of the scores of agreements negotiated between the governments, and between the governments and the private participants, were made public. See Caspian Development and Export, www.caspiandevelopmentandexport.com/ASP/Home.asp.
34. Steven Mann, interview, September 2005.
35. President Woodrow Wilson coined the phrase in his April 2, 1917, address to Congress seeking a declaration of war.
36. White House, *The National Security Strategy*, 2002, 1.
37. White House, *The National Security Strategy*, 2006, 1. The words echo President Bush's second inaugural address, given January 21, 2004: "It is the policy of the United States to seek and support the growth of democratic movements and institutions in every nation and culture with the ultimate goal of ending tyranny in our world."
38. Adams, *The Education of Henry Adams*, 852.
39. "The goal of transformational diplomacy is defined as follows: a world of democratic well-governed states that respond to the needs of their citizens, reduce widespread poverty, and behave responsibly toward their people and toward the international system." Department of State, Summary and Highlights International Affairs Function 150, Fiscal Year 2009 Budget Request, 5.
40. Rice, Remarks at Georgetown School of Foreign Service.
41. Rice, Opening remarks before the House Committee.
42. Quoted in Shane Harris, "New Order," *Government Executive* 38, no. 13 (August 1, 2006): 31, www.govexec.com/features/0806-01/0806-01s1.htm.
43. Rea Brazeal, interview, January 2006; Katherine Canavan, interview, September 2005; Betsy Whitaker, interview, December 2005.
44. Shea, *Saudi Publications on Hate Ideology*, 2–4.
45. The fifteen focus countries are Botswana, Cote d'Ivoire, Ethiopia, Guyana, Haiti, Kenya, Mozambique, Namibia, Nigeria, Rwanda, South Africa, Tanzania, Uganda, Vietnam, and Zambia. In those countries, PEPFAR's objectives are summarized and quantified as "2-7-10": treat two million people suffering from AIDS, prevent seven million new infections, and care for ten million people affected by HIV/AIDS, including orphans. All three objectives are to be met by FY 2008.
46. Jimmy Kolker, interview, May 2007.
47. The Census Bureau, working with epidemiologic models developed by the World Health Organization and the Joint United Nations Program on AIDS, produces "without AIDS" and "with AIDS" demographic projections for selected countries (Botswana, Cameroon, Haiti, Kenya, Lesotho, Malawi,

Mozambique, Russia, Tanzania, Uganda, Ukraine, and Zambia, as of 2006) that allow the office of the global AIDS coordinator to project the effect of treatment, prevention, and care on future rates on infection. See http://www.census .gov/ipc/www/idb/aidsproj.html. For the PEPFAR budget request, see Congressional Budget Justification, Foreign Operations, Fiscal Year 2009, Department of State, pp. 841–45.

Chapter 5

1. Elizabeth Williamson, "How Much Embassy is Too Much?" *Washington Post*, March 2, 2007.
2. Tobin Bradley, interview, November 2005.
3. Vincent Campos, interview, February 2007.
4. See Perito, "Provincial Reconstruction Teams in Iraq." The civilian leadership of the PRTs in Iraq stands in contrast to Afghanistan, where the PRTs have a military commander (usually a lieutenant colonel) and a staff in which military personnel outnumber civilians. The PRTs in Afghanistan report, effective 2007, to the International Security Assistance Force, a NATO operation.
5. Stephenson, Presentation; U.S. Department of State, "Provincial Reconstruction Teams."
6. See, for example, U.S. Department of State, *FY 2008 Congressional Budget Justification, Foreign Operations*, 128.
7. Speckhard, "Provincial Reconstruction Team leaders discuss progress"; U.S. Department of State, "On-the-Record Briefing," March 30, 2007.
8. U.S. Department of State, "On-the-Record Briefing," March 30, 2007.
9. U.S. Department of State, *FY 2008 Budget in Brief*, 175: "Funds will be used to stand up new PRTs and to support and augment existing PRTs. The funds requested will be used to cover the costs of salaries, life and other operational support, offices and housing (and furnishings for both), vehicles, communications, and leases not covered by other agencies. This funding also will cover security costs for the stand-alone PRTs that will not be co-located with a brigade combat team or on a forward operating base."
10. U.S. Department of State, "On-the-Record Briefing."
11. Ann Scott Tyson, "Applying Diplomacy to Conflict," *Washington Post*, September 29, 2006. "Ex-Envoy Says Iraq Rebuilding Plan Won't Work," *Reuters*, February 17, 2007, www.nytimes.com.
12. U.S. Department of State, "On-the-Record Briefing," March 30, 2007.
13. Ibid.
14. Ibid.
15. U.S. Department of State, "Briefing on Reconstruction Progress," November 30, 2007.
16. See Elizabeth Williamson, "How Much Embassy Is Too Much?" *Washington Post*, March 7, 2007; U.S. Department of State, "On-the-Record Briefing," February 7, 2007.
17. Numbers from U.S. Department of State, *Goal for Arabic Speakers*. Forty percent is a reasonable figure, assuming a twenty-seven-year career with five years spent in entry-level positions and two years in Arabic language training.

18. U.S. Department of State, "Daily Press Briefing," June 19, 2007.

19. Helene Cooper, "Few Veteran Diplomats Accept Mission to Iraq," *New York Times*, February 8, 2007.

20. U.S. Department of State, "Foreign Service Assignments" (provided to the author by the American Foreign Service Association).

21. U.S. Government Accountability Office, "U.S. Public Diplomacy: Strategic Planning Efforts," 14. As of March 31, 2007, 199 of 887 public diplomacy positions in the United States and abroad were vacant.

22. U.S. Department of State, "Daily Press Briefing," November 1, 2007, response to taken question.

23. Karen De Young, "U.S. to Cut Ten Percent of Diplomatic Posts Next Year," *Washington Post*, December 13, 2007. According to AFSA President John Naland, the effect of Thomas's order is to remove about eighty positions—mainly FS-3 and FS-2 generalist (officer) positions—from the list of jobs opening in the summer of 2008 (Private communication, December 2007).

24. According to unpublished data from the State Department's Bureau of Human Resources, only 5.5 percent of foreign service officers and generalists left the service in 2005, and 4.5 percent in 2006.

25. Reuters, "State Department to Order 250 to Iraq Posts," *New York Times*, October 27, 2007, www.nytimes.com/2007/10/27/washington/27diplo.html.

26. Karen DeYoung, "Envoys Resist Forced Iraq Duty," *Washington Post*, November 1, 2007; Helene Cooper, "Foreign Service Officers Resist Mandatory Iraq Postings," *New York Times*, November 1, 2007; Farah Stockman, "Diplomats Angry over Forced Posts in Baghdad," *Boston Globe*, November 1, 2007; U.S. Department of State, "Daily Press Briefing," October 31, 2007.

27. Ralph Peters, "Strip for Action," *New York Post*, December 26, 2006.

28. Helene Cooper, "Few Veteran Diplomats Accept Mission to Iraq," *New York Times*, February 8, 2007.

29. Max Boot, "Send the State Department to War," *New York Times*, November 14, 2007.

30. www.blogs.state.gov.

31. Ibid. The response did not indicate how many of those who served were on temporary duty. In the spring of 2007 the Bureau of Human Resources identified a total of 585 foreign service generalists (officers), 8.9 percent of the total, who had served in Iraq or Afghanistan. Most of those had been on temporary duty.

32. The department can order foreign service officers and generalists to any post, in accordance with the needs of the service, but such directed assignments are rare. Anyone who accepts an assignment without being ordered to do so is considered a volunteer.

33. Private communication, November 5, 2007, provided to the author by Director General Henry Thomas

34. Robert Gates, Landon Lecture.

35. See U.S. Department of State, *FY 2008 Budget in Brief*, 22–24. Specifically, 104 positions for training enhancement, fifty-seven for reconstruction and stabilization programs, seventy-three to handle increased overseas workload, and twenty to represent the United States in new and nontraditional locations.

36.   Leahy, Statement at hearing on FY 2008 budget request, May 10, 2007.
37.   Gingrich, "Rogue State Department," 45. Gingrich is a member of Secretary Rice's Advisory Committee on Transformational Diplomacy, and he has made similar recommendations in that context.
38.   Dorman, "Iraqi Service and Beyond," 37.
39.   Name withheld, private correspondence, August 2006.

Chapter 6

1.   Johnstone, "Strategic Planning and International Affairs," 1997.
2.   Kissinger, *Years of Upheaval*, 445.
3.   Gingrich, "Transforming the State Department."
4.   Kissinger, *Years of Upheaval*, 434. Dr. Kissinger speaks on this point with authority. As President Nixon's national security advisor in the years before he became secretary of state, Kissinger traveled secretly to China in 1971 and arranged President Nixon's visit there that ended twenty years of Chinese isolation. Secretary of State Rogers was not told of Kissinger's trip until after it had been successfully concluded.
5.   Acheson, *Present at the Creation*, 162–63.
6.   Baker, *The Politics of Diplomacy*, 31–32.
7.   Haig, *Caveat*, 62.
8.   Kissinger, *Years of Upheaval*, 445.
9.   Ibid., 442.
10. Haig, *Caveat*, 27. Thomas O. Melia of Georgetown University, in an unpublished October 2002 study, "Congressional Staff Attitudes toward the Department of State and Foreign Service Officers," notes that "both Republicans and Democrats say they generally *presume* that FSOs are Democrats at heart because FSOs are by definition internationalists, and the Republican Party is often seen as something else" (p. 7, emphasis in original).
11. Schedule C positions are excepted from the competitive service because they have policy-determining responsibilities or require the incumbent to serve in a confidential relationship to a key official. Appointments to Schedule C positions require advance approval from the White House Office of Presidential Personnel and OPM, but appointments may be made without competition. OPM does not review the qualifications of a Schedule C appointee—final authority on this matter rests with the appointing official. See www.opm.gov/transition/trans20r-ch5.htm.
12. Kissinger, *Years of Upheaval*, 442–43.
13. Marshall, *The Armed Forces Officer*, 8.
14. Tony Motley, interview, 2006.
15. Freeman, *Arts of Power*, 127.
16. Name withheld, interview, 2006.
17. Mark Fitzpatrick, quoted in Glenn Kessler, "Administration Critics Chafe at State Dept. Shuffle," *Washington Post*, February 21, 2006.
18. Craig Kelly, e-mails to author, September 28 and October 7, 2006.

19. Kashkett, "On Dissent and Disloyalty," 3. Regulations on the dissent channel are in 2 FAM 071, available at www.state.gov/s/p/of/abt/18676.htm.

20. Craig Kelly, e-mail to author, September 28, 2006.

21. Eagleburger, remarks, *All Things Considered*, NPR, June 28, 2007.

22. See http://careers.state.gov/specialist/faqs/index.html and http://careers.state.gov/officer/faqs/index.html.

23. Deborah Ann McCarthy, interview, 2006.

24. Name withheld, interview, 2006.

25. Resignations over Balkan policy included Steven Walker, desk officer for Croatia; Marshall Freeman Harris, desk officer for Bosnia; and George Kenney, deputy head of the Yugoslav desk. Jon Western, a State Department civil servant, also resigned over Balkan policy. John Brady Kiesling, a political officer in Athens, Mary Ann Wright, deputy chief of mission in Mongolia, and John Brown, a cultural affairs officer in Moscow, resigned over Iraq.

26. See www.state.gov/s/h/tst/ and www.usaid.gov/press/spe_test/testimony.

27. Some appointees on special temporary missions may be accorded the personal rank of ambassador without Senate confirmation for a period not to exceed six months. See U.S. Department of State, *Foreign Affairs Handbook*, 3FAH-1 H-2432.1-2.

28. Representative Jeff Fortenberry, comments to meeting of Diplomatic and Consular Officers Retired (Washington, DC, September 26, 2006). The phrase *A committee* is a term of art. By custom, members do not serve on two A committees. In the Senate, unlike the House, the Committee on Foreign Relations is considered an A committee.

29. See www.state.gov/s/h/org/css.

30. Melia, "Congressional Staff Attitudes," 16–17.

31. Jennifer Butte-Dahl, interview, April 2007.

32. Leahy, statement at hearing on FY 2008 budget request, May 10, 2007.

33. In 2007, on the Senate side, the chairman and ranking member of the Foreign Relations Committee had thirty-four and thirty years seniority, the chairman and ranking member of the Appropriations Committee had forty-eight and twenty-eight years, and the chairman and ranking member of the appropriations subcommittee on State, foreign operations, and related programs had thirty-two and fourteen years seniority. On the House side, the figures for the same positions were twenty-six, twenty-one, thirty-eight, twenty-nine, twenty-four, and twelve.

34. Name withheld, interview, 2006.

35. The Pearson program also includes one-year assignments to state and local government offices. The American Political Science Association also provides congressional fellowships that are open to foreign service personnel.

36. Authorizing legislation for entitlement programs like Social Security usually does include budget authority, called direct or mandatory spending. Mandatory spending, which also covers interest on the national debt, does not require separate appropriation. Although mandatory spending now amounts to about 60 percent of all federal outlays, it is a trivial element in spending on

international affairs, coming into play only with regard to pensions for foreign service personnel.

37. For the State Department's budget presentation to those subcommittees, see www.state.gov/s/d/rm/rls/bib. For AID's budget presentation, see www.usaid .gov/policy/budget.

38. Jim Morhard, Remarks at a forum for business leaders organized by the Business Council for International Understanding, Rosslyn, Virginia, May 5, 2003.

39. Steve Dietz, interview, April 2007.

40. For a more detailed presentation, see www.state.gov/f/releases/iab/fy2009cbj.

41. State receives appropriations for U.S. participation in international border and fisheries commissions under Function 300, Natural Resources and Environment; the rest of State's budget and all of AID's is in Function 150. Other government agencies in Function 150 include Export-Import Bank, the Overseas Private Investment Corporation, the Trade and Development Agency, and the Peace Corps. Nongovernmental organizations include the U.S. Institute of Peace, the Inter-American Foundation, the Asia Foundation, the National Endowment for Democracy, the Millennium Challenge Corporation. Agencies principally funded elsewhere that receive some funds through the 150 account include the Department of Agriculture for food aid, the Treasury Department for international technical assistance and debt relief, and the Department of Defense for support for foreign military sales and international exchange and training programs.

42. Craig Johnstone, interview, February 2006.

43. Steve Dietz, interview, April 2007.

44. Katherine Canavan, interview, September 2005.

45. Shultz, *Turmoil and Triumph*, 35. Shultz served in four cabinet posts (secretary of state, labor, and treasury, and director of the Office of Management and Budget). He was also chief executive officer of Bechtel Corporation, a global construction and engineering company with forty thousand employees.

46. For the 2001 directive establishing the NSC committees, see www.fas.org/ irp/offdocs/nspd/nspd-1.htm. For a 2005 NSC staffing memorandum and organization chart, see www.fas.org/irp/news/2005/03/nsc-reorg.pdf.

47. Barbro Owens-Kirkpatrick, interview, September 2005.

48. Hugo Llorens, interview, August 2005.

49. James Durham, interview, June 2005.

50. Name withheld, interview, August 2005.

51. John Ritchie, interview, August 2005.

52. Sean Murphy, interview, August 2006.

53. Name withheld, interview, August 2005.

54. Foreign Service Act of 1980, sect. 207.

55. U.S. Department of State, *Foreign Affairs Manual*, 2 FAM 113.1. www.state .gov/documents/organization/84388.pdf

56. Ibid., 2 FAM 111.1-5.

57. National Security Decision Directive 38, June 2, 1982. www.state.gov/m/r/ nsdd/45148.htm.

58. U.S. Department of State, *Foreign Affairs Manual*, 2 FAM 112.

59. Committee on Foreign Relations, *Embassies as Command Posts*, 9.

60. See www.rand.org/pubs/monographs/MG607. The European command (EU-COM), for example, operates the websites www.magharebia.com and www.setimes.com, intended to encourage support for the United States and its policies in northern Africa and southeast Europe. The *Washington Post* reported that "in an April 23, 2007, interview with the national security blog IntelliBriefs, Maj. Gen. David P. Fridovich said the Special Operations approach includes providing 'civil affairs assets to assist in humanitarian and civic assistance' and offering 'information operations resources to aid the host nation in countering violent ideological threats.'" Walter Pincus, "Pentagon Hopes to Expand Aid Program," May 12, 2007.

61. Committee on Foreign Relations, *Embassies as Command Posts*, 7.

62. Priest, *The Mission*, 71n. The intention to establish a sixth area command, AFRICOM, was announced in 2007.

63. The programs, called Section 1206 programs after the relevant clause of the National Defense Authorization Act, are aimed at strengthening the capacity of foreign militaries to interdict terrorists and drug traffickers. In 2006 programs were operating in fourteen countries: Algeria, Chad, the Dominican Republic, Indonesia, Lebanon, Morocco, Nigeria, Pakistan, Panama, São Tomé and Principe, Thailand, Yemen, Senegal, and Sri Lanka. See Committee on Foreign Relations, *Embassies as Command Posts*, 7. In the president's budget, Section 1206 programs are in Function 050 (national defense), not Function 150 (international affairs), which shifts congressional authorization, appropriations, and oversight away from committees that deal with State and USAID to committees that deal with the Department of Defense.

64. Pincus, "Pentagon Hopes to Expand Aid Program," *Washington Post*, May 12, 2007; and Pincus, "Taking Defense's Hand Out of State's Pocket," *Washington Post*, July 9, 2007.

65. U.S. Senate, *Embassies Grapple to Guide Foreign Aid*, appendix I, 1.

66. U.S. Department of the Army, *Counterinsurgency*, 2–9.

67. Ibid. Anne Witkowski of the Center for Strategic and International Studies alerted the authors to this publication. David Galula is the author of *Counterinsurgency Warfare: Theory and Practice* (Praeger, 1964), in which this citation originally appeared.

68. Barry Blechman, interview, June 2006.

69. Richard Miles, interview, March 2006.

70. Steve Dietz, interview, April 2007.

71. Name withheld, interview, April 2007.

72. Vincent Campos, interview, February 2007.

73. See www.dod.mil/policy/sections/policy_official/index.html and www.jcs.mil/j5/organization.

74. See www.state.gov/t/pm/polad/c18485.htm for a current State Department list of current POLADs with contact information online.

75. Robert Loftis, interview, September 2006. Loftis was U.S. ambassador to Lesotho from 2001 to 2004.

76. Testimony of Theresa Whelan, Senate Committee on Foreign Relations, *Exploring the U.S. Africa Command*, 110th Cong., 1st sess., 3.

77. U.S. Department of the Army, *Counterinsurgency*, A-3.

78. Loftis refers to Robert Kaplan's book *Imperial Grunts*.
79. President Truman to Secretary James F. Byrnes, October 1945, cited in Acheson, *Present at the Creation*, 158.
80. Acheson, *Present at the Creation*, 127, 157–63. The description of OSS personnel as collectivists and do-gooders is a citation in Acheson from 1954 testimony by Spruille Braden, a three-time ambassador who in 1945 was assistant secretary for Latin American affairs (160). Another account of this episode appears in Weiner, *Legacy of Ashes*, 15.
81. James Pavitt, interview, 2007.
82. Newsom, *Diplomacy and the American Democracy*, 39.
83. See the official website of the intelligence community, www.intelligence.gov.
84. Name withheld, interview, June 2007.

Chapter 7

1. See Nakamura, *The Foreign Service*.
2. See http://careers.state.gov/officer/benefits/index.html.
3. J. Christian Kennedy, interview, July 2005.
4. See http://careers.state.gov/officer/roles/index.html.
5. The six questions in the personal narrative are linked to the six areas of competence identified in precepts that guide the evaluation of foreign service officers and specialists: leadership skills, managerial skills, interpersonal skills, communication skills, intellectual skills, and substantive knowledge. The precepts appear in appendix B.
6. The thirteen dimensions were distilled from the competencies and precepts that appear in appendix B. The department's intention is to replace the thirteen dimensions with a set of pre-employment precepts now being drafted as part of the Diplomat of the Future project described in chapter 10. In time a single set of precepts should guide all personnel decisions, including hiring, assignments, and promotions.
7. See http://careers.state.gov/officer.
8. For vacancy announcements, see www.careers.state.gov/specialist/opportunities.
9. See www.usajobs.opm.gov.
10. Debi Fairman, interview, March 2007.
11. The Arlington campus of the Foreign Service Institute is the George P. Shultz National Foreign Affairs Training Center. Secretary Shultz worked hard with the Congress to obtain the funds to create the center, on a campus that was once a girls' school and later, during the Second World War, the home of the Army Security Agency, forerunner of today's National Security Agency (NSA).
12. Salary and allowances are paid every two weeks, in arrears, so long as the Congress appropriates the necessary funds.
13. Marcos Mandojana, interview, February 2006.
14. Richard Miles, interview, March 2006.
15. Clayton Hays, interview, August 2005.

16. Name withheld, interview, March 2006.
17. Deborah Ann McCarthy, interview, August 2005.

Chapter 8

1. Marcos Mandojana, interview, February 2006.
2. Under a visa waiver program that started in 1986, visitors from twenty-seven countries may enter the United States without a visa if they meet certain requirements. Without this program, the demand for visas would be dramatically greater.
3. Marcos Mandojana, interview, February 2006.
4. Name withheld, interview, June 2007.
5. Robert Batchelder, interview, August 2005.
6. Gregory Schiffer, interview, February 2006.
7. Marcos Mandojana, interview, February 2006.
8. Sean Murphy, interview, March 2006.
9. David Caudill, interview, June 2007.
10. Name withheld, interview, March 2006.
11. Sean Murphy, interview, March 2006.
12. Alan Larson, interview, July 2007. The full title of the position is undersecretary for economic, business, and agricultural affairs.
13. Deborah Ann McCarthy, interview, August 2005.
14. Bill McCahill, interview, August 2007.
15. Aid and military sales to Pakistan were restricted under the Symington (1978), Pressler (1990), and Glenn (1998) amendments, which imposed sanctions aimed at curtailing Pakistan's nuclear weapons program. President Bush waived these restrictions after the September 11 attacks.
16. Alan Larson, interview, July 2007.
17. Ibid.
18. Maryanne Myles and David Dlouhy, interview, July 2007. See chapter 10.
19. Frank Coulter, interview, November 2005.
20. Russ King, interview, February 2007.
21. Eric Khant, interview, February 2007.
22. Richard Miles, interview, March 2006.
23. The Myers-Briggs Type Indicator is a psychological or personality test administered to entering foreign service officers during their basic A-100 training. Whether the test, based on Jungian ideas, offers more insight than a skillful reading of the Tarot is a matter of debate.
24. Harry Kamian, interview, August 2006.
25. See http://careers.state.gov/officer/employment.html#PO.
26. The Government Accountability Office has issued several reports on public diplomacy since 1999. See *U.S. Public Diplomacy: Strategic Planning Efforts Have Improved, But Agencies Face Significant Implementation Challenges,* GAO-07-795T (April 26, 2007), www.gao.gov/new.items/d07795t.pdf; *Foreign Assistance: Actions Needed to Better Assess the Impact of Agencies' Marking and Publicizing Efforts,* GAO-07-277 (March 12 2007), www.gao.gov/new.items/

d07277.pdf; *U.S. Public Diplomacy: State Department Efforts to Engage Muslim Audiences,* GAO-06-535 (May 3, 2006), www.gao.gov/new.items/d06535.pdf; *U.S. Public Diplomacy: State Department Efforts Lack Certain Communication Elements,* GAO-06-707T (May 3, 2006); *U.S. Public Diplomacy: Interagency Coordination Efforts Hampered,* GAO-05-323 (April 4, 2005), www.gao.gov/new.items/d05323.pdf; and *U.S. Public Diplomacy: State Department and Broadcasting Board of Governors Expand Post-9/11 Efforts but Challenges Remain,* GAO-04-1061T (August 23, 2004), www.gao.gov/new.items/d041061t.pdf.

27. Marcia Bosshardt, interview, August 2007.
28. See www.publicdiplomacy.org.
29. See www.state.gov/www/global/general_foreign_policy/rpt_981230_reorg6.html and www.state.gov/s/d/rm/rls/bib/2008. The same words appear almost verbatim in part III of the reorganization plan President Clinton submitted to the Congress in 1998, and on page 14 of the department's budget in brief for fiscal year 2008.
30. Caryn Danz, interview, July 2007.
31. Betsy Whitaker, interview, December 2005.
32. See http://exchanges.state.gov/education/evaluations.

Chapter 9

1. U.S. Department of State, "Daily Press Briefing," November 1, 2007, response to taken question.
2. Sylvia Bazala, interview, August 2006.
3. Name withheld, interview, April 2007.
4. In April 2007, according to the Bureau of Human Resources, there were 589 tandem couples (1,178 employees) in the foreign service agencies of State, USAID, the Foreign Commercial Service, and the Foreign Agricultural Service. The total includes couples in which husband and wife work for different agencies.
5. Philo Dibble, interview, October 2005. Places with more than one mission include Brussels, home to the U.S. Mission to the European Union, the U.S. Mission to NATO, and the U.S. Embassy to the Kingdom of Belgium; Geneva, which houses the U.S. missions to UN agencies and to the World Trade Organization; Vienna, with the embassy to Austria, a mission to UN organizations, and a mission to the Organization for Security and Cooperation in Europe; and Paris, with an embassy and a mission to the Organization for Economic Cooperation and Development.
6. Robin Byrd, interview, August 10, 2006.
7. Lewis Byrd, interview, August 10, 2006.
8. James Derham, interview, July 2005.
9. Not at all. Derham later became ambassador to Guatemala.
10. Chris Midura, interview, April 2007.
11. Name withheld, interview, June 2007.

12. The department's inspector general noted some of the problems with stretch assignments in "Strengthening Leadership and Staffing at African Hardship Posts," referenced in U.S. Department of State, Office of the Inspector General, *Semiannual Report to Congress*, 18.

13. Sometimes an assignment changes during a rating period, or a new rating officer takes over. In such cases an interim report must be filed to cover any period of 120 days or more. Raters can also prepare voluntary reports covering shorter periods. Interim and voluntary reports do not have to use the full EER form.

14. U.S. Department of State, *Foreign Affairs Handbook*, 1 (composition).

15. Rob Nolan, interview, May 2005.

Chapter 10

1. The full list includes the Department of Agriculture, Department of Commerce, Department of Defense (including the Office of the Secretary and the Joint Staff), Department of Energy, Environmental Protection Agency, Health and Human Services (including the Centers for Disease Control and Prevention), Department of Homeland Security, Department of Labor, Millennium Challenge Corporation, Office of the Director of National Intelligence, Department of State, Department of the Treasury, U.S. Agency for International Development, National Defense University, and National Security Council staff.

2. Sidney Kaplan, interview, May 2007.

3. Marianne Myles, interview, August 2007.

4. David Dlouhy, interview, August 2007.

5. The precepts appear as appendix 2. Plans call for replacing the thirteen dimensions with a fourth column of pre-entry level precepts in each of the six skill areas. Unlike precepts used for decisions on tenure and promotion, those used for decisions on entry need not be negotiated with AFSA.

6. Marianne Myles, interview, August 2007.

7. Members of the Advisory Committee include Barry Blechman, John Breaux, Steven Case, Johnetta Cole, Kenneth Derr, Jennifer Dunn, John Engler, Carly Fiorina, Yousif Ghafari, Newt Gingrich, Maria Elena Lagomasino, Harold McGraw III, Gen. Richard Myers, Tom Pickering, Pamela Thompson, and Charles Vest. Under Secretary of Management Henrietta Fore guided the committee's work.

8. Senior fellow Anne Witkowsky of the Center for Strategic and International Studies led the 2006–2007 study, which was funded by the Una Chapman Cox Foundation and conducted with the cooperation of the Department of State. Charles A. Gillespie, coauthor of this book, served on the twenty-five member commission that guided the project. The study is available at http://www.csis.org/media/csis/pubs/embassy _of_the_fu ture.pdf. Other recent studies include "A Smarter, More Secure America" by the CSIS Commission on Smart Power, November 2007, at www .csis.org/media/csis/pubs/071106_csissmartpowerreport.pdf, and "Beyond As-

sistance," by the HELP Commission on Foreign Assistance Reform, December 2007, at http://helpcommission.gov/portals/0/Beyond%20Assistance_HELP_Commission_Report.pdf.

9. White House, *The National Security Strategy*, 2006, 44. President Bush repeated the call for a civilian reserve corps in his 2007 State of the Union address. See www.whitehouse.gov/stateoftheunion/2007.

10. Foreign Affairs Council, *Managing Secretary Rice's Department*, 3. The Foreign Affairs Council is an umbrella group of eleven nonpartisan organizations (see chapter 2, note 62).

11. The bill is S.613. See Senator Lugar of Indiana, February 15, 2007, introducing the bill and the text of the bill S. 613, *Congressional Record* 153, pt. 29:S2039–42. See also the statement of John E. Herbst, coordinator for the Department of State, Office of Reconstruction of and Stabilization, before the House Armed Services Subcommittee on Oversight and Investigations, October 30, 2007; Richard Lugar and Condoleezza Rice, "A Civilian Partner for our Troops," *The Washington Post*, December 17, 2007.

12. Kopp, *Commercial Diplomacy*, 5–7.

13. Ambassador Pickering testified that USAID "has become largely, in my view, a contract management organization rather than one directly representing the U.S. in development." Testimony, January 23, 2008.

14. Maria Elena Lagomasino and Governor John Engler chair a working group on private sector partnerships of the Secretary's Advisory Committee on Transformational Diplomacy.

15. David Sanger, "Propping Up the Weak as a Policy," *The New York Times*, September 2, 2007.

16. The *Embassy of the Future* (Witkowsky et al.) draft report proposes that the State Department develop the capacity to deploy foreign service nationals outside their home country.

17. Newsom, *Diplomacy and the American Democracy*, 74.

18. "Truck Stop Confidential," *The New York Times*, August 14, 2007.

Glossary

13 dimensions	Traits and skills measured during the oral assessment of foreign service candidates (State)
150 account	Section of the federal budget, as prepared by the Office of Management and Budget, dealing with international affairs
360° review	Evaluation by superiors, subordinates, and peers
A-100	Basic training and orientation course for new foreign service officers (State)
AEP	Ambassador Extraordinary and Plenipotentiary: full diplomatic title of an ambassador sent by one head of state to another and commissioned to represent and act on behalf of the sending state
AFRICOM	See *combatant command*
AFSA	American Foreign Service Association: the professional association and collective bargaining agent (union) for members of the foreign service. www.afsa.org
AID, USAID	U.S. Agency for International Development
Aide-mémoire	Text summarizing a document or (more often) an oral presentation, often left with officials after a démarche
Ambassador	Highest diplomatic rank
Ambassador at large	Ambassador not accredited to any foreign state or international organization
APEC	Asian Pacific Economic Cooperation
Area combatant command	See *combatant command*
ARB	Accountability Review Board, a panel convened by the secretary of state to investigate incidents at U.S. posts abroad that result in loss of life or serious injury
Assistant secretary	At the Department of State, the official in charge of a bureau; assistant secretaries and higher officials require Senate confirmation, deputy assistant secretaries and below do not
Attaché	An official assigned to an embassy to perform a specific task (for example, military attaché, agricultural attaché)
Backstopping	Bureaucratic jargon for providing support
Base pay	Basic salary prescribed by law for a given rank or pay grade; may be increased by various allowances and bonuses

Bid list	A list of preferred assignments that a member of the service submits to the Bureau of Human Resources
Bureau	Basic organization unit of the Department of State; headed by an assistant secretary
Cable	Electronic communication sent through official channels requiring *clearance*; also called telegram—cables originating at an overseas post bear the signature of the officer in charge, those originating in the Department of State bear the signature of the secretary of state or acting secretary
CDO	Career development officer
CENTCOM	See *combatant command*
Chancery	Embassy building in which the ambassador's office is located
Chargé, chargé d'affaires	Diplomatic title given to an embassy official in charge of a mission in the absence of an ambassador; if temporary, chargé d'affaires ad interim
Chief of mission	Head of a diplomatic mission
Chief of party	Project leader (USAID)
CIA	Central Intelligence Agency
Civil service	Corps of civilian public employees, other than members of excluded services (such as the foreign service)
Clearance	Approval of a document by offices with an interest in the topic; whoever drafts a document obtains the clearances
Coalition Provisional Authority	Governing body in Iraq from April 2003, until June 2004
Codel	State Department jargon for a congressional delegation on official overseas travel
COIN	Counterinsurgency
COM	Chief of mission
Combatant command	One of nine U.S. military unified combatant commands involving more than one service; five are area commands—CENTCOM (central), EUCOM (European), NORTHCOM (northern), PACOM (Pacific), and SOUTHCOM (southern)—with a sixth, AFRICOM (African), scheduled to come into being in 2008
Cone	One of five functional specializations for foreign service officers: consular affairs, economic affairs, management, political affairs, public diplomacy, also called *track*
ConGen	Consulate general: a relatively large post headed by a consul general; subordinate to an embassy
Constituent post	Overseas post separate from and subordinate to an embassy

Consul	Diplomat accredited to perform consular functions, including protection and welfare of citizens of the sending state, representation of commercial interests, and administration of travel controls (visas)
Control officer	Member of embassy or consular staff designated to take care of an official delegation or important visitor
COPs	Country operating plans
CORDS	Civil Operations and Revolutionary Development Support, an element of the U.S. pacification program during the Vietnam War
Counselor	(1) Diplomatic title of an embassy officer responsible for supervising the work of a section (such as, agricultural counselor, political counselor, counselor for consular affairs); (2) lowest rank in the senior foreign service; (3) title of a confidential adviser to the secretary of state, the highest-ranking office in the department of state not requiring Senate confirmation. Not to be confused with consular, which pertains to the work of consuls.
CPA	See *Coalition Provisional Authority*
DACOR	Diplomatic and Consular Officers Retired, a private association, www.dacorbacon.org
DATT	Defense attaché, normally the senior military member of an embassy
DCM	See *deputy chief of mission*
DEA	Drug Enforcement Administration
Démarche	An official diplomatic representation to a foreign government, conducted in person
Deputy chief of mission	Second-highest-ranking official in a diplomatic mission
Desk officer	An officer in a regional *bureau* of the Department of State responsible for a specific country or group of countries
DG	See *director general*
DIA	Defense Intelligence Agency
Diplomatic corps	All the accredited diplomats at a post or in a country
Diplomatic immunity	Protection from taxation, arrest, or prosecution accorded to accredited diplomats as representatives of sovereign powers. See *Vienna Convention*.
Diplomatic list	Official list of all the accredited diplomats in a country
Diplomatic note	A formal written communication between governments, generally from a foreign ministry to a diplomatic representative, or from a diplomatic representative to a foreign ministry
Director general (DG)	Head of the U.S. Foreign Service and of the State Department's Bureau of Human Resources; by law must be a career foreign service officer

DNI	Director of National Intelligence
DOD	Department of Defense
DOJ	Department of Justice
Drafter	Principal author of a document
DRI	Diplomatic Readiness Initiative
DS	Bureau of Diplomatic Security (State)
DSS	Diplomatic Security Service (State)
EAP	Bureau of East Asia and Pacific Affairs (State)
EEOC	Equal Employment Opportunity Commission
EER	Employee evaluation report, also called efficiency report
ELO	Entry-level officer
EO	Executive order: a presidential document establishing or implementing regulations.
EUCOM	See *combatant command*
FAH	Foreign affairs handbook with procedures of the *Foreign Affairs Manual*
FAM	Foreign affairs manual setting out the regulations and procedures of the foreign service
FAS	Foreign Agricultural Service, the foreign service of the Department of Agriculture
FBI	Federal Bureau of Investigation
FCS	Foreign Commercial Service, the foreign service of the Department of Commerce, part of the U.S. Commercial Service.
FMF, FMS	See foreign military financing, foreign military sales
Foreign military financing, foreign military sales	U.S. government programs to support the sale of U.S.-made weaponry abroad
Foreign Service Act	Unless otherwise stated, the 1980 legislation
FSI	Foreign Service Institute, the training arm of the foreign service
FSN	Foreign service national: non-American employee of the U.S. service, ordinarily a national of the country in which employed
FSO	Foreign service officer
FSR	Foreign service reserve, a personnel category (1946–1980, State)
FY	Fiscal year; in the U.S. government it begins October 1 and ends September 30; designated by its ending date (FY 2010 is the year ending September 30, 2010)
GPOI	Global Peace Operations Initiative: program run by the Department of Defense to provide training for foreign forces engaged in international peacekeeping
GS	General schedule: pay schedule for members of the civil service
GSO	General services officer: an embassy officer responsible for the housing stock, transportation, contracts and procurement, supplies, and the like

Hardship allowance, differential	Supplemental pay, a percentage of base pay, for members of the foreign service serving in places designated by the Department of State
HR/CDA	Bureau of Human Resources, Career Development and Assignments Office (State)
ICASS	International Cooperative Administrative Support Services
IDCA	International Development and Cooperation Agency: an umbrella agency that included *USAID* (1979–1998)
IED	Improvised explosive device
IMET	International Military Education and Training, a U.S. military-to-military exchange program
INR	Bureau of Intelligence and Research (State)
Inspector general	Senior official in an agency, authorized to conduct internal reviews and investigations to promote good management and prevent waste, fraud, and abuse
ITA	International Trade Administration: unit of the Department of Commerce that is home to the U.S. Commercial Service, formerly the U.S. and Foreign Commercial Service
IV, NIV	Immigrant visa, nonimmigrant visa
JAG	Judge advocate general (U.S. Navy)
JCS	Joint chiefs of staff
KGB	Internal security and foreign intelligence service of the Soviet Union (acronym for Committee on State Security, in Russian)
Legal attaché	Title used by an FBI agent assigned to an embassy abroad
LES	Locally engaged staff, includes FSNs and other persons hired locally by a U.S. mission, including third-country nationals, resident U.S. citizens, and family members of foreign service or other embassy personnel
Locality pay	Adjustments to base pay to account for local differences in living costs
Main State	The Harry S Truman Building at 22nd and C Streets NW, Washington, D.C.
MCC	Millennium Challenge Corporation, a U.S. provider of foreign assistance
Mid-level officer	Foreign service officer in grade three, two, or one
Mission	(1) The broadest word for a diplomatic post; the U.S. mission to a country includes the embassy, all subordinate posts, and all personnel subject to the authority of the chief of mission (ambassador); (2) U.S. representation to an international organization, such as the U.S. Mission to the United Nations or the U.S. Mission to

	the European Union; (3) the AID presence in a country, headed by a mission director
MOU	Memorandum of understanding
NATO	North Atlantic Treaty Organization
NFATC	(George P. Shultz) National Foreign Affairs Training Center: the Arlington, Virginia, campus of the Foreign Service Institute
NGO	Nongovernmental organization
NIV, IV	Nonimmigrant visa, immigrant visa
Nodel	State Department jargon for members of Congress traveling abroad unofficially (see *Codel*)
Noncareer	See *political appointee*
NORTHCOM	See *combatant command*
Note verbale	An unsigned diplomatic note in the third person, less formal than a signed note, more formal than an aide-mémoire
NSA	National Security Agency
NSC	National Security Council
OECD	Organization for Economic Cooperation and Development
OEO	Office of Economic Opportunity, a U.S. domestic agency closed in 1974
OER	Officer evaluation report, subsumed in EER (employee evaluation report)
Office of Personnel Management	Federal agency that operates the civil service
OJT	On-the-job training
OMB	Office of Management and Budget
OMS	Office management specialist
OPAP	Overseas Presence Advisory Panel (State, 1999)
OpenNet	State Department intranet
OPM	See *Office of Personnel Management*
OSAC	Overseas Security Advisory Council, a federal advisory committee promoting cooperation between private entities and the Department of State on security matters. www.osac.org
OSS	Office of Strategic Services, the wartime predecessor of the *CIA*, closed in 1945
OUDS(P)	Office of Under Secretary of Defense for Policy
PACOM	See *combatant command*
PAO	Public affairs officer
PCS	Permanent change of station (not temporary duty) transfer
PEPFAR	President's Emergency Program for AIDS Relief
PNG	Persona non grata. Literally, unwelcome person, a designation applied by a receiving government when it

	strips a diplomat of accreditation and evicts him or her from the country
POLAD	Political adviser
Political appointee	Office holder named by and serving at the pleasure of the president or the agency head and exempt from the rules of competitive service; positions designated by law, executive order, or action of the Office of Personnel Management. See *Schedule C.*
Post	Any U.S. diplomatic or consular establishment
Principal officer	Senior officer at a post
Protocol	Accepted way of doing things
Provincial Reconstruction Team	Mixed military-civilian unit engaged in civil affairs, economic reconstruction, and political stabilization in Iraq and Afghanistan
PRT	Provincial reconstruction team
Public diplomacy	Diplomatic action intended to affect public opinion in a foreign country
Reclama	State Department jargon for an appeal for reversal of a decision
REO	Regional embassy office (State, Iraq)
Residence	The ambassador's living quarters
RIF	Reduction in force: federal employment jargon for layoffs
RNet	Intranet for State Department retirees
Rotational tour	For entry-level foreign service officers, includes service in more than one section of an embassy
RSO	Regional security officer
Schedule C	Personnel category designating a *political appointee* serving at the pleasure of the agency head and not subject to Senate confirmation
SCO	Senior commercial officer, title used by the senior foreign commercial service representative at an overseas post
Security clearance	Authorization of access to classified information
SES	Senior executive service, the top grades of the civil service
Seventh floor	The leadership of the Department of State, location in *Main State* of the offices of the secretary, deputy secretary, and under secretaries of state
SFS	Senior foreign service: the top grades of the foreign service
SOCOM	See *combatant command*
SOUTHCOM	See *combatant command*
Special envoy	Person appointed to represent the United States with respect to a particular topic, not accredited to any government or international organization (for example,

	special envoy for Holocaust issues, special envoy for Korean peace talks)
Staffdel	Congressional staff delegation on official travel
Tandem	Foreign service employees on active duty who are married to each other
TDY	Temporary duty (not permanent change of station)
TIC	Time in class
Track	One of five functional specializations for foreign service officers: consular affairs, economic affairs, management, political affairs, public diplomacy; also called *cone*
Undersecretary	Subcabinet rank below deputy secretary and above assistant secretary
UNODIR	Unless otherwise directed
USAID, AID	U.S. Agency for International Development (1961)
USDA	Department of Agriculture
USIA, USIS	United States Information Agency, the locus of U.S. public diplomacy from 1953 to 1999. Outside the United States, USIA was called the U.S. Information Service, apparently to reduce confusion with the Central Intelligence Agency (CIA).
USICA	U.S. Information and Communications Agency (1978–1982)
USTR	U.S. Trade Representative
Vienna Conventions	1961 and 1963 conventions on diplomatic relations and consular relations, respectively, codifying international law with respect to treatment of diplomatic and consular personnel and property. Signatories to the conventions agree that diplomats and property covered by the conventions are immune from arrest, prosecution, taxation, and similar forms of state coercion.
WAE	"When actually employed": a retired member of the foreign service available to work under a short-term contract
WTO	World Trade Organization

Bibliography

Acheson, Dean. *Present at the Creation.* New York: W. W. Norton, 1969.

Adams, Henry. *The Education of Henry Adams.* 1918. Reprint, New York: Library of America, 1983.

Bacchus, William. *Staffing for Foreign Affairs: Personnel Systems for the 1980s and 1990s.* Princeton, NJ: Princeton University Press, 1983.

Baker, James A., III, with Thomas M. DeFrank. *The Politics of Diplomacy: Revolution, War, and Peace, 1989–1992.* New York: G. P. Putnam's Sons, 1995.

Barnes, William, and John Heath Morgan. *The Foreign Service of the United States: Origins, Development, and Functions.* Washington, DC: U.S. Department of State, Historical Office, 1961.

Berridge, G. R. *Diplomacy: Theory and Practice.* 3rd ed. Basingstoke, Hampshire, UK: Palgrave Macmillan, 2005.

Bierce, Ambrose. *The Devil's Dictionary.* 1911. Reprint, New York: Dover, 1993.

Carlucci, Frank C., III. The U.S. Foreign Affairs Oral History Collection. Association for Diplomatic Studies and Training. Arlington, VA, CD-ROM, 2000.

Davies, John Paton. "The Personal Experience." In *The China Hands' Legacy: Ethics and Diplomacy,* edited by Paul Gordon Lauren, 37–57. Boulder, CO: Westview, 1987.

Destler, I. M., Haruhiro Fukui, and Hideo Sata. *The Textile Wrangle: Conflict in Japanese-American Relations, 1969–1971.* Cornell, NY: Cornell University Press, 1979.

Dorman, Shawn. "Iraqi Service and Beyond." *Foreign Service Journal* 83, no. 3 (March 2006): 17–41.

Eagleburger, Lawrence. "U.S. Diplomat Gets 'Constructive Dissent' Award." *All Things Considered,* NPR, June 28, 2007. www.npr.org/templates/story/story.php?storyId=11630586&ft=1&a

Ford, Charles A. "Final Thoughts on the Foreign Service at the Commerce Department." *AFSA News,* May 2005, 4.

Foreign Affairs Council. *Managing Secretary Rice's Department: An Independent Assessment.* Task Force Report, June 2007. Washington, DC: American Foreign Service Association, June 2007. www.afsa.org/fac/foreign_affairs.pdf.

———. *Secretary Colin Powell's State Department: An Independent Assessment.* Task Force Report. Chapel Hill, NC: American Diplomacy Publishers, 2004. www.diplomatsonline.org/taskreport0303.html.

Foreign Service Act of 1980, PL 96-465, as amended, 22 U.S.C. sec. 3901 et seq. http://www.usaid.gov/policy/ads/400/fsa.pdf.

Freeman, Charles W., Jr. *The Arts of Power: Statecraft and Diplomacy.* Washington, DC: U.S. Institute of Peace Press, 1997.

Gallucci, Robert, Daniel Poneman, and Joel Wit. *Going Critical: The First North Korean Nuclear Crisis.* Washington, DC: Brookings Institution Press, 2004.

Gates, Robert M. Landon Lecture, Kansas State University. November 22, 2007. www.defenselink.mil/speeches/speech.aspx?speechid=1199.

Gingrich, Newt. "Rogue State Department." *Foreign Policy* 137 (July/August 2003): 42–48.

———. "Transforming the State Department: The Next Challenge for the Bush Administration." Speech at the American Enterprise Institute. April 22, 2003. http://www.aei.org/publications/pubID.16992,filter.all/pub_detail.asp.

Goodwin, Doris Kearns. *Team of Rivals: The Political Genius of Abraham Lincoln.* New York: Simon & Schuster, 2005.

Grove, Brandon. *Behind Embassy Walls: The Life and Times of an American Diplomat.* Columbia: University of Missouri Press, 2005.

Haig, Alexander M., Jr. *Caveat: Realism, Reagan, and Foreign Policy.* New York: Scribner, 1984.

Humphrey, David C., ed. *Foreign Relations of the United States, 1969–1976.* Vol. II, *Organization and Management of U.S. Foreign Policy, 1969–1972.* Washington, DC: Government Printing Office, 2006. http://www.state.gov/documents/organization/77830.pdf.

Johnstone, L. Craig. "Strategic Planning and International Affairs in the 21st Century." Remarks at opening session of the Conference Series on International Affairs in the 21st Century. U.S. State Department, Dean Acheson Auditorium, Washington, DC, November 18, 1997. http://www.state.gov/www/policy_remarks/971118_johnstone_stratplan.html.

Kahn, E. J. *The China Hands.* New York: Viking, 1972.

Kaplan, Robert. *Imperial Grunts: The American Military on the Ground.* New York: Random House, 2005.

Kashkett, Steve. "On Dissent and Disloyalty." *AFSA News*, December 2005, 3. www .afsa.org/fsj/dec05/AFSANEWSDec2005.pdf

Kennan, George. *Memoirs, 1950–1963.* Boston: Little, Brown, 1972.

Kissinger, Henry. *Diplomacy.* New York: Touchstone, 1995.

———. *White House Years.* Boston: Little, Brown, 1979.

———. *Years of Renewal.* New York: Simon & Schuster, 1999.

Kopp, Harry W. *Commercial Diplomacy and the National Interest.* Washington and New York: American Academy of Diplomacy and Business Council for International Understanding, 2004.

Lauren, Paul Gordon, ed. *The China Hands' Legacy: Ethics and Diplomacy.* Boulder, CO: Westview Press, 1987.

Leahy, Patrick. "Statement of Senator Patrick Leahy, Chairman, State Foreign Operations, and Related Programs Subcommittee." Hearing on FY 2008 State, Foreign Operations Budget Request, May 10, 2007. http://leahy.senate.gov/press/200705/051007.html.

Lutkins, LaRue R. Interview by Charles Stuart Kennedy. The Foreign Affairs Oral History Collection of the Association for Diplomatic Studies and Training. Washington, DC: Library of Congress, Manuscript Division, October 18, 1990. http://hdl.loc.gov/loc.mss/mfdip.2004lut01.

Marquardt, Niels. "The DRI Rides to the Rescue." *Foreign Service Journal* 81, no. 4 (April 2004): 20–28.

Marshall, S.L.A. *The Armed Forces Officer.* Department of the Army Pamphlet 600-2. Washington, DC: Government Printing Office, 1950.

Mee, Charles L., Jr. *The Marshall Plan: The Launching of the Pax Americana.* New York: Simon and Schuster, 1984.

Melia, Thomas O. "Congressional Staff Attitudes toward the Department of State and Foreign Service Officers: A Report Based on 25 One-on-One Interviews with Key Congressional Staff." Unpublished paper prepared for the Una Chapman Cox Foundation, Washington, DC, 2002.

Morgan, William, and Charles Stuart Kennedy, eds. *American Diplomats: The Foreign Service at Work.* Lincoln, NE: iUniverse, 2004.

Nakamura, Kennon H. *The Foreign Service and a New Worldwide Compensation System.* CRS Report for Congress RL33721. Washington, DC: Government Printing Office, November 16, 2006. http://fas.org/sgp/crs/misc/RL33721.pdf

Nathan, James, and James Oliver. *Foreign Policy Making and the American Political System.* 3rd ed. Baltimore: Johns Hopkins University Press, 1994.

Newsom, David. *Diplomacy and the American Democracy.* Bloomington: Indiana University Press, 1988.

Nicolson, Harold. *The Evolution of Diplomatic Method.* London: Constable and Co., 1953.

Perito, Robert. "Provincial Reconstruction Teams in Iraq." Special Report 185. Washington, DC: United States Institute of Peace, March 2007. www.usip.org/pubs/specialreports/sr185.pdf.

Perkins, Dexter. "The Department of State and American Public Opinion." In *The Diplomats: 1919–1939,* Vol.1, *The Twenties,* edited by Gordon A. Craig and Felix Gilbert. New York: Atheneum, 1963.

Pickering, Thomas R. Testimony before the House Subcommittee on National Security and Foreign Affairs of the House Committee on Oversight, January 23, 2008. http://nationalsecurity.ovresight.house.gov/documents/20080123123433.pdf.

Priest, Dana. *The Mission.* New York: W. W. Norton, 2003.

Random House Unabridged Dictionary of the English Language, 2nd ed. New York: Random House, 1987.

Rice, Condoleezza. Confirmation hearings before Senate Foreign Relations Committee, opening statement as prepared for delivery. Washington, DC, January 18, 2005. www.state.gov/secretary/rm/2005/40991.htm.

———. Opening remarks before the House Committee on Appropriations Subcommittee on Science, State, Justice, and Commerce, and Related Agencies, as prepared for delivery. *President's FY 2006 Budget Request.* Washington, DC, March 9, 2005. www.state.gov/secretary/rm/2005/43184.htm.

———. Remarks at Georgetown School of Foreign Service. "Transformational Diplomacy." Washington, DC, January 18, 2006. www.state.gov/secretary/rm/2006/59306.htm.

———. Remarks at Town Hall Meeting. U.S. State Department, Dean Acheson Auditorium, Washington, DC, January 31, 2005. www.state.gov/secretary/rm/2005/41414.htm.

Seitzinger, Michael V. *Conducting Foreign Relations without Authority: The Logan Act.* CRS Report for Congress RL33265. Washington, DC: Government

PrintingOffice,February1,2006.http://opencrs.cdt.org/rpts/RL33265_20060201 .pdf.

Shea, Nina, ed. *Saudi Publications on Hate Ideology Invade American Mosques.* Washington, DC: Freedom House, Center for Religious Freedom, 2005. www .freedomhouse.org/uploads/special_report/45.pdf.

Shultz, George P. *Turmoil and Triumph.* New York: Scribner, 1993.

Speckhard, Daniel. "Provincial Reconstruction Team leaders discuss progress." PRT Press Briefing. Baghdad, Iraq: Operation Iraqi Freedom, January 12, 2007. www .mnf-iraq.com/index.php?option=com_content&task=view&id=8787&Item id=30.

Steigman, Andrew. *The Foreign Service of the United States: First Line of Defense.* Boulder, CO: Westview Press.

Stephenson, Barbara. Presentation at U.S. Institute of Peace, Washington, DC, February 22, 2007.

Transition Center of the Foreign Service Institute. *Protocol for the Modern Diplomat.* Washington, DC: U.S. Department of State, 2005. www.state.gov/documents/ organization/15742.pdf.

Trask, David. *A Short History of the U.S. Department of State, 1781–1981.* Washing- ton, DC: Government Printing Office, 1981.

United States and Bobby Ray Inman. *Report of the Secretary of State's Advisory Panel on Overseas Security.* Washington, DC: U.S. Department of State, 1985. www. fas.org/irp/threat/inman.

U.S. Congress. Senate. *Congressional Record.* 110th Cong., 1st sess., 2007. Vol. 153, No. 29, daily ed. (February 15, 2007): S2039–2042.

———. Committee on Foreign Relations. *Embassies as Command Posts in the Anti- Terror Campaign.* 109th Cong., 2nd sess., 2006. Committee Print 109-52. www.fas .org/irp/congress/2006_rpt/embassies.pdf.

———. *Exploring the U.S. Africa Command and a New Strategic Relationship with Af- rica.* 110th Cong., 2st sess., August 1, 2007. http://foreign.senate.gov/hearings/ 2007/hrg070801a.html.

———. *Embassies Grapple to Guide Foreign Aid.* 110th Cong., 1st sess., 2007. Com- mittee Print 111-33. www.gpoaccess.gov/congress/index.html.

U.S. Department of the Army. *Counterinsurgency.* U.S. Army Field Manual 3-24 and Marine Corps Warfighting Publication 3-33-5. Washington, DC: Government Printing Office, December 2006. www.fas.org/irp/doddir/army/fm3-24.pdf.

U.S. Department of State. *America's Overseas Presence in the 21st Century: The Report of the Overseas Advisory Panel.* Washington, DC: Government Printing Office, 1999.

———. *Department of State's Goal for Arabic Speakers.* Office of the Spokesman. Question Taken at the June 19, 2007. Daily Press Briefing. www.state.gov/r/pa/ prs/ps/2007/jun/86803.htm.

———. *Final Report and Recommendations of the President's Commission on Hostage Compensation.* Unpublished paper. Washington, DC: U.S. Department of State Library, September 21, 1981.

———. *Foreign Affairs Handbook, vol. 3, Personnel Operations Handbook.* Wash- ington, DC: Government Printing Office, 2003. http://foia.state.gov/master docs/03fah01/03fah012430.pdf.

————. *Foreign Affairs Manual, vol. 2, General.* Washington, DC: Government Printing Office, 2006. www.state.gov/documents/organization/84388.pdf.

————. "Foreign Service Assignments: The Future Is Now." State Department cable 133427, unclassified. August 15, 2006.

————. *FY 2008 Budget in Brief.* Bureau of Resource Management. U.S. Department of State website, February 5, 2007. www.state.gov/s/d/rm/rls/bib/2008/html/79744.htm.

————. FY 2009 Budget in Brief. Bureau of Resource Management. U.S. Department of State website, February 4, 2008, www.state.gov/s/d/rm/rls/bib/2009/.

————. "New Direction for Foreign Assistance." Fact sheet, Office of the Spokesman. U.S. Department of State website, January 19, 2006. www.state.gov/r/pa/prs/ps/2006/59398.htm.

————. *Summary and Highlights: International Affairs Function 150.* Fiscal Year 2008 Budget Request. Washington, DC: Government Printing Office, 2007. www.state.gov/documents/organization/80151.pdf.

————. *Summary and Highlights, International Affairs Function 150.* Fiscal Year 2009 Budget Request. Washington, D.C.: Government Printing Office, 2008. www.state.gov/documents/organization/100014.pdf.

————. Bureau of Diplomatic Security. *Partnerships for a Safer World.* 2006 Year in Review. Publication 11423. Washington, DC: Government Printing Office, 2007. www.state.gov/documents/organization/86789.pdf.

————. Bureau of Public Affairs. "Provincial Reconstruction Teams: Building Iraqi Capacity and Accelerating the Transition to Iraqi Self-Reliance." Fact sheet. Washington, DC: Government Printing Office, March 28, 2007. ww.state.gov/documents/organization/82244.pdf.

————. David M. Satterfield. "On-the-Record Briefing on Provincial Reconstruction Teams (PRTs) in Iraq." Washington, DC: Video Teleconference, February 7, 2007. www.state.gov/p/nea/rls/rm/2007/80216.htm.

————. James Knight, Steven Buckler, John Melvin Jones, and Charles Hunter. "On-the-Record Briefing with Provincial Reconstruction Team (PRT) Leaders on Iraq." Washington, DC: Digital Video Conference, March 30, 2007. www.state.gov/p/nea/rls/rm/2007/82501.htm.

————. Sean McCormack. "Daily Press Briefing." DPB #109. Washington, DC: Bureau of Public Affairs, Public Relations Office, June 19, 2007. www.state.gov/r/pa/prs/dpb/2007/jun/86611.htm.

————. Sean McCormack. "Daily Press Briefing." DPB #192. Washington, DC: Bureau of Public Affairs, Public Relations Office, June 19, 2007. http://www.state.gov/r/pa/prs/dpb/2007/oct/94402.htm.

————. Sean McCormack. "Daily Press Briefing." DPB #193. Washington, DC: Bureau of Public Affairs, Public Relations Office, November 1, 2007. www.state.gov/r/pa/prs/dpb/2007/nov/94478.htm.

————. Steven Buckler, Dave Bailey, and Michael McBride. "Briefing on Reconstruction Progress in Salah ad Din." Special Briefing #2007/1069, via Satellite. Washington, DC: Bureau of Public Affairs, Public Relations Office, November 30, 2007. www.state.gov/r/pa/prs/ps/2007/nov/96029.htm.

————. Office of Inspector General. *Semiannual Report to the Congress: April 1, 2004 to September 30, 2004.* Publication 11193. Washington, DC: Government Printing Office, 2004. http://oig.state.gov/documents/organization/39596.pdf.

———. John E. Herbst. "Stabilization and Reconstruction Operations: Learning from the Provincial Reconstruction Team (PRT) Experience." Statement before House Armed Services Subcommittee on Oversight and Investigations. Washington, DC: Office of Reconstruction and Stabilization, October 30, 2007. www.state.gov/s/crs/rls/rm/94379.htm.

U.S. General Accounting Office. *State Department: Minorities and Women Are Underrepresented in the Foreign Service.* Report B-232884 to Congress. Washington, DC: Government Printing Office, 1989.

U.S. Government Accountability Office. *Staffing and Foreign Language Shortfalls Persist Despite Initiatives to Address Gaps.* GAO-06-894. Washington, DC: Government Printing Office, August 2006.

———. *U.S. Public Diplomacy: Strategic Planning Efforts Have Improved, but Agencies Face Significant Implementation Challenges.* GAO-07-795T. Washington, DC: Government Printing Office, April 26, 2007. www.gao.gov/new.items/d07795t.pdf.

Vance, Cyrus. *Hard Choices: Critical Years in America's Foreign Policy.* New York: Simon & Schuster, 1983.

Weiner, Tim. *Legacy of Ashes: The History of the CIA.* New York: Doubleday, 2007.

White House, The. *The National Security Strategy of the United States of America.* Washington, DC: Government Printing Office, September 2002. www.whitehouse.gov/nsc/nss.pdf.

———. *The National Security Strategy of the United States of America.* Washington, DC: Government Printing Office, March 2006. www.whitehouse.gov/nsc/nss/2006/nss2006.pdf.

Witkowsky, Anne, project director; George L. Argyros, Marc Grossman, Felix G. Rohatyn, project cochairs. *The Embassy of the Future.* Washington, D.C.: Center for Strategic and International Studies, 2007.

About the Authors

Harry W. Kopp is a former foreign service officer and consultant in international trade. He was Deputy Assistant Secretary of State for International Trade Policy in the Carter and Reagan administrations and his foreign assignments included Warsaw and Brasília. He is now president of Harry Kopp, LLC, a consulting company. He is the author of *Commercial Diplomacy and the National Interest.*

Charles A. Gillespie was a former foreign service officer and was Deputy Assistant Secretary of State for Inter-American Affairs; American ambassador to Grenada, Colombia, and Chile; and Special Assistant to the President on the National Security Council Staff. He was a principal in The Scowcroft Group, a consulting company. He was also a member of the American Academy of Diplomacy, the Business Council for International Understanding, and the Forum for International Policy.

Index

Note: Page numbers followed by t or f indicate tables and figures in the text. Page numbers followed by n indicate endnotes.

A-100 (basic training), 147–49
accountability review board (ARB), 28–29
accreditation, 57–58
Acheson, Dean, 10, 16, 17, 90, 123
advertising vs. public diplomacy, 60
affirmative action, 23
Afghanistan conflict, accountability review
    board regulations, 29
Afghanistan–U.S diplomatic relations
    economic support, 158
    military assumption of foreign relations role,
      116
    Taliban, 157–58, 195
Africa
    AFRICOM (area combatant command),
      121
    AIDS relief in, 71–73
    as assignment destination, 21, 221n34
    Nigeria, 160–61
    terrorist incidents, 29, 31
African Americans in foreign service, 20–22,
    23t, 221n34
AFRICOM, 121
AFSA. See American Foreign Service
    Association (AFSA)
agencies, 41–42
    consolidation, 193–94
    domestic, 109–11
    fragmentation, 14
    interagency conflict and coordination, 106–7,
      108–9, 187–88
    clearance, 107–8
    foreign service and intelligence community,
      122–27
    foreign service and the military, 117–22
    Foreign Service Board, 34
    Mexican–U.S. border, 109–11
    overseas posts, 111–17, 162
    See also specific agencies

Agency for International Development (AID).
    See U.S. Agency for International
    Development (USAID)
agrément, 55, 225n11
agriculture. See Foreign Agricultural Service
    (FAS); U.S. Department of Agriculture
    (USDA)
AID. See U.S. Agency for International
    Development (USAID)
AIDS relief programs, 71–73
Albright, Madeleine, 32
Alexander, Chuck, 47
amateurs, as diplomats, 7, 11, 52, 91
ambassadors
    authority and roles, 111–17, 114f, 124, 191
    distinction between chief of mission, 112–13
    influence on policy, 60
    personnel/project examples, 51–52, 60, 72, 74
    social protocol, 56–57
    See also specific ambassadors
American Citizen Services, 152–55
American Foreign Service Association (AFSA),
    42, 51, 85, 94, 96, 133, 180
analysis, 209
    economic, 156
    intelligence, 125–27
anti-Communist sentiment, 16
antiterrorism measures, 26, 28, 116, 118, 157,
    195, 233n63
appropriations, 30t, 99–103
    Defense vs. State Department, 86, 117–18
    foreign aid, 15, 43–44, 47
    2009 international affairs request, 104–5t
    Iraq war budget, 80, 228n9
    PEPFAR program, 72–73
    recruitment and hiring, 33, 192
    security, 26, 28–29, 118
Arabic language skills, need for, 76, 78, 82–83,
    136, 141, 228n17

ARB. *See* accountability review board (ARB)

Armitage, Richard, 52, 93, 97

assignments, global, 8, 13t, 35, 48, 87, 168
  for deputy chiefs of mission, 171–73
  exclusive benefits to, 134–35
  first-time, 149, 150, 154–55, 163–64, 169
  formal process, 168–71
  future needs and trends, 71, 159, 175–76, 194
  priority-based distribution, 83–84, 170–71,
    175–76, 229n32
  volunteer aspect, 84–86

attachés, 41, 56, 115–16, 123, 224n8

attitudes, American, on foreign service
  on consuls, 19th century, 12
  following Iranian hostage crisis, 25
  mistrust, 5–6, 10, 53, 90–92
  negotiation-related, 61
  representation dissatisfaction, 12–13
  stereotypes, 92, 119, 120, 122

attrition, 29, 31–33, 43
  due to disagreement with policy, 95
  plans to combat, 191–92

authorization vs. appropriation legislation, 100

background checks, 146

Baker, James P., 90

basic training (A-100), 147–49

Bazala, Sylvia, 171

Beers, Charlotte, 60

benefits. *See under* pay/compensation

Bierce, Ambrose, 11

bipartisanship, 88, 91–92, 230n10

blacks. *See* African Americans in foreign service

Blackwater, 81

Blechman, Barry, 119, 190

boards
  commissioning and tenure, 180–81
  selection, 181–83

Boeing, 52–53

border, U.S.–Mexico, 109–11

Bosshardt, Marcia, 165–66

Boyatt, Tom, 70

Bradley, Toby, 75–78

Brazeal, Rea, 70

Broome, Douglas, 43, 44

Bryan, William Jennings, 12

Buckler, Steven, 80, 82

budgets. *See* appropriations

buildings
  Department of State, 36–38, 39, 147,
    223–24n3

management of, 159
  security, 30–31, 36
  USAID, 43

bureaucracy
  as foreign service obstacle, 90–91, 92, 107
  lighter levels, overseas posts, 111–12
  See also hierarchy

Bureau of Administration, 159

Bureau of Diplomatic Security (DS), 26–27,
  223n49

Bureau of Human Resources
  examination involvement, 22, 140, 141
  management positions, 159
  post assignment, 168–70
  promotion administration, 180–81, 182

Bureau of Intelligence and Research (INR),
  125–27

Bureau of Legislative Affairs (H bureau), 97–99

Bureau of Resource Management, 101, 159, 190

Burns, Nicholas, 39

Bush, George H. W., 90

Bush, George W., 90, 93, 235n15

business vs. diplomatic negotiations, 60

Butte-Dahl, Jennifer, 97–98

Byrd, Lewis, 174

Byrd, Robin, 174

Byrnes, James F., 123

Callières, François de, 53

Campos, Vincent, 78–79, 120

candor, 92–95

career development (commissioning and tenure),
  180–83, 196

career development officers (CDOs), 169–70

career tracks
  choosing, 139, 141
  consular affairs, 150–55
  economic affairs, 155–59, 189–90
  management, 159–62
  political affairs, 162–65
  promotion competition within, 181, 182
  public diplomacy, 165–67
  trajectory examples, 8, 98, 132–34, 135–39,
    171–72
    pay scale, 134t

Carlucci, Frank, 63–66, 69, 117

Carter, Jimmy, 20, 24–25, 90

Caspian Basin pipeline project, 66–68

Caucasus, 66

Caudill, David, 154–55

Central Asia, 66

Central Intelligence Agency (CIA), 19, 26, 123, 125–26
changes in foreign service
  career, 131, 196
  institution, 191–95
  pressure for, 187
  profession, 195
  transformational diplomacy expectation, 70–71, 190–91
  See also future scenarios/studies
chargé d'affaires, 24, 56
chief of mission (COM), 112–15, 114f
  deputy, 123, 171–73, 179
  distinction between ambassador, 112–13
  responsibilities, 27, 171
China hands, 17, 221n25
China–U.S. diplomatic relations, 17, 52–53, 156–57
Christopher, Warren, 90
CIA (Central Intelligence Agency), 19, 26, 123, 125–26
civilian reserve corps, 192–93, 195, 238n11
Civil Operations and Revolutionary Development Support (CORDS) program, 19
civil service
  aspect of Foreign Agricultural Service, 48
  employee diplomatic status, 57
  foreign service opportunities, 145–46
  foreign service relationship, 18, 40–41
  foreign service similarities and differences, 34–35
  part of H bureau, 98
  reform, under Carter, 20, 41
Civil Service Commission, 12, 21
Civil Service Reform Act of 1978, 20, 41
clandestine information, 124–25, 163
classes. *See* ranks
classified information, 17, 27, 204
clearance
  ambassadorial control, 113, 115
  classified material, 204
  exploitation, 107–8
  medical, 146
Clinton, Bill, 90
Coalition Provisional Authority (CPA) (Iraq), 75, 77
codels (congressional delegations), 98–99
cold war policy, American, 60, 124, 165
COM. *See* chief of mission (COM)
combatant commands, 116–18, 121

Commerce Department. *See* U.S. Department of Commerce
commissioning and tenure boards, 180–81
committees, congressional, 96–98, 100, 107, 116–17
communications, Iraq, 76, 81
communication skills, precepts, 207–8
communism, fears of, 17, 63–64
compromise, 60, 61, 106
cones. *See* career tracks
Congress
  career risks, foreign relations involvement, 96–97
  influence over foreign service, 8, 87, 95–99
  seniority levels, 231n33
  support/funding
    foreign aid, 43, 72, 73, 118, 158
    recruitment and hiring, 33, 192
    security, 26, 28–29, 30t, 33, 118
  travel by, 98–99
  See also appropriations; House Foreign Affairs Committee; Senate Foreign Relations Committee
Congress of Vienna (1815), 54
consolidation, of agencies, 193–94
consular affairs, as career track, 150–55
consuls, 11, 56, 219n7
  job duties, 150–55
  staffing levels, 13t
contractors
  private, in Iraq, 81, 195
  USAID use of, 194, 224n10, 238n13
conversion programs, 145–46
CORDS (Civil Operations and Revolutionary Development Support program), 19
Coulter, Frank, 160
counseling, in promotion system, 177
counselors, 56, 132, 181
counterinsurgency field manual, 118, 121–22
country operating plans, 72–73
country teams, 72, 111–16, 114f, 124
couples as foreign service officers, 173–75, 236n4
CPA. *See* Coalition Provisional Authority (CPA) (Iraq)
crisis management, 138–39, 153–54, 160
  See also Iranian hostage crisis
Crumpton, Henry, 195
cultural affairs, 166
cultural centers, 30, 165
cultural sensitivity, 148, 212

danger in profession, 25, 37, 81, 153, 197, 222n44, 224n4
Danz, Caryn, 166, 167
D committee, 171
debt relief, 157–58, 158
de Callières, François, 53
defense attachés, 115–16
Defense Intelligence Agency (DIA), 115, 126
democracy via transformational diplomacy, 69–70, 76–78, 79
Democratic party, 91, 230n10
demographic representation, foreign service members, 20, 22, 23t
Department of Agriculture. *See* U.S. Department of Agriculture (USDA)
Department of Commerce. *See* U.S. Department of Commerce
Department of Defense. *See* U.S. Department of Defense
Department of Homeland Security, 110, 111
Department of State. *See* U.S. Department of State
Department of State 2012/2025 project, 190–91
deputy chiefs of mission (DCM), 123, 171–73, 179
deputy secretary of state, 171
Derham, James, 109, 174–75
Derham, Joleen, 174–75
development, as component of national security, 43–44
DG (director general), 41
Dhi Qar province (Iraq), reconstruction, 75–77
DIA (Defense Intelligence Agency), 115, 126
Dibble, Elizabeth, 173–74
Dibble, Philo, 173–74
Dietz, Steve, 101, 103, 119–20
diplomacy
    European traditions, 53, 54–55, 57
    negotiation within, 60–61
    as profession, 6–7, 12–14, 51–52
    public
        as career track, 166–67
        diminished program support, 165
        growing importance of, 190–91
    traditions and protocol, 53–58
    transformational, 5, 9, 44, 66, 69–73, 163
        Advisory Committee on, 190
        defined, 227n39
        Iraq elections example, 76–78, 79
        and military, 118–19
        PEPFAR example, 71–73

U.S. nineteenth-century, 11–12
    See also operations, as mission; policy, as mission; representation, as mission
diplomatic immunity, 54–55
Diplomatic Readiness Initiative (DRI), 22, 32–33, 83, 187
Diplomatic Security. *See* Bureau of Diplomatic Security (DS)
Diplomatic Security Service (DSS), 26–27, 223n50
Diplomat of the Future project, 189–90
diplomats
    foreign/domestic differences, 7, 13
    future needs/predictions, 189–93
    harm to, American, 25, 37, 81, 153, 197, 222n44, 224n4
    professionalism, 6–7, 11, 52, 197
    public opinion and stereotypes, 10, 53, 85, 92, 119, 122
    responsibilities, 58–63
        intelligence-related, 124
        Iraq-specific, 74–87
    social standing, 11, 56–57
    titles and ranking, 56, 59
    See also foreign service officers (generalists) (FSOs); skills, diplomatic
director general (DG), 41
director of national intelligence (DNI), 123, 126
discrimination, 20–23
dissent, 92–95, 201
diversity issues, 20–23, 203
Dlouhy, David, 189
domestic policy, informed by foreign, 109–10
DRI (Diplomatic Readiness Initiative), 22, 32–33, 83, 187
DS (Bureau of Diplomatic Security), 26–27, 223n49
DSS (Diplomatic Security Service), 26–27, 223n50
Dulles, John Foster, 18

Eagleburger, Lawrence, 39, 94
early retirement, 35–36
economic affairs, as career track, 155–59, 189–90
Economic Cooperation Administration, 220n16
EEOC. *See* Equal Employment Opportunity Commission (EEOC)
efficiency reports, 177–80
Eisenhower, Dwight, 17
elections, Iraq, 76–78, 79
eligibility requirements, 140, 145–46

El Salvador, 164
embassies, 30, 111–17
    attacks on, 26, 29, 31
    hosting responsibilities, 99
    intelligence component, 123–24, 157
    military component, 115–16
    record keeping and management, 57, 159–60
    security, 26, 27–28, 30–31, 115–16
    staff, 40, 113, 114f
    strategic plan/budget requests, 102–3
    suspicion of, 53
    U.S. embassy, Baghdad, 74, 78, 82
Embassy of the Future study, 191, 237–38n8,
        238n16
employee evaluation reports (EER), 177–80
employees. *See* members of the foreign service
energy affairs, 66–68
entertaining, 4, 28
entrance exams
    alternatives to, 145–46
    cancellation, 32
    for generalists, 132, 139–40
        oral, 141–43, 142t
        preparation, 143
        registration, 140
        written, 21, 140–41
    for specialists, 134, 143–45
    and women/minorities, 21–23
Equal Employment Opportunity, 203
Equal Employment Opportunity Commission
        (EEOC), 21–22
European diplomacy, 53, 54–55, 57
evaluation, in promotion system, 177–80, 202
evaluations, personnel, 123
exequatur, 56
exports, U.S., 45, 47

float, in staffing, 32–33, 83, 161, 191
Ford, Charles, 46, 225n15
Foreign Affairs Council, 192, 223n62
Foreign Affairs Manual, 113
Foreign Agricultural Service (FAS), 14–15, 41,
        47–48, 101
foreign aid funding, 15, 43–44, 47
    Carlucci/Portugal example, 64
    debt relief, 158
    diverted to security assistance, 118
    PEPFAR program, 72, 73
Foreign Commercial Service (FCS), 14–15, 41,
        45–46
foreign intelligence. *See* intelligence

foreign language skills, 33, 78, 82–83, 141
    "hard" languages, 136, 137, 141
    precepts, 208
    training and testing, 136–37, 138
Foreign Operations Administration, 220n16
foreign policy. *See* policy
Foreign Service Act of 1946, 19
Foreign Service Act of 1980, 5, 20, 23, 32, 34, 43
    ambassadorial responsibility, 112, 221n33
    employment rules, 42, 48, 176
    privacy guidelines, 179
Foreign Service Board, 34
foreign service exams. *See* entrance exams
Foreign Service Institute training programs, 33,
        147–49
    consular, 151
    language, 136–37, 138
    leadership, 139
foreign service nationals (FSNs), 40, 41, 57,
        221n33
    management, 159, 167
    under USAID, 42, 43
foreign service officers (generalists) (FSOs), 40,
        132, 139
    career tracks, 139, 141, 150
        consular affairs, 150–55
        economic affairs, 155–59
        management, 159–62
        political affairs, 162–65
        public diplomacy, 165–67
    congressional opinions on, 97
    diplomatic status, 57
    interagency work, 108–9, 120–21
    See also diplomats; training
foreign service specialists, 40, 134, 143
    assignment process, 169
    diplomatic status, 57
    jobs and categories, 144t, 161–62
    operational role, 61–62
    as political advisors, 121
    reserve officers, 19
    security, 27, 223n50
fragmentation by agencies, 14
France, diplomatic system, 53–54
    See also terminology, foreign language origins
Franklin, Benjamin, 11
Freeman, Chas, 93
FS levels. *See* ranks
FSNs. *See* foreign service nationals (FSNs)
FSOs. *See* foreign service officers (generalists)
        (FSOs)

Function 150, 102, 103, 104–5t, 232n41
funding. *See* appropriations
future scenarios/studies, 188, 190
    Department of State 2012/2025, 190–91
    Diplomat of the Future, 189–90
    Embassy of the Future, 191, 237–38n8, 238n16
    Project Horizon, 187–88

Galbraith, Peter, 52
Gallogly, Steve, 67
Gallucci, Robert, 52, 61
GAO. *See* General Accounting Office (GAO);
    Government Accountability Office
    (GAO)
gaps, staffing. *See under* staffing
Gates, Bill, 52–53
Gates, Robert, 31, 83, 86
gender bias, 20–23
General Accounting Office (GAO), 22
generalists. *See* foreign service officers
    (generalists) (FSOs)
Germany, 164
Giambastiani, Edmund, 85
Gibson, Hugh, 13–14
Gingrich, Newt, 87, 90
globalization, 159
Global Peace Operations Initiative (GPOI), 116
Government Accountability Office (GAO),
    235–36n26
grades. *See* ranks
Grossman, Marc, 23, 32–33, 93

Haig, Alexander, 91–92, 117
Hamas, 195
"handshake" assignment agreements, 170
"hard" languages, 136, 137, 141
hardship posts, 84, 87, 112, 169, 170–171
Hay, John, 11–12
Hays, Clayton, 148
H bureau, 97–99
hierarchy
    military, 119–20
    of precedence, 56–57
    State Department, 37–39, 198–99
high-priority posts, 83–84, 170–71, 175–76
hiring. *See* recruitment and hiring
Hiss, Alger, 16, 221n21
Holbrooke, Richard, 52
hostages, 24–25, 222n43
House Foreign Affairs Committee, 96

Hughes, Karen, 60
Hu Jintao, 52–53
Hull, Cordell, 15
human resources. *See* staffing
Hunter, Chuck, 81

immigration policy, 109–11, 150–52
immunity, diplomatic, 54–55, 57
information-related services, 15, 166–67
information technology, 159
Inman, Bobby Ray, 26
Inman Report, 26–27, 28, 29, 30
INR. *See* Bureau of Intelligence and Research
    (INR)
institutional characteristics, 6
intellectual skills, precepts, 209–10
intelligence
    analysis, 125–27
    community and foreign service, 122–27
    sharing, military, 116
    sources, 66, 123, 124–25, 157
interagency relationships. *See under* agencies
International Affairs, budget request, 104–5t
International Broadcasting Bureau (IBB), 41
International Cooperative Administrative
    Support Services (ICASS) system, 162
International Military Education and Training
    (IMET), 116
International Trade Administration (ITA), 45
    See also Foreign Commercial Service (FCS)
interpersonal skills, precepts, 205–6
Iranian hostage crisis, 23–25, 222n43
Iranian revolution, 1979, 24
Iraq–U.S. diplomatic relations, Iraq War (2003-)
    accountability review board regulations, 29
    consular work, 154
    debt relief, 158
    expectations of foreign service, 74, 85, 195
    foreign relations, by military, 116, 120
    impact on foreign service, 82–87
    political work, 2005, 77–79
    provincial reconstruction, 2003, 75–77
    provincial reconstruction, 2005-2007, 79–82

Jenner, William, 17
job offers, 146–47
    See also assignments, global
Johnstone, Craig, 44, 88, 102–3
Jones, John Melvin, 81
journalism vs. foreign service reporting, 59–60

Kamian, Harry, 164
Kaplan, Sid, 188
Kelly, Craig, 93, 94, 172
Kennan, George, 16, 17, 60, 226n19
Kennedy, John F., 42, 112
Kennedy, Robert F., 10
Khalilzad, Zalmay, 51
Khant, Eric, 161, 162
Khomeini, Ruholla, 24
kidnapping, 25, 81, 153
King, Russ, 161, 162
Kissinger, Henry, 10, 64–65, 90, 91–92
    missions, 230n4
    quotations, 59
Kolker, Jimmy, 72–73
Kuwait, 153–54

Laingen, L. Bruce, 24
Lange, John, 72
languages, foreign, as skill, 33, 78, 82–83, 141
    "hard," 136, 137, 141
    precepts, 208
    training and testing, 136–37, 138
Lanpher, Gib, 29, 223n54
Lansing, Robert, 12
Larson, Alan, 155, 156, 157–59
Latin terminology, 56
law
    authorization vs. appropriation, 100
    enforcement, domestic, 109–11
    foreign service execution of, 96
    international, 190
    vs. diplomatic negotiations, 60
layoffs, 43
Leahy, Patrick, 87, 98
Llorens, Hugo, 108–9
locally employed staff, 40, 41, 57, 221n33
    management, 159, 167
    under USAID, 42, 43
Loftis, Robert, 121, 122
Logan Act of 1799, 225n1
low ranking, in performance evaluation, 182–83
loyalty and dissent, 92–95, 101

Main State building, 36–38, 39, 165
management, as career track, 159–62
managerial skills, precepts, 202–4, 210
mandatory retirement, 20, 35, 48, 137, 183
Mandojana, Marcos, 148, 151–52, 153, 155
Mann, Steven, 68

Marine Corps, 27
Marine Security Guards, 27–28
Marshall, George C., 16, 117
Marshall, S. L. A., 92–93
Marshall Plan, 88
McCahill, Bill, 156–57
McCarthy, Deborah Ann, 149, 156
McCarthy, Joseph, and McCarthyism, 16–17,
    91
media
    introduced in Iraq, 81, 82
    press relations and information, 166–67
members of the foreign service, 3–4, 40–48
    demographic representation, 20, 22, 23t
    marginalization, 90–92
    pay scales, 133t, 134, 134t
    political surroundings, 88–103, 106–27
    See also diplomats; foreign service nationals
        (FSNs); foreign service officers
        (generalists) (FSOs); foreign service
        specialists; U.S. Foreign Service
memoranda of understanding (MOU), 115
Mexico–U.S. border issues, 109–11
Midura, Chris, 175–76
Miles, Richard, 119, 163, 164
Miley, Stephanie, 82
military
    idealization and stereotyping, 119, 120, 122
    intelligence, history, 122–23
    organization and methods, 32, 85, 87, 119
military colleges, 120–21
military/diplomatic links, 11, 72, 117–22
    combatant commands, 116–17
    within embassies, 115–16, 124
    in Iraq, 74–75, 78–82, 120
    personnel, 52, 117, 119–20
    political advisor role, 121
    See also Iraq–U.S. diplomatic relations, Iraq
        War (2003–)
Millennium Challenge Corporation (MCC),
    72, 220n16
minorities, 22–23, 23t
mistrust, 5–6, 10, 53, 90–92
Motley, Tony, 29, 89–90, 93
Munshi, Kiki, 80–81
Murphy, Sean, 153–54, 155
Musharraf, Pervez, 157–58, 165
Mustang program, 145–46, 161
Myers-Briggs Type Indicator, 163, 235n23
Myles, Marianne, 189–90

Naland, John, 85
National Defense Authorization Act, 2004, 72,
    233n63
National Intelligence Council, 126
National Oceanic and Atmospheric
    Administration, 45
national security
    consular work as, 155
    development as component, 43–44
    enabled by foreign service, 61, 69–73
National Security Act, 1947, 107
National Security Council (NSC), 107
The National Security Strategy, 2002 and 2006
    (reports), 69, 192
nation-building. *See* transformational diplomacy
NATO, politics of member countries, 64–65
negotiation, 60–61, 205
Negroponte, John D., 39, 123
new countries, challenges, 31, 66
Newsom, David, 124–25, 197
Nicolson, Harold, 53
Nigeria, 160–61
Nineteenth-century diplomacy, 11–12
Nixon, Richard, 5, 10, 64, 90
Nolan, Rob, 135, 182, 183
noncareer appointees. *See* political appointees
nonprofessionals, as diplomats, 11, 52, 91
nonstate actors, 70, 193
NSC (National Security Council), 107

oath of office, 147–48
office designation shorthand, State Department,
    38, 44
Office of Management and Budget (OMB), 102
Office of Personnel Management, 41, 230n11
Office of Security, 27, 223n49
Office of Strategic Services (OSS), 122–23,
    234n80
Office of the Undersecretary for Management,
    159
Office of the U.S. Trade Representative
    (USTR), 15
Office of War Information, 15, 220n15
officer tracks, of foreign service, 139, 141, 150
    consular affairs, 150–55
    economic affairs, 155–59
    management, 159–62
    political affairs, 162–65
    public diplomacy, 165–67
oil interests, 66–68
OMB (Office of Management and Budget), 102

Omnibus Diplomatic Security and
    Antiterrorism Act of 1986, 26
operations, as mission, 4, 61–62
OPM (Office of Personnel Management), 41,
    230n11
oral assessment, entrance exam, 141–43, 142t
organization charts
    country teams, 114f
    Department of State, 37, 39, 198–99
orientation, basic, 147–49
origins, of diplomacy, 53–54
OSAC. *See* Overseas Security Advisory Council
    (OSAC)
outsiders, as diplomats, 7
Overseas Presence Advisory Panel (OPAP), 32
Overseas Security Advisory Council (OSAC),
    26
oversight, congressional, 96, 100
Owens-Kirkpatrick, Barbro, 60, 108

Pahlavi, Reza, 24
Pakistan–U.S. diplomatic relations, 157–58,
    235n15
Palmer, Alison, 21, 22, 23
Passen, Andy, 86
patriotism, 53, 95, 197
Pavitt, Jim, 124
pay/compensation, 13–14, 20, 34, 35, 182
    base pay, 133
    benefits, 131, 134–35
    of consuls, 11, 12
    scales, 133t, 134, 134t
Peace Corps, 41
Pearson program, 99, 230n35
PEPFAR. *See* President's Emergency Program
    for AIDS Relief (PEPFAR)
performance evaluations, 176–80, 202
personal narrative, exam registration, 140, 234n5
persona non grata, 56
personnel systems, 19–20, 34, 42
    See also staffing
Philippines, 151, 153
physical security. *See* security
Pickering, Tom, 190
POLADs (political advisors), 121
policy
    affected by diplomacy/foreign service, 62–63,
        88, 90
    clearance processes exploited, 107–8
    and dissent, 92–95
    political affairs, 163, 164–65

public diplomacy, 166–67
    reporting, 59–60
domestic, 109–10
by Foreign Agricultural Service, 47
military engagement, 118–20
as mission, 4, 62–63, 89–90
USAID role in, 44
See also transformational diplomacy; specific
    countries
political advisors (POLADs), 121
political affairs, as career track, 162–65
political appointees
    ambassador title, 113
    assignment, 92, 98
    assumptions about, 51, 91
political surroundings, of foreign service, 88–90
    ambassador role, 111–17, 114f
    budgets, 99–103, 104–5t
    clearance, 107–9
    Congress, 95–99
    dissent implications, 92–95
    intelligence community, 122–27
    interagency relations, 106–7
    military, 117–22
    Secretary of State and management, 90–92
Portugal–U.S. diplomatic relations, 63–65, 69
posts. *See* assignments, global
Powell, Colin, 22, 32–33, 90, 93, 97, 117
precedence, 56–57, 225–26n12
precepts, for career progression, 135–36, 183,
    189, 200–212, 237n5
President of the United States, relationship with
    State Department, 90
    See also specific presidents
President's Emergency Program for AIDS
    Relief (PEPFAR), 71–73, 227n45
press relations and information, 166–67
pride, 196–97
private sector, partnerships with, 26, 194–95,
    238n14
professionalism, 88–90, 205
profession of diplomacy, 6–7, 51–52
    changes to, 195–96
    creating, 12–14
Project Horizon, 187–88
promotions, 22, 44–45
    within agencies, 123
    as alternative to adding staff, 87
    congressional approval, 96, 132, 134
    consequences of non-promotion, 137, 181,
        182–83

formal system, 176–80
    prerequisites, 170, 172
    selection boards, 180–83
    See also precepts, for career progression
protocol, diplomatic, 53–58
provincial reconstruction teams, (PRTs) (Iraq),
    75, 80–82, 84, 86, 228n4
    See also reconstruction
public diplomacy
    as career track, 166–67
    diminished program support, 165
    growing importance of, 190–91

racial bias, 20–23
ranks
    diplomatic, 56, 132
    personal, 35, 39, 55–58, 131–32, 134, 224n6
    progression through, 135–36, 137–38, 196
    promotion considerations, 181–82
reconstruction, 74, 75–77, 192–93
    See also provincial reconstruction teams,
        (PRTs) (Iraq)
recruitment and hiring, 32–33
    conversion programs, 145–46
    by Foreign Agricultural Service, 47–48
    by Foreign Commercial Service, 46
    future considerations, 189–90
    hiring timeframe, 146–47
    for specific posts, 170
    of women and minorities, 22–23
    See also entrance exams
regional bureaus, 98
regional embassy offices (REOs) (Iraq), 78, 79–80
regional security officers (RSO), 27, 159–60
reporting, 47, 59–60
    economic affairs, 156
    political affairs, 163, 164
    source of intelligence, 124, 157
representation
    as mission, 4, 59–61
    and professionalism, 89–90, 206
Republican party, 91, 230n10
reserve officers
    civilian corps, 192–93, 195, 238n11
    specialists, 19
resignations over policy, 95, 231n25
retirees as employees, 40
retirement
    in civil service, 36
    early, 35–36
    mandatory, 20, 35, 48, 137, 183

Rewards for Justice program, 26
Rice, Condoleezza, 5, 44, 66, 70, 93, 118
Richelieu, Cardinal, 53
Ritchie, John, 110
Rogers, John Jacob, 12
Rogers, William P., 90, 230n4
Rogers Act (1924), 12–14
Roosevelt, Franklin D., 15
Roosevelt, Theodore, 11
Ross, Dennis, 52, 195
Russia–U.S. diplomatic relations, 66–68

salaries. See pay/compensation
Schedule C positions, 92, 230n11
Shultz, George P., 26, 58, 60, 106, 226n23,
    232n45, 234n11
Scowcroft, Brent, 60
screening. See entrance exams
second careers, 154–55
Secretary of State, 34, 90–92
    Acheson, Dean, 10, 16, 17, 90
    Albright, Madeleine, 32
    Baker, James P., 90
    Bryan, William Jennings, 12
    Byrnes, James F., 123
    Christopher, Warren, 90
    Dulles, John Foster, 18
    Eagleburger, Lawrence, 39, 94
    Haig, Alexander, 91–92, 117
    Hull, Cordell, 15
    Kissinger, Henry, 10, 59, 64–65, 91–92
    Lansing, Robert, 12
    Marshall, George C., 16, 117
    Powell, Colin, 22, 32–33, 90, 93, 97, 117
    Rice, Condoleezza, 5, 44, 66, 70, 93, 118
    Rogers, William P., 90, 230n4
    Shultz, George P., 26, 58, 60, 234n11
    Vance, Cyrus, 24, 25, 90
Section 1206 programs, 118, 233n63
security
    architecture planning, 30–31, 36
    congressional support/funding, 26, 28–29,
        30t, 33
    enhancement, 1980s–90s, 26–27, 29–31
    in Iraq, 75, 79, 80–81, 82
    by Marine guards, 27–28
    portion of foreign aid, 118
    specialists, 27, 223n50
    See also national security; specific agencies
selection out, 19, 35, 136, 137, 137t
Senate Foreign Relations Committee, 116–17

senior officers, 19, 20
    career path, 136, 137–39, 171
    executive level pay scale, 133t
    as political advisors, 121
    rank, 56, 132
September 11, 2001, terrorist attacks, influence,
    62, 69, 151, 157–58, 193, 235n15
Shah, Iran, 24
skills, diplomatic, 6–7, 51, 65, 166
    future trends, 189–91
    languages, 33, 78, 82–83, 136–37, 141, 208
    measurement via entrance exams, 141, 142t,
        144, 234n6
    needed for promotion, 138–39, 172, 178,
        200–212
    negotiation, 60–61, 205
    on-the-job learning, 161, 163–64
    problem-solving, 77
social protocol, 53–58
sovereign power, 54
Soviet Union
    Kennan report, 60, 226n19
    political changes, 31, 66
special envoys, 67–68
specialists. See foreign service specialists
Special Operations Command (SOCOM), 116
spending. See appropriations
spies, 16–17, 56, 124
    See also intelligence
spoils system, 11, 12
spouses, 21, 55, 145, 152, 173, 236n4
stabilization, 74, 192–93
staffing
    bloat, 19
    budgeting requests, 192
    exchanges, foreign service/military, 120
    gender and race issues, 20–23, 23t
    shortages, State Department, 29, 31–33,
        86–87, 175–76
        due to disagreement with policy, 95
        Foreign Agricultural Service, 48
        Iraq posts, 83–84, 86–87
        plans to combat, 191–92
        USAID, 43, 192
    statistics, 13t, 35t, 40, 42
State Department. See U.S. Department of State
Steigman, Andy, 25
stereotypes, 92, 119, 120, 122
Stoessel, Walter, 39
strategic plans, 102–3, 187–88, 191
stretch assignments, 176

substantive knowledge, precepts, 211–12
Sullivan, William, 24

Taliban, 157, 158, 195
tandem couples, 173–75, 236n4
technology
    infrastructure, 27
    skills, as precepts, 212
    State Department intranet, 169, 177
    virtual U.S. presence posts, 194
tenure, 134, 135–37, 150, 180–81
terminology, foreign language origins, 55, 56, 57, 224n8
terrorist attacks, 26, 29, 36
    See also antiterrorism measures; September 11, 2001, terrorist attacks, influence
tests. See entrance exams
thirteen dimensions (oral assessment), 141, 142t, 234n6
Thomas, Harry, 84–85
Thomas, Walter, 21–22
time-in-class limits, 137, 137t, 183
Tobias, Randall, 72
tracks. See career tracks
trade-related services, 14–15, 41, 45–48, 219n14
traditions, diplomatic, 53–58
training, 33, 192
    basic (A-100), 147–49
    cross-training, 120–21, 138
    International Military Education and Training (IMET), 116
    lack of, Iraq preparation, 82–83
    language, 136–37, 138
    on-the-job, 161, 163–64
    See also skills, diplomatic
trajectory, career, 8, 98, 132–34, 135–39, 171–72
transformational diplomacy, 5, 9, 44, 66, 69–73, 163
    Advisory Committee on, 190
    defined, 227n39
    Iraq elections example, 76–78, 79
    and military, 118–19
    PEPFAR example, 71–73
Truman, Harry, 16, 122–23
Tutwiler, Margaret, 60
2025 project, 190–91

Udall, Mo, 10
unaccompanied posts, 170
United Kingdom, diplomatic system, 57
up or out, 19, 35, 136, 137, 137t

U.S. Agency for International Development (USAID), 3, 19, 41, 42–45, 220n16
    budget, 100–101, 102
    Bureau of Legislative and Public Affairs, 97
    staffing levels, 31, 42, 43, 45, 146, 192
    use of contractors, 194, 224n10, 238n13
U.S. Census Bureau, 45, 73
U.S. Commercial Service, 41, 45
    See also Foreign Commercial Service (FCS)
U.S. Department of Agriculture (USDA), 3, 46–47, 101
    See also Foreign Agricultural Service (FAS)
U.S. Department of Commerce, 3, 45–46
    See also Foreign Commercial Service (FCS)
U.S. Department of Defense, 116–17
    budget, 86, 117–18, 125
    filling civilian positions, Iraq, 83
    See also military/diplomatic links
U.S. Department of State, 34
    budget, 99–103, 104–5t, 228n9, 229n35, 232n41
        compared with Defense Department, 86, 117–18
        military program funding, 116
        staffing requests, 33, 192
    building layout, 36–38, 39, 147, 223–24n3
    civil service relationship, 18, 40–41
    foreign aid ownership, 15, 43
    intelligence community relationship, 122–27
    organization charts, 37, 39, 198–99
    perceived failures, 15, 193
        in Iraq, 85
        of leadership, 17–18, 91
        in recruitment, 32
    personnel system, 19, 34, 42
    target of anti-Communist attacks, 16–17, 221n21
    during WWI and WWII, 12, 15
    See also specific bureaus and offices
U.S. Foreign Service
    defined, 3–4, 34
    historical developments, 6, 193
    mission, 4–5
    See also foreign service officers (generalists) (FSOs); foreign service specialists; members of the foreign service; specific departments and agencies
U.S. Information Agency (USIA), 15, 31, 165, 220n15
U.S. Information Communications Agency (USICA), 220n15

U.S. Information Service (USIS), 220n15
U.S. Patent and Trademark Office, 45
USAID. *See* U.S. Agency for International
    Development (USAID)
USDA. *See* U.S. Department of Agriculture
    (USDA)
USTR (Office of the U.S. Trade
    Representative), 15

vacancies. *See under* staffing
Vance, Cyrus, 24, 25, 90
Vandenberg, Arthur, 88
Vienna, Congress of (1815), 54
Vienna Convention on Consular Relations,
    1963, 54–55
Vienna Convention on Diplomatic Relations,
    1961, 54–55
Vietnam War, 19
    dissent expression, 94
    training during, 83
visas, 111, 151–52
volunteer aspect of service assignments,
    84–86, 146

WAE (when actually employed) personnel,
    40, 161
weapons sales, 116, 163
website, of State Department, 140, 143, 169,
    177, 234n4
Whitaker, Betsy, 166–67
Wilson, Woodrow, 12
wives. *See* spouses
women
    bias against, 20, 21
    percentage of total officers, 23t
    recruitment and hiring, 22–23
World Trade Organization (WTO), 156–57
Wriston, Henry, 18
writers, as consuls, 219n7
written portion, entrance exams, 21, 140–41, 144

Yamauchi, Emi, 172–73
yes-men, 93
youth staff revitalization, 33